'An urgent and passionate call for architecture to awaken from its current dogmatic slumber, Nadir Lahiji's *Architecture or Revolution* is also a stunning attempt to re-read Marx as our contemporary. Against the defeatist consolations of so-called "post-critical" theory and neoliberal fantasies of capitalist progression, this remarkable book shows how we need Marx's critical and emancipatory perspective more than ever. The lesson is that a critical theory of architecture will be Marxian, or it will not be at all.'

David Cunningham, Institute for Modern and Contemporary Culture, University of Westminster

'In his latest book, *Architecture or Revolution*, architectural philosopher Nadir Lahiji argues cogently and fiercely for what he calls the "right to shelter". Shelter is more than a roof over one's head, more than what Le Corbusier described as "a primal instinct". It's a human right inherently linked to a political philosophy—to a fundamental commitment to equality. Starting from a rereading of Marx and the French Revolution, Lahiji calls for architecture to move beyond capitalist complaisance and nihilism and take a revolutionary stance, one that conjoins aesthetics and ethics with a critique of political economy. A fervent cry from the contemporary barricades.'

Joan Ockman, Vincent Scully Visiting Professor of Architectural History, Yale University

'With *Architecture or Revolution*, Nadir Lahiji provides the most thorough attempt to conceive an emancipatory theory of building that anyone has yet tried. His book doesn't just propose a Marxist theory of architecture, but engages architecture as itself a form of Marxist practice. The insights are stunning, and the ramifications are far-reaching.'

Todd McGowan, University of Vermont

'In Lahiji's *Architecture or Revolution*, le Corbusier's pronouncement, "Architecture or Revolution" is, perhaps for the first time, analyzed seriously. Examined in the context of the French Revolution and the revolutions projected by Corb's philosophic contemporaries, "revolution" is shown to be the logical option that Corb so incorrectly dismisses. Lahiji makes the argument that, starting with Corb, architects, especially in the academy, have eradicated both the idea of a true revolution and the critical framework we need to articulate its necessity.'

Peggy Deamer, Yale School of Architecture, emerita

Architecture or Revolution

By linking building theory to the *emancipatory project of critique* advanced by radical thinkers in our time, this work investigates the key conceptual and historical elements that culminate in an *emancipatory theory of building* entitled: 'Toward a philosophy of shelter'. Taking Marx as its *only* resource, this work proceeds with the conviction that our era is contemporaneous to Marx's historical era. This means 'not judging the validity of Marx from the perspective of the historical situation', but rather, 'demonstrating the validity of a Marxian perspective for a singular historical situation', as ours. This work will therefore translate this perspective into seeing the situation of architecture through the eyes of Marx.

All those concerned with the predicament in our current condition in which architecture must play a major social role in upholding the universal value of what Alain Badiou calls *'generic humanity'* will take an interest in this work. In particular, architects, critics, scholars, and students inside the field of architecture who would be seeking the application of this universal value to a new theory of building will be a welcoming audience for this work.

Nadir Lahiji is an architect. He is most recently the author of *An Architecture Manifesto: Critical Reason and Theories of a Failed Practice* (Routledge, 2019). His previous publications include, among others, *Adventures with the Theory of the Baroque and French Philosophy*, and the co-authored *The Architecture of Phantasmagoria: Specters of the City*.

Architecture or Revolution

Emancipatory Critique After Marx

NADIR LAHIJI

LONDON AND NEW YORK

First published 2021
by Routledge
2 Park Square, Milton Park, Abingdon, Oxon OX14 4RN

and by Routledge
52 Vanderbilt Avenue, New York, NY 10017

Routledge is an imprint of the Taylor & Francis Group, an informa business

© 2021 Nadir Lahiji

The right of Nadir Lahiji to be identified as author of this work has been asserted by him in accordance with sections 77 and 78 of the Copyright, Designs and Patents Act 1988.

All rights reserved. No part of this book may be reprinted or reproduced or utilised in any form or by any electronic, mechanical, or other means, now known or hereafter invented, including photocopying and recording, or in any information storage or retrieval system, without permission in writing from the publishers.

Trademark notice: Product or corporate names may be trademarks or registered trademarks, and are used only for identification and explanation without intent to infringe.

British Library Cataloguing-in-Publication Data
A catalogue record for this book is available from the British Library

Library of Congress Cataloging-in-Publication Data
Names: Lahiji, Nadir, 1948– author.
Title: Architecture or revolution / Nadir Lahiji.
Description: New York: Routledge, 2020. | Includes bibliographical references and index.
Identifiers: LCCN 2020002859 (print) | LCCN 2020002860 (ebook) | ISBN 9780367425470 (hardback) | ISBN 9780367425487 (paperback) | ISBN 9780367853372 (ebook)
Subjects: LCSH: Architecture–Philosophy. | Marx, Karl, 1818–1883.
Classification: LCC NA2500.L3454 2020 (print) | LCC NA2500 (ebook) | DDC 720.1–dc23
LC record available at https://lccn.loc.gov/2020002859
LC ebook record available at https://lccn.loc.gov/2020002860

ISBN: 978-0-367-42547-0 (hbk)
ISBN: 978-0-367-42548-7 (pbk)
ISBN: 978-0-367-85337-2 (ebk)

Typeset in Univers
by Deanta Global Publishing Services, Chennai, India

We may affirm absolutely that *nothing great in the World* can be accomplished without *passion*.
    —**G. W. F. Hegel**, *Philosophy of History*

I said *virtue*! It is a natural passion, no doubt about it ... But there do exist, I can assure you, souls that are feeling and pure; it exists, that tender imperious and irresistible passion, the torment and delight of magnanimous hearts; that deep horror of tyranny, that compassionate zeal for the oppressed, that sacred love for the homeland, that even more sublime and holy love for humanity, without which a great revolution is just a noisy crime that destroys another crime; it does exist, that generous ambition to establish here on earth the world's first Republic.
    —**Maximilien Robespierre**, 'From Speech of 8 Thermidor Year II—26 July 1794'

As at the time it was a monk, so now it is the philosopher in whose brain the revolution begins.
    —**Karl Marx**, 'A Contribution to the Critique of Hegel's *Philosophy of Right*—Introduction'

Contents

List of figures   xi
Acknowledgments   xii

Apologue: Revolution, critique, and return to philosophy   1

Exordium: Learning from Valéry reading Marx   20

Critical pedagogy: Architecture or Revolution   26

PART I   45

1 The Blank Wall: Architecture and the French Revolution   47

    Architecture and bourgeoisie   48
    Invention of the Blank Wall   53
    Theses on the Blank Wall   61
    Virtue and Terror   67
    The Blank Wall and the philosophy of revolution   76
    Notes   88

2 The architecture of (Neo)Bonapartism — 102

Corbusianism and Bonapartism — 102
Keynesianism and Corbusianism — 118
Neo-Bonapartism and specters of Le Corbusier — 126
Notes — 130

PART II — 135

3 Marx and Critique — 137

Critique and Enlightenment — 137
Transcritique — 144
Critique and the Unconscious — 169
Notes — 188

4 Transcritique of architecture — 200

The sublime object of critique — 200
Phantasmagoria of architecture — 216
Architecture and the capitalist Unconscious — 227
Notes — 242

PART III — 251

5 Toward a philosophy of shelter — 253

Shelter, not a lofty tower — 254
Universality of shelter and the philosophy of right — 264
Notes — 275

Coda: In defence of Marx — 280

Notes — 287

Bibliography — 289
Index — 301

Figures

0.1	Le Corbusier, *Sketch for book cover with the working title 'ARCHITECTURE OU RÉVOLUTION', 1923*	26
0.2	Le Corbusier: *Publicity Flyer for VERS UNE ARCHITECTURE, 1923*	27
1.1	Jacques Louis David, *The Death of Marat*	47
5.1	Le Corbusier, *Maison Dom-Ino* (Dom-Ino House), 1914	253

Acknowledgments

I would like first to express my gratitude to my publisher Francesca Ford for embracing the initial proposal for this book and giving it her support throughout its approval process. I thank the reviewers of the proposal for their constructive comments and suggestions.

My sincere thanks go to Trudy Varcianna, the Senior Editorial Assistant, for her invaluable help throughout the process and for her kindness answering all my email inquiries promptly and taking care of all the problems.

I thank Kristina Wischenkamper for reading the early draft of the manuscript with her excellent editorial intervention.

Apologue

Revolution, critique, and
return to philosophy

> Theory is capable of seizing the masses once it demonstrates *ad hominem,* and it demonstrates *ad hominem* once it becomes radical.
>
> —Karl Marx[1]

The Left, according to Fredric Jameson, had once a political project by the name of 'revolution'. No more. If that project is in shambles, the intellectual program of Left Critique is well and thriving. It got an impetus with the renewed interest in the French Revolution after its bicentennial in 1989. As the title of a book by Eric Hobsbawm in 1990 attests, there are 'Echoes of the Marseillaise', after 200 years, that are being heard louder, despite revisionist historians issuing its death certificate.[2]

The echoes of that revolutionary song did not penetrate the thick walls of the architecture academy. The logic of its pedagogy is well constructed against Revolution making sure that the echoes of that noisy song do not disturb its tranquility. In this work I challenge the conformist academic pedagogy and the *hegemonic apparatus*—a Gramscian term—abetting it from the outside. The distinct feature of the academic pedagogy is its regressive Romanticism, insofar as Romanticism is an anti-modernist attack on Enlightenment reason. This ideology is in conformity with the 'irrationality' of the global *postmodern* capitalism. I enter into a 'discursive struggle' with this academic discourse.[3] By deploying the notion of Critique I intend to rudely *awaken* the academy from its *dogmatic slumber*—invoking Kant's term—called 'critical criticism'. Here I confront 'criticism' with the conceptual resources in the idea of *Critique* for which Marx is the *only* source, insofar as the project of *Critique* must not only confront but overcome capital.

It is important to take Marx as *the* name for the completion of Enlightenment and the *unfinished* French Revolution. From the Enlightenment, the idea of critique was born, first with Kant and then Marx. In a specific sense, Marx is the continuation of Kantian critique, although he was 'rather ungenerous with Kant'.[4] If Marx, as we are told, is the 'child of the French Revolution',[5] then the *Critique* is his brainchild. Marx stands for what Jameson once characterized as the 'proletarian Enlightenment'.[6] The latter fulfills but goes beyond the 'bourgeois Enlightenment' that preceded it.[7] Accordingly, I propose to reconfigure a pedagogy that will find its resources in the Marxian legacy of the *proletarian* Enlightenment. After the miserable failure of Social Democracy and reformism and the defeat of the 'really existing socialism', the Left must stand for the 'Idea of communism'. The latter term is credible only if it 'returns to philosophy'. According to Agon Hamza, a 'return to philosophy' has 'a double role today: one, it is a means to reinvent the critical powers needed in order to transform the world; and two, it is the first movement of constructing something that has no place in our world'.[8] Going back to Marx's much misinterpreted 'eleventh thesis' on Feuerbach, that

'The philosophers have only *interpreted* the world in various ways; the point, however, is to change it', it must be said that the task of critique is to interpret the world in order to change it. In this sense, the architecture academy suffers from the 'poverty *of* philosophy', to paraphrase Marx's famous inversion of Monsieur Proudhon's *The Philosophy of Poverty* into *The Poverty of Philosophy*.[9] In this work, I allow the notion of 'poverty' to enter architecture discourse within the dialectic of *freedom* and *necessity*, first through Hegel's *Philosophy of Right* and then Marx's critique of it. As will become clear, one term emphatically occupies the center in this discourse: the Proletariat.

The notion of 'proletarian Enlightenment' is only an Idea, in the Hegelian sense. Its project remains unfinished. It should not therefore be *ontologized*. There cannot be a Left political project without this Idea. If it sounds *utopian*, it is only in the sense of *practical* utopia and not a utopian *fantasy*, which underpins all sorts of political-technological 'utopias' in *postmodern* global capitalism. It is in fact against the latter that I will invoke Walter Benjamin's famous 'pulling the emergency break' in order to derail the train of 'progress' heading headlong into a catastrophe. There is no *light* at the end of tunnel, for what we see, as Slavoj Žižek once put it, is actually the blinding light of the train speeding toward us from the opposite direction.

For reading Marx, I take Kojin Karatani's advice: 'It is crucial to read Marx's corpus as *critique*'.[10] It is this *critique* that I deploy to explore architecture's tangled relation with Revolution—(capital R) Revolution designating the French Revolution. This entanglement came to the consciousness of architecture at the moment when Le Corbusier in 1923 pronounced his famous declaration: 'Architecture or

Revolution'. Almost a century later, his 'defensible dilemma' has to be rendered *indefensible*. Therefore a central thesis the premise of which goes by this: *philosophy is an impulse to Revolution.* Critique is under the spell of this impulse. This thesis is indebted to Hegel who in his *Philosophy of History* wrote: 'We should not, therefore, contradict the assertion that the [French] Revolution received its first impulse from Philosophy'.[11] Here we must recall that Kant is named as *the* philosopher of the French Revolution. Recall the great poet Heinrich Heine, a friend of Marx and a fellow exile, who once said that 'Kant is our Robespierre'.

But *Why* Marx? And its corollary question: *Which* Marx? To the latter I come in a moment. A short answer to the former is simply this: *Marx is our contemporary.*[12] A longer version would go as follows: global capitalism has reached a stage of *barbarism* that *necessitates* a return to Marx. The co-authors of *Reading Marx*, a timely book, have suggested a tautology: instead of 'socialism or barbarism' the choice is now, sadly, between '(capitalist) barbarism or (barbaric) capitalism'.[13] To put it even more radically I would adopt Alain Badiou's words: 'As to barbarism, we are already there, and are rapidly going to sink further into it'.[14] Badiou reserves a short-hand definition for the contemporary capitalist regime: 'It is a regime of gangsters'. What else can it be called, Badiou asks, when the fate of people is entrusted to the 'financial appetites of a tiny oligarchy [...] whose only norms is profit'.[15] As the late Daniel Bensaïd in his *Marx for Our Time* wrote, more than 150 years have passed since the declaration of the *Communist Manifesto* but no 'specter of communism' haunts Europe anymore.[16] It has vanished from the scene behind the 'really-existing capitalism', and has been conjured away. But as Jacques Derrida in *Specters of Marx* wrote: 'Not without Marx, no future without Marx, without the memory and inheritance of Marx: in any case of a certain Marx, of his genius, of at least one of his spirits ... *there is more than one of them, there must be more than one of them*'.[17]

A *certain* Marx then, *one* of his *spirits* at least *must* come to haunt architecture. It must come to haunt an architecture that is exposed to capitalist *barbarism*. In this architecture has taken a specific but unmistakable form: the *barbarism of technological image* engendering a general *psychosis*. In this clinically incurable psychosis the *anaesthetization* of the subject is well accomplished and is total. It comes with its consequence: architecture is that *agency* which has emptied the subject of its *political* constitution. Unlike film in the early twentieth century that *caused* psychosis but also found its *cure*, as Benjamin memorably analyzed in 'The Work of Art in the Age of Its Technical Reproducibility', architecture cannot ever find its own cure for what it has caused in the subject. It is appropriate to cite the relevant passage from the 'second version' of the Artwork essay here:

> *If one considers the dangerous tension which technology and its consequences have engendered in the masses at large—tendencies which at critical stages take on a psychotic character—one also has to recognize that this same technologization [Technisiering] has created the possibility of psychotic immunization against such mass psychoses. It does so by means of certain films in which the forced development of sadistic fantasy or masochistic delusions can prevent their natural and dangerous maturation in the masses.* Collective laughter is one such preemptive and healing outbreak of mass psychosis.[18]

Such a possibility cannot be obtained in architecture. For this condition, a definition grounded in psychoanalytical theory may be suggested: Architecture has turned into the *jouissance of the mage*. The 'lust for image', a quintessentially capitalist property, is a 'cult' emanating from a *certain* religion, the *religion* of capitalism. Benjamin called it 'Capitalism as Religion'—the title of a short fragment he penned in 1921. It is a religion with no 'specific body of dogma, no theology', Benjamin wrote, but only a *utilitarianism* which 'acquires its religious overtones'.[19]

The 'criticism of religion', the young Marx said, 'is the premise of all criticism'. In 'A Contribution to the Critique of Hegel's *Philosophy of Right*—Introduction' he wrote:

> Man is *the world of man*, the state, society. This state and this society produce religion, which is an *inverted consciousness of the world*, because they are an *inverted world*. Religion is the generalized theory of this world, its encyclopedic compendium, its logic in popular term, its spiritualistic point d'honneur, its enthusiasm, its moral sanction, its solemn complement, its general ground of consolation and justification. It is the *fantastic realization* of the human essence inasmuch as the *human essence* possesses no true reality. The struggle against religion is therefore indirectly the struggle against *that world* whose spiritual *aroma* is religion.[20]

The next paragraph is an oft-cited one but much misinterpreted:

> *Religious* suffering is the *expression* of real suffering and at the same time the *protest* against real suffering. Religion is the sigh of the oppressed creature, the heart of a heartless world, as it is the spirit of spiritless conditions. It is the *opium*

of the people. The abolition of religion as people's *illusory* happiness is the demand for their *real* happiness. The demand to abandon illusions about their condition is a *demand to abandon a condition which requires illusions*. The criticism of religion is thus in *embryo a criticism of the vale of tears* whose *halo* is religion.[21]

Karatani offers a novel interpretation of this passage based on the Kantian difference between the 'theoretical reason' and the 'practical reason' and the primacy of the latter over the former. He thus points out that what Marx in essence is saying is that it is impossible to 'dissolve any religion unless the "real suffering" upon which every religion is based is dissolved. *There is no reason to criticize religion theoretically, because it can only be dissolved practically*' [emphasis mine].[22] Further, 'While philosophers of the Enlightenment criticize religion through reason', Marx had said that such a '*criticism of religion* has been essentially completed'.[23] Karatani remarks that 'Religion, albeit as *Schein*, has a certain necessity inasmuch as man is an existence of passivity (pathos); it functions "regulatively" as a protest against reality, if not a "constitution" of reality'.[24]

This confirms Benjamin's insight in what he said in 'Capitalism as Religion', in which in part he refutes Max Weber's argument in his *Protestant Ethics and the Spirit of Capitalism* to the effect that capitalism is not, 'a formation conditioned by religion', but rather, 'as a religious phenomenon' that 'serves essentially to allay the same anxieties, torments, and disturbances to which the so-called religion offered answers'.[25] Accordingly, I amend my claim above about the 'religion of the image' and its *cult* through the architectural agency. All these constitute a *Schein* of global capitalism and its 'New Spirit'. We might say that they are in fact the 'things-in themselves' of the world of capitalism, to put it in Kantian terms, or otherwise, they can be conceived as the Real of capitalism. In any case, architecture conceived as *Schein* in contemporary culture, *subjectifies* the Subject through the *logic of ideological fantasy*. This comes with its political consequences. In rare moments in the twentieth century certain intellectual attempts were made to *interrupt* this capitalist subjectivity, notably in the 1960s—and although laudable, they failed. Mainly because they lacked a conceptual category against this capitalist subjectivity. This category is the Idea of communism. Contrary to a common misreading, Marx never intended to project a utopian communist society into the future in which all forms of antagonisms and all variants of subjective and social alienations dissolved or went away, let alone for an 'ideal' to be superimposed on the 'reality'. Against this misunderstanding, we must recall the remarks Marx (with Engels) made in *German Ideology* which are unmistakably clear:

> Communism is for us not a *state of affairs* which is to be established, an *ideal* to which reality [will] have to adjust itself. We call communism the *real* movement which abolishes the present state of things. The conditions of this movement result from the now existing premise.[26]

Communism for Marx was not merely a historical necessity, but an ethical intervention.[27]

Projecting the category of 'communism' as a category of critique I commit a *salto mortale*—a fatal leap I am willing to take in this work. A tripartite structure of categories will constitute it, namely: *theory, critique,* and *ethics*. The kernel of this triadic structure is to be found in a famous passage that the young Marx wrote in the same work cited above:

> The weapon of criticism certainly cannot replace the criticism of weapons; material force must be overthrown by material force; but theory, too, becomes a material force once it seizes the masses. Theory is capable of seizing the masses once it demonstrates *ad hominem*, and it demonstrates *ad hominem* once it becomes radical. To be radical is to grasp matters at the root. But for man the root is man himself. The manifest proof of the radicalism of German theory, and thus of its practical energy, is the fact of its issuing from a resolute positive transcendence [*Aufhebung*] of religion. The critique of religion ends in the doctrine that man is the highest being for man; thus it ends hence with the categorical imperative to overthrow all conditions in which man is a debased, enslaved, neglected, contemptible being—conditions which cannot be better described than by the Frenchman's exclamation about a proposed tax on dogs: 'poor dogs! They want to treat you like men!'[28]

In this astonishing passage, the term 'categorical imperative' is borrowed from Kant. Stathis Kouvelakis, whose *Philosophy and Revolution* I will be following in this work, takes this passage to be a 'fine example of Marx's style' and offers his analysis:

> the contrast between the two parts of the sentence (almost without exception, commentators ignore the second) produces an irresistible effect of ironic distantiation that tempers the pathos created by evoking the categorical imperative—or, rather, encourages us to see in it less a first-person appropriation of Kantian humanism than a lucid acknowledgment

Apologue

> of the debt practical criticism owes the Enlightenment. This acknowledgment comes at the moment in which criticism realizes that its object has changed: from the critique of religion to that of law and politics, and also—let us not forget—from '*man* [as] an abstract being [*abstraktes Wesen*] encamped outside the world', a being [*Wesen*] who is, among other things, to that of the categorical imperative *à la* Kant, to the world of man, the state, society.[29]

And further,

> Let us also note that when he talks about 'positive abolition' of religion, Marx once again introduces the Hegelian theme of the superiority of the German *Aufklärung* to the French Enlightenment. The suggestion is that the French Enlightenment did not go beyond the unmediated negation of religion, because it was incapable of grasping religion's essential determinations in their internality. The balance of the text confirms this: Marx maintains that Luther and Reformation set the stage, theoretically and practically, for the moment of German philosophy, and puts the whole of this movement under the banner of the revolution.[30]

In the course of the investigation in this work I will take up the points Kouvelakis has brought up in Marx's passage. The triadic structure that I adopt forms a *Borromean Knot*—in Lacanian theory—that ties the categories of theory, critique, and ethics. Once it is brought to the order of thought, this structure will constitute an *epistemological break*—in the Althusserian sense of the term—with academic 'criticism', on the ruins of which I construct a new foundation for Marxian pedagogy of Critique.

I can now return to the second question posed above: '*Which* Marx'? First, I must reiterate the *twofold* return that structures the philosophical inquiry I undertake in this work, which is (1) a return to Marx and (2) a return to *critique*. The post-1960s discourse of criticism in architecture never offered a conception of 'critique' in its specific terms I explore here. Nor, for that matter, did any systematic reading of *Capital*. In the absence of this reading, the dominant pedagogy of criticism in the academy from the 1990s to the present accords with the 'deconstructive' movement of capitalism, exemplified in relativism, aesthetic affirmation of the present, empiricism, utilitarianism, and above all, passive-reactive *nihilism* in the service of the ideology of *normalization*. In the contemporary global-capitalist disorder, nihilism is confused with a new 'freedom'. The hedonistic culture in this notion of 'freedom' promotes all sorts of *transgressions*.[31] 'Permanent transgression' has become the norm legitimizing liberation from tradition and all kinds of constraints. 'Freedom' translates itself imperceptibly into a superego *obligation* to transgress, as Žižek notes.[32] Not only contemporary art but more determinately architecture has become the locus for exercising a *transgressive aesthetics*. I will explore the relation between this aestheticization, or '*sensibilization*' and 'moral' sentiments under the 'ethical critique' in this study.

The question after all boils down to this: 'Where do we stand today?' It is posed by the same co-authors of *Reading Marx*, and they offer a precise answer.[33] They indicate that in our present philosophical and political conjuncture, 'there is a conceptual need that is yet to be determined. A need for Marx'.[34] This is a need which compels us to return to Marx's oeuvre, as they like to emphasize. They leave no ambiguity that this return to Marx can only be a *philosophical one*, which means that the 'need for philosophy is directly related to the need for Marx'.[35] This is because the present historical situation has foreclosed all the possibilities of any *emancipatory* alternatives. In the present conjuncture, Marx has been repeatedly declared *dead*, in the same fashion that every decade Freud's work is pronounced dead. It is a tiring ritual that every once in a while Marx and Freud are 'proved' to be wrong. It is also customary that Marx is held responsible for the history of 'Marxism' and the tragic turn in twentieth-century 'communism'. We must recall the oft-quoted short memo that Marx handed to Paul Lafargue written in French: *Ce qu'il y a de certain c'est que moi, je ne suis pas Marxiste.* ('What is certain is that I am not a Marxist.') Thus Marx must be saved from his 'Marxism' which troubled the twentieth century so much—and still does. A project for which Engels carries a certain responsibility.

The authors of *Reading Marx* cite Lenin who in *State and Revolution* mocked those reactionary 'social chauvinists' who presented themselves as emancipators, who 'are now Marxists (do not laugh!)'. It is that Marx was suspended of his radicality. Marx became 'canonized, a sacred name'. They further note that

> The transformation of 'Marx' into 'Saint Marx' consequently manifested itself in the form of a harmless idolatry that, for Lenin, enabled the gathering of the political groups around his name that have no real connection whatsoever to the idea of emancipation or revolution.[36]

Once again, in the manner of Lenin in *State and Revolution*, it seems imperative that the name Marx be 'de-sacralized' in order to bring out the relevance of his thought to the specific situation in our present conjuncture. The truth of his name can be restored if

> it becomes effective as a truth of this specific concrete and singularly historical situation [...] This means not judging the validity of Marx from the perspective of the historical situation, but demonstrating the validity of a Marxist perspective for a singular situation. The principle is thus not what Marx is as seen through the eyes of the situation, but what the situation is as seen through the eyes of Marx.[37]

This is a 'methodological' advice I will be taking in 'judging the validity of Marx' for a critique of state of architecture and its pedagogy in the present conjuncture but with specific reference to Revolution.

It is instructive to compare our present situation, as the co-authors of *Reading Marx* further point out, with the period in the 1960s

> when Marxism was still an integral and constitutive element of philosophical, political, and cultural debate, an element whose relevance and scope were also supposed to be constantly reassigned within, and through, the historical practice and debates that reflected on and directed it. This is no longer the case.[38]

We must recall the famous intellectual circle formed around Louis Althusser at the prestigious École Normale Supérieure in Paris, whose intellectual work resulted in the collection entitled *Reading Capital*. Today's task of philosophical reinterpretation of Marx, we are reminded, is happening outside the academic institutional supports that once it enjoyed. But

Apologue

the result is no less impressive. It is the *philosophical* reading of Marx that constitutes this continuity, notwithstanding the fact that the co-authors of *Reading Marx* take an exception to Althusser's problematic notion of 'science' and his entrenched position in Spinozan philosophy coupled with his anti-Hegelianism. But Althusser taught us a valuable lesson: that there is a philosophical foundation in the *Capital* that has to be reconstructed. His notable contribution to this was his conception of '*symptomatic*' reading. In *Reading Capital* he noted: 'But as there is no such thing as an innocent reading, we must say what reading we are guilty of'.[39] An important lesson in the applied methodology of the symptomatic reading consists in the fact that in every text there is a 'repressed' element that returns that must be subsequently reconstructed. This reconstruction constitutes *the unconscious of the text itself*. Althusser was, of course, indebted to Jacques Lacan who was in the same circle at the École Normale Supérieure. It was Lacan who first said that Marx, long before Freud, was the inventor of 'Symptom'. As the work of Slavoj Žižek has abundantly shown, the psychoanalytical theory is now an integral part of any 'new' reading of Marx.

In this book, I will be following the same *philosophical* reading of Marx from Althusser to our radical thinkers today. This reading is the foundation on which I base the notion of Critique, which is directed, as I stated above, against the practice of 'criticism' in the academy. Here I would like to recall the subtitle Marx and Engels added to their *The Holy Family* which reads '*Or Critique of Critical Criticism*'—intended as a sarcastic polemic against the Young Hegelians, notably Bruno Bauer among them, a former friend of Marx, that was addressed to the German academy at that time. I use the same phrase in my confrontation with the architecture academy in our time. What is called 'critical theory' and 'criticism' in the discipline—with no noticeable ground in the tradition of the Critical Theory of the Frankfurt School—is no more than a facile use of 'criticism' which takes pleasure in the '*tranquility of knowledge*', to invoke the phrase in *The Holy Family*. This 'tranquility' in the intellectual comfort zone of our architecture academy which has yet to be disturbed.

According to Karatani, 'Critique is impossible without moves'.[40] For the task at hand, the critique must move in multiple directions. In one direction it moves toward a *philosophical* reading of Marx integrated into German Idealism, mainly Kant and Hegel. And in other direction, it moves toward a reading of Marx that must be integrated in psychoanalytical theory in Freud and Lacan. A *transcendental* frame marks and unifies these moves. It frames the *condition of the possibility of critique*. Our radical thinkers remind us that if we are to understand Marx's *Capital* we have to first understand Hegel's *Science of Logic*—no doubt a daunting task. Žižek among them has made an astonishing remark in his *Like a Thief in Broad Daylight* that must be taken seriously. He writes:

> As for the relationship between Hegel's *Logic* and Marx's *Capital*, we should not be sentimental and awed by Lenin's statement that anyone who didn't read Hegel's *Logic* cannot understand *Capital*: Lenin himself read Logic but he didn't really understood it (his limit was the category of *Wechselwirkung* [meaning 'interaction', 'reciprocity', 'correlation', or 'interplay'], plus he didn't really understand *Capital*. Here one should be precise: what Lenin did not understand was the—let's risk this term—'transcendental' dimension of Marx's critique of political economy, the fact that Marx's *Critique of Political Economy* is not just a critical analysis of

economics but simultaneously a kind of transcendental form which enables us to articulate the basic contours of the entire social being (inclusive of ideology) in capitalism.[41]

In this work, I am willing to take the same *risk* and heed Žižek's call for this 'transcendental form', on which I venture to base the philosophical understanding of the conception of Critique. Marx's *Critique of Political Economy* will occupy the center of this conception. In this sense, Marx's *critique* must perhaps be considered to be a *fourth* Critique after Kant's three *Critiques*.[42]

Taking up Marx for my critical investigation in this work will result in a general thesis that I name 'philosophy of shelter'; the last part of the book is devoted to its explication. Underlying it will be the conviction that the academy by betraying the 1968 radical moment has *also* betrayed the legacy of the French Revolution as the founding moment of our modernity and democratic idea, which amounts to the *non-knowledge* of the dialectic of the Enlightenment. Immanuel Wallerstein once said, that 'The post-1789 consensus on the normality of change and the institutions it bred has now at last ended perhaps. Not in 1917, however, but rather in 1968'. He further notes that 'If we are to clarify our options and our utopias in the post-1968 world system, perhaps it would be useful to reread the trinitarian slogan of the French Revolution: liberty, equality, fraternity'.[43] Jameson, for his part, would say that *utopia* must perhaps be constructed on the same Marxian 'proletarian Enlightenment' mentioned above.

Notes

1 In Karl Marx, *Critique of Hegel's 'Philosophy of Right'* (Cambridge: Cambridge University Press, 1970), 137.

Apologue

2 I am referring to E.J. Hobsbawm, *Echoes of the Marseillaise: Two Centuries Look Back on the French Revolution* (London and New York: Verso, 1990).

3 I adopt the term 'discursive struggle' that Fredric Jameson uses and attributes to Stuart Hall; see Fredric Jameson, 'An American Utopia', in *An American Utopia: Dual Power and the Universal Army*, ed. Slavoj Žižek (London and New York: Verso, 2016). Jameson explains: 'Discursive struggle—a phrase that originated in the defeat of the Thatcher years and the interrogations around the victory—discursive struggle posited the process whereby slogans, concepts, stereotype, and accepted wisdoms did battle among each other for preponderance, which is to say, in the quaint language of that day and age, hegemony', 6.

4 Here I am following the incisive argument by Kojin Karatani in his *Nation and Aesthetics: On Kant and Freud* (New York: Oxford University Press, 2017); see the chapter on 'Transcritique on Kant and Freud'.

5 See Sven-Eric Liedman, *A World to Win: The Life and Works of Karl Marx* (London and New York: Verso, 2018), 21.

6 See Fredric Jameson, 'An American Utopia', in *An American Utopia: Dual Power and the Universal Army*.

7 In my use of these terms I am following Fredric Jameson in his provocative 'An American Utopia', in *An American Utopia: Dual Power and the Universal Army*. Jameson writes that Marx's critique of what Adorno and Horkheimer called 'instrumentalization' must not be confused with the reactionary anti-modernist attack on the Enlightenment.

8 See Agon Hamza's 'From the Other Scene to the Other State: Jameson's Dialectic of Dual Power', in *An American Utopia: Dual Power and the Universal Army*, 150.

9 In this I am following Hamza in his 'From the Other Scene to the Other State: Jameson's Dialectic of Dual Power', in *An American Utopia: Dual Power and the Universal Army*.

10 See Kojin Karatani, *Transcritique: On Kant and Marx*, trans. Sabu Kohso (Cambridge: The MIT Press, 2005), 134. I come back to this seminal text in later chapters in this book.

11 See G.W.F. Hegel, *Philosophy of History*, intro. C.J. Friedrich (Dover: New York: 1956), 446. For a comprehensive extension of Hegel's assertion see Stathis Kouvelakis, *Philosophy and Revolution, from Kant to Marx* (London and New York: Verso, 2003). See also Steven B. Smith, 'Hegel and the French Revolution: An Epitaph for Republicanism', in *French Revolution and the Birth of Modernity*, ed. Ference Feher (Berkeley: University of California

Apologue

> Press, 1990). Also see the book by Geoff Mann, *In the Long Run We Are All Dead: Keynesianism, Political Economy, Revolution* (London and New York: Verso, 2017). I will discuss the latter book extensively in later chapters of this book.

12 For my reasoning and what follows I am following Žižek, Ruda, and Hamza in their *Reading Marx* (Cambridge: Polity, 2018).

13 Žižek, Ruda, Hamza, in their *Reading Marx*, 10.

14 Alain Badiou, *The Rebirth of History: Times of Riots and Uprisings* (London and New York: Verso, 2012), 14.

15 Alain Badiou, *The Rebirth of History*, 12.

16 See Daniel Bensaïd, *Marx for Our Time: Adventures and Misadventures of a Critique*, trans. Gregory Eliott (London and New York, 2009), see 'Preface to the English Translation: Archipelago of a Thousand Marxisms'.

17 See Jacques Derrida, *Specters of Marx: The State of the Debt, the Work of Mourning, and the New International*, trans. Peggy Kamuf, intro. Bernard Magnus and Stephen Cullenberg (New York and London: Routledge, 1994), 13. Also see Daniel Bensaïd, *Marx for Our Time*.

18 Walter Benjamin, 'The Work of Art in the Age of Its Technological Reproducibility, second version', in *Walter Benjamin: Selected Writings, vol. 3, 1935–1938*, ed. Michael W. Jennings (Cambridge: The Belknap Press of the Harvard University Press, 2002), 118.

19 Walter Benjamin, 'Capitalism as Religion', in *Walter Benjamin, Selected Writings, Volume 1, 1913–1926* (Cambridge: The Belknap Press of Harvard University Press), 288.

20 Karl Marx, 'A Contribution to the Critique of Hegel's "Philosophy of Right": Introduction', in *Karl Marx: Selected Writings*, ed. Lawrence H. Simon (Indianapolis: Hackett, 1994), 28. For a slightly different translation see 'A Contribution to the Critique of Hegel's "Philosophy of Right": Introduction', in Karl Marx, *Critique of Hegel's 'Philosophy of Right'*, ed. and intro. Joseph O'Malley (Cambridge: Cambridge University Press, 1970).

21 Karl Marx, 'A Contribution to the Critique of Hegel's "Philosophy of Right": Introduction', 28.

22 See Kojin Karatani, *Architecture as Metaphor, Language, Number, Money*, trans. Sabu Kohso, ed. Michael Speaks (Cambridge: The MIT Press, 1995), 186.

23 Kojin Karatani, *Architecture as Metaphor, Language, Number, Money*, 186.

24 Kojin Karatani, *Architecture as Metaphor, Language, Number, Money*, 186–187.

25 Walter Benjamin, 'Capitalism as Religion', 288.
26 Karl Marx with Friedrich Engels, *The German Ideology: Includes Theses on Feuerbach and Introduction to the Critique of Political Economy* (New York: Prometheus Books, 1998), 57.
27 For more on this point see Kojin Karatani, *Transcritique: On Kant and Marx* (Cambridge: The MIT Press, 2005).
28 See Karl Marx, 'Critique of Hegel's "Philosophy of Right"', 137.
29 Stathis Kouvelakis, *Philosophy and Revolution*, 323.
30 Stathis Kouvelakis, *Philosophy and Revolution*, 323.
31 Here I am following Slavoj Žižek's diagnostic assessment of the present situation in his recent *Like a Thief in Broad Daylight: Power in the End of Post-Humanity* (UK: Allen Lane, 2018), see specially the 'Introduction'.
32 In Slavoj Žižek's 'Introduction' to his *Like a Thief in Broad Daylight.*
33 See Žižek, Ruda and Hamza, *Reading Marx* (Cambridge: Polity 2018).
34 Žižek, Ruda and Hamza, *Reading Marx*, 3.
35 Žižek, Ruda and Hamza, *Reading Marx*, 3.
36 Žižek, Ruda and Hamza, *Reading Marx*, 5.
37 Žižek, Ruda and Hamza, *Reading Marx*, 7.
38 Žižek, Ruda and Hamza, *Reading Marx*, 7.
39 See Althusser et al., *Reading Capital: The Complete Edition* (London and New York: Verso, 2015), 12; also see *Reading Marx*, 12.
40 See Kojin Karatani, 'Critique is impossible without moves', An Interview with Kojin Karatani by Joel Wainwright, in *Human Geography*, 2012, 2 (1).
41 Slavoj Žižek's, *Like a Thief in Broad Daylight*, 217.
42 For this point see Kojin Karatani, *Transcritique: On Kant and Marx*, especially the chapter on 'Transcritique'. I will deal with this seminal work extensively in later chapters of this book.
43 See Immanuel Wallerstein, 'The French Revolution as a World-Historical System', in *The French Revolution and the Birth of Modernity*, ed. Ference Fehér (Berkeley: University of California Press, 1990), 130.

Exordium

Learning from Valéry reading Marx

Paul Valéry in one of his extensive correspondences with his life-time friend André Gide wrote the following on 11 May 1918 that I quote in part.

> Last night reread… (a little…) *Das Kapital!* I am one of the rare men who has read it. It seems that even [Jean]
> Jaurès himself …[1]
> While I was reading it, I worked up an article on the side.
> Which makes the third in two weeks. An article in the mind—that is, a five-and-ten article.
> One on the *Mémoire Lichnowski*. The other on a masterpiece that I once read a great deal, and the author of which has just been made a member of the Academy of Science. It is M. Koenigs. I could see in it a method for *Le Mercure*. One day I'll talk to you about that little book, which I value tremendously—and have for the last ten years.
> As for *Das Kapital*, that fat book contains very remarkable things. One has only to find them. It shows a rather heavy-handed pride. Is often very inadequate as far as rigor is concerned, or very pedantic for nothing, but certain analyses are

terrific. I mean that the manner of grasping things is similar to the one I use rather often, and that I can translate rather often his language into mine. The objective is of no importance, and at bottom it's the same.[2]

How would Valéry 'translate' the language of *Das Kapital* 'rather often' into his own? In his 'Reflections on Art', in a highly didactic style but perhaps not 'very pedantic', he wrote:

After all, a work of art is an object, a human product, made with a view to affecting certain individuals in a certain way. Works of art are either objects in the material sense of the term, or sequences of acts, as in the case of drama or dance, or else summations of successive impressions that are also produced by acts, as in music. We may attempt to define our notion of art by an analysis based on these objects, which may be taken as the only positive elements in our investigations: considering these objects and progressing on the one hand to their authors and on the other hand to those whom they affect, we find that the phenomenon of art can be represented by two quite distinct transformations. (*We have here the same relation as that which prevails in economics between production and consumption.*) [emphasis mine].

What is extremely important is to note that these two transformations—the author's modification of the *manufactured objects* and the change which the object or work brings about in the consumer—are quite independent. It follows that *we should always consider them separately.*

Any proposition involving all three terms, an author, a work, a spectator or listener, is meaningless—for you will never find all three terms united in observation.[3]

And further:

> I shall go further—and here I come to a point you will no doubt find strange and paradoxical, if you have not come to that conclusion about what I have already said: art as *value* (for basically, we are studying a problem of value) depends essentially on this nonidentification, this need for an intermediary between producer and consumer. It is essential that there should be something irreducible between them, that there should be no direct communication, and that the work, the medium, should not give the person it affects anything that can be reduced to an idea of the author's person and thinking.[4]

Valéry undoubtedly would not have come to his notion of art as '*value*', or the 'problem of value'—or the 'value form', to put it more accurately—if not through his reading of *Capital*.[5] I imagine he would have brought to Gide's attention the following passage from the 'Chapter 1: The Commodity' in *Capital*:

> Men do not therefore bring the products of their labour into relation with each other as values because they see these objects merely as the material integuments of homogenous human labour. The reverse is true: by equating their different products to each other in exchange as values, they equate their different kinds of labour as human labour. They do this without being aware of it. Value, therefore, does not have its description branded on its forehead; it rather transforms every product of labour into a *social hieroglyphic*. Later on, men try to decipher the hieroglyphic, to get behind the *secret* of their own social product: for the characteristic which objects of utility have of being values is as much man's social product as is their language.[6] [emphasis mine]

On a similar path, if the architect had picked up *Capital* for a reading as Valéry did, he might have arrived at a certain notion of 'building' as '*value form*', on 'the same relation as that which prevails in economics between production and consumption' in the era of capitalism. The critic would have to conceive it as a 'social hieroglyphic'. The architect could have tried to translate Marx's language into his own, similar to what Valéry attempted to do. But there is absolutely no evidence that the architect ever did, or had any inclination to do so, for that matter. He is oblivious of the Marxian notion of 'value' in the bourgeois society to which he renders his service. Not being schooled in critical philosophy and radical social theory, or critique of political economy, the whole thing remains a mystery to the architect. This is nothing short of *poverty of philosophy* in architectural thinking. And the architect is its *subjective* agency. But the architect-critic must be told what Marx wrote at the end of his '*Preface*' to the 'Critique of Political Economy'. There, reflecting on his own view on the realm of political economy as 'the result of conscientious and lengthy research', he made the extraordinary remark that 'over the entrance to science, as over the entrance to hell, this demand must be registered':

> Here you must leave all wariness behind;
> All traces of cowardice must be extinguished.
> (Dante, *The Divine Comedy*, III. 14–15)[7]

This demand must not escape the architect-critic upon the entry to the architecture academy no matter whether it is an entrance to science or an entrance to hell. In any event, it is the demanding lesson of '*value form*' for a *labor theory of building*, that must not fail to be registered by a 'conscientious and lengthy research'. This book begins with this Exordium taking Marx's dictum of *extinguishing all traces of cowardice*—rampant in the discipline—seriously.

Etymologically, the word 'exordium' means 'beginning of a discourse', from Latin *exordiri*, formed of, *ex + ordiri*, related to *ordo*, Order.[8] It means 'a beginning to a discourse or composition'. Accordingly, I begin with a lengthy exploration on Marxian pedagogy on *critique* and its 'uses' in the critique of architecture that will lead to a discourse on the 'Philosophy of Shelter' composed as a Treatise with which I end the investigation in this work.

Notes

1 Jean Jaurès (1859–1914) was the head of the Socialist Party in France from 1905 until his assassination in 1914. He remains an important historical figure of the French Left. See *Self-Portrait: The Gide/Valéry Letters 1890–1942*, ed. Robert Mallet, abridged and trans. June Guicharnaud (Chicago and London: The University of Chicago Press, 1966), 290–291. The ellipses (…) in front of Jaurès's name must be read as '[has not read it]'. This Exordium is informed by my reading of Kojin Karatani's seminal book, *Transcritique: on Kant and Marx* (Cambridge: The MIT Press, 2005), where Karatani mentions the book of correspondences between Valéry and Gide, 339, n. 18.
2 See *Self-Portrait: The Gide/Valéry Letters 1890–1942*, 290–291.
3 Quoted in Kojin Karatani, *Transcritique: On Kant and Marx*, 232–233. Also see Paul Valéry, *Aesthetics*, trans. Ralph Manheim (New York: Pantheon, 1964), 142–143.
4 Kojin Karatani, *Transcritique: On Kant and Marx*, 233.
5 Karatani comments that Valéry points to the 'ultimate ground upon which the value of artwork arises in the separation of two processes (production and consumption), and the impenetrability of the gap'. Karatani points out further that the target of Valéry's critique is 'evidently Hegelian aesthetics, which stands in the position to subsume both processes, and claims that history has no opacity', in Kojin Karatani, *Transcritique: On Kant and Marx*, 233.

6 See Karl Marx, *Capital, Volume 1* (London: Penguin, 1976), 167.
7 Karl Marx, 'A Contribution to the Critique of Political Economy—Preface', in *Marx, Later Political Writings*, ed. Terrell Carver (Cambridge: Cambridge University Press, 1996), 162.
8 From *The Oxford Dictionary of English Etymology*.

Critical pedagogy

Architecture or Revolution

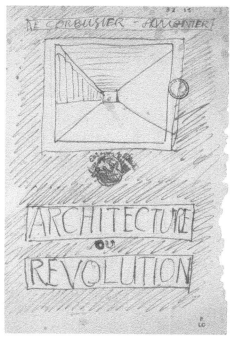

Figure 0.1 Le Corbusier, *Sketch for book cover with the working title 'ARCHITECTURE OU RÉVOLUTION'*, 1923. Credit: © F.L.C. / ADAGP, Paris / Artists Rights Society (ARS), New York 2019

Figure 0.2 Le Corbusier: *Publicity Flyer for VERS UNE ARCHITECTURE, 1923*. Credit: © F.L.C. / ADAGP, Paris / Artists Rights Society (ARS), New York 2019

In a moment in 1923 the specter of revolution had to be conjured away. Le Corbusier, the 'architect of the century', titled the last chapter of his *Vers une architecture* as 'Architecture ou Révolution', a phrase that was originally envisioned to be the title of his book.[1] He famously ended the book by a rhetorical declaration:

Architecture or Revolution.
Revolution can be avoided.

The last chapter of the book begins with this declaration: '*it is a question of building that is key to the equilibrium upset today: 'Architecture or revolution'*.[2] The penultimate chapter entitled 'Mass Production Housing' had already ended with a 'Conclusion' that runs as follows:

> What is in question is a problem of the era. More than that: *the* problem of the era. Social equilibrium is a question of building. We conclude with this defensible dilemma: *Architecture or Revolution.*[3]

With an obsessive habit of repeating his declarations, Le Corbusier leaves no doubt that 'revolution' is not a solution. Rather, it is *building* that is the saving agency of '*social equilibrium*'. A propaganda leaflet for *l'Esprit nouveau* had been issued in which the forthcoming publication of '*Architecture ou Révolution*' (1922) had been announced. There he warned the reader: 'the housing shortage will lead to revolution. Be alert to housing'.[4] He further noted: 'There are too many wretched, disgraceful, scandalous neighborhoods in old cities, which are worm-eaten and impossible to disinfect'.[5]

In his mind, achieving an 'architectural revolution' would render revolution *unnecessary*. But, just what 'revolution', we might ask, did he have in mind that could be 'avoided'? Was it the 'bourgeois' revolution or the 'proletarian' revolution? Did he mean *political* revolution or *social* revolution? If he had in mind the French Revolution, was it the 'mild' moment of 1789, or the Terror of 1792–1794? Whatever is the case, let us imagine him sitting in the crowd and listening to the exasperated Robespierre who in a heated moment during the French Revolution asked the bourgeois convention of 1792: 'Citizens! Would you have a revolution without revolution?'[6] I am fashioning this scene on the model described by Geoff Mann in his book on John Maynard Keynes. Mann contemplates that not just Keynes himself but all the 'Keynesians' born before him, who heard Robespierre, thought to themselves: 'Yes, actually. That sounds just right'.[7] I want to suggest that, analogically, not only the *citizen* Le Corbusier but all 'Corbusians' before and after him, would similarly think to themselves to say the same: 'Yes—actually, that sounds just right, count us in'! Later in Chapter 2 I will bring out certain confluences of ideas, linked to revolution, between Le Corbusier and Keynes.

Le Corbusier thought to himself that industrial capitalism *in potentia* alone is able to make 'An Architecture' possible. In *Toward An Architecture* he wrote: '*if we set ourselves against the past, there is revolution in the methods and the magnitude of enterprises*'.[8] Further he said: '*In every domain of industry, new problems have been posed, tools capable of solving them have been created. If we set this fact against the past, there is revolution*'.[9] In other words, as Mann puts it in the case of Keynes, equally applicable to our architect, all that is needed is a 'problem solver's intuition' combined with 'wise expert administration'. 'An Architecture' can build this new brave world that is radically different from what we had in the past. The problem of the past, for Le Corbusier, was, of course, the problem of the past 'styles'. He said: '*If we set ourselves against the past, we determine that the "style" no longer exists for us, that the style of an era has been elaborated; there has been a revolution*'.[10]

It was, therefore, an '*architecture révolution sans révolution*' Le Corbusier was contemplating. From this I draw a central thesis which goes as follows: Not just in the moment of 1923, but in the entire epoch of liberal capitalist modernity, a latent '*architecture sans révolution*' is the operative axiom. Which means that in this era, architecture *disavows* Revolution—(capital-R) Revolution is used for the French Revolution. Le Corbusier's 'defensible dilemma' is to be rendered *indefensible:*

Architecture or Revolution.
Yes, Please!

Dismissing his rhetorical declaration is a reminder to our Architect that he owes his *modernity* to the French Revolution. In this book, I contend that the critique of architecture in the epoch of liberal capitalist modernity must begin with an *affirmation:* the French Revolution is the founding moment of our modernity. This thesis is grounded in speculative thought that moves between the poles of *freedom* and *necessity*. Hegel in *Philosophy of History* put forward the view that 'Reason governs the world, and has subsequently governed its history' and claimed that 'The Union of Universal Abstract Existence generally with the Individual—the Subjective—that this alone is Truth, belongs to the department of speculation, and is treated in this general form in Logic'.[11] He then crucially noted:

The question also assumes the form of the union of *Freedom* and *Necessity*; the latent abstract process of Spirit being regarded as *Necessity* while that which exhibits itself in the conscious will of man, as their interest, belongs to the domain of *Freedom*.[12]

In Marxian terms, Le Corbusier must be understood to be a figure in the lineage of the bourgeois 'myth of the savior from on high'[13] built upon the infrastructure of private property and the laws of the capitalist economy grounded in the 'kingdom of necessity' in a dialectical conflict with the 'kingdom of freedom'.[14] 'Saint' Le Corbusier is an embodiment of this 'myth of the savior' filled with a demiurgic drive to save architecture from revolution by *revolutionizing* it. He indeed succeeded—in spite of his detractors. But, within the political and economic imperatives of liberal capitalism on which he—as an 'intellectual' architect, as Manfredo Tafuri called him—could not exert any *control*. His *success* was bound to end in *failure*. His 'revolution' failed to meet its objectives. His Project ran into conflict with basic imperatives of liberal capitalism. It left him disillusioned in the years that followed the 1920s. It was the revolution's failure that failed him. This is nothing short of being *tragic*, an 'architectural tragedy' we might say, ensuing on the political tragedy. Paradoxically, in the dialectic between *necessity* and *freedom*, Le Corbusier, the 'revolutionary' architect, in one respect and unwittingly, or rather oddly, comes close to the revolutionary Robespierre whom every bourgeois liberal, Republican or reactionary, loves to hate. This statement would come as a surprise to Le Corbusier's detractors and admirers both. As for Robespierre, in respect of the rights of the *sans-culottes* that were the *necessity* of 'dress, food and the reproduction of their species', the foundation of freedom had to be abandoned, so for

Le Corbusier, in respect of the right to the *necessity* of 'shelter'—with which he was passionately concerned—the foundation of freedom in political revolution had to be sacrificed: 'revolution', therefore, 'can be avoided'. Not *freedom* but rather the *happiness of the people* for which the revolution had to change its direction. Le Corbusier took this direction. He was not a *fool* himself, but he might have been the fool of history. Nor was he a conservative, or a reactionary, or a reformist—contrary to what we are told by our 'radicals' in the discipline. Instead, it is more pertinent, as I suggest, that we scrutinize him under the notion of Bonapartism, as I will explain in the next chapter.

We might find certain affinities between Le Corbusier and Saint Simonians. The word 'industrialist' was the word coined by Saint-Simon. The 'industrialists' were 'productive entrepreneurs', bankers, scientists, technologists, artists, and intellectuals, but also laboring people. It is significant that, as Eric Hobsbawm notes, Saint-Simon's doctrines 'attack poverty and social inequality, while he totally rejects the French Revolution's principles of liberty and equality'.[15] While the 'industrialists' are technocratic planners they 'oppose not only the idle and parasitic ruling classes, but also the anarchy of bourgeois-liberal capitalism'[16] of which Saint-Simon provides an earliest critique. The Swiss architectural historian Sigfried Giedion, a fellow traveler of Le Corbusier, in 1928 wrote that: 'INDUSTRY anticipates society's inner upheaval just as construction anticipates the future expression of building'.[17] He further pointed out that

> Even before industry existed in the present sense—around 1820—Henri de Saint-Simon (1760–1825) understood that it was the central concept of the century and that it was destined to turn life inside out: 'The Whole of society rests upon industry'.[18]

Giedion surmised that

> the force of Saint-Simon's influence on the school and tendencies of the century lay, above all, in his ability to grasp the emerging reality and to transform it into a utopia. It is the opposite method to the cultural idealism that dominated Germany at the time, which neglected reality in order to pursue emanations of pure spirit.[19]

He further remarks that

> Saint-Simon foresaw the great concentrations of labor, the urban centers, and the factories with thousands of workers and transferred the result of research directly into action. As a consequence of an industrial economy he foresaw the dawn of a classless society, the end of war, and the end of national borders: a single army of workers spanning the globe. The end of man's exploitation of man (*l'exploitation de l'homme par l'homme*) will have been achieved.[20]

Giedion is quick to remind us that, 'The eye of the visionary no doubt simplifies and leaps over intermediary stages: Saint Simon never reckoned with the century's divided soul, which in architecture as in society imposed the old formal apparatus on the new system'. And further, 'The anonymous process of production and the interconnected procedures that industry offers only now fully take hold of and reshape our nature'.[21]

The influence of Saint-Simon on 'pre-Marx socialism' has been noted. Giedion's remarks in the block quotation above is a page taken from Friedrich Engels's *Anti-Dühring* book. Engels wrote that 'in Saint-Simon we find the breath of view of genius, thanks to which almost all ideas of later socialists, which are not strictly economic, are contained in his work in embryo'.[22] The 'exploitation of man by man' is a Saint-Simonian phrase.[23] 'Implicit in him', Hobsbawm remarks, 'is the recognition that industrialization is fundamentally incompatible with an unplanned society'.[24] A consistent doctrine underlies the 'theory of industrial revolution' that 'productive industry' must make the 'productive elements in society into its social and political controllers' that would shape the future of society.[25] In this we might recognize Le Corbusier's obsession with the 'plan' and the French term '*planisme*', fashionable terms in the 1930s, which would later prompt Georges Bataille to take an interest in our Architect.[26]

But I am not interested in dwelling more than this on the tired subject of 'affiliation' between Le Corbusier and Saint-Simon, nor am I interested in a hagiography of Le Corbusier in this work. Rather, my intention is to confine him to the problematic of the failed political revolution in his time and see him as a representative of the transformation of a thought when it was stripped of its historical necessity and energy. He is a representative of the shift in the conception of historical possibility and the limits of historical agency that makes room for an *architectural agency*. Le Corbusier is the *name* for this architectural agency in the twentieth century. He *revolutionized architecture without revolution*. Even the architects in the Soviet Union looked at him as a model to emulate, in spite of the fact that he was scornful of them.[27]

We must therefore consider Le Corbusier's declaration in the context of the failed revolution of 1918–1920 in Europe, exactly at a time when liberal-industrial capitalism needed an architectural 'revolution' to avoid a political revolution. The following is a concise account by John Willet of the dominant situation of the period in question in Europe:

By the end of 1920, at the latest, it was evident that their hopes of a genuine social revolution extending beyond Russia's borders would not yet be realized. The Spartacist revolt in January 1919 was stillborn, a defeat paid for with the death of Karl Liebknecht, Rosa Luxemburg and Leo Jogiches, assassinated by the Freikorps ['Free Crops'—German rightwing militia and mercenary group in Berlin] with official complaisance. In May, the Bavarian Soviet Republic was crushed by government troops and their allies in the Freikorps: the anarchist scholar Gustave Landauer was beaten to death; Toller and his fellow-poet Erich Mühsam ended up in prison. A month later, in Vienna, a smaller small-scale Communist insurrection was put down; those arrested included the journalist Egon Erwin Kisch, the former commandant of the Red Guard. Without the support from Austria or southern Germany, and withdrawing from Slovakia, in August Hungary's revolutionary government fell to an invading force of White Hungarians, Romanians and French. There followed a White Terror, and in November Admiral Horthy was appointed regent, acting for a king who did not exist. Things did not turn much better for the Russians. In June 1920 their ill-judged attack on Warsaw failed, apparently because Polish workers were not disposed to support it. The International and German Communist leadership embarked on further fruitless actions in the autumn of 1923, but for others it was not hard to see that the revolution was over...

...while, at the Bauhaus, Gropius, who in Spring 1920 was proposing a monument to the nine workers killed in the resistance to the Kapp putsch, chose henceforward to refuse all political commitment—which of course did not stop reactionaries from associating him and his school with the cause of the republic and revolution.[28]

It is significant that Le Corbusier added the last chapter to *Vers une architecture*, the only chapter that had not previously appeared in his journal *L'Esprit nouveaux*. In the dialectics between the bourgeois Stability *and* 'violence' of Revolution, Le Corbusier chose the *synthesis of architecture*.

Le Corbusier stands for an 'architectural revolution' in the era of liberal-capitalist modernity, however, *unrealizable, unfulfillable and unachievable*. To assess Le Corbusier's unique position, he must be saved from two opposing camps: from those who enthusiastically canonize him into 'Saint Le Corbusier' in their various hagiographies, *and* from those who are too eager to heap scorn on him for his alleged reactionary 'political' missteps and 'faulty' architectural schemes, or distrusting him for serving the 'elite managerialism' of the industrial capitalism. Against both camps, we must instead locate him in the actual *conflictual avant-garde moment* in the twentieth century. Walter Benjamin memorably captured this moment when in his *The Arcades Project* he wrote: 'To encompass both Breton and Le Corbusier—that would mean drawing the spirit of contemporary France like a bow, with which knowledge shoots the moment in the heart'.[29] This 'spirit of contemporary France', we must note, has deep roots in the legacy of the French Revolution. Not only Le Corbusier but our own generation is its heir. Moreover, Le Corbusier belongs to that moment of thought in the early twentieth century that Benjamin analyzed in his important essay 'Experience and Poverty' written in 1933.[30]

The name Le Corbusier must *also* be considered in a historical trajectory that I label as 'Corbusianism' whose genealogy goes back to the Second Empire under Napoleon III. This is a lineage that continues to our present moment in the twenty-first century, under a political system that I will call Neo-Bonapartism—a *bourgeois* absolutism ruling under the 'absolute monarchy of capital', to use Kojin Karatani's apt term. I explore this genealogy in Chapter 2.

Freedom is the founding principle of modernity. Le Corbusier was *thinking* in the terms of *emancipatory modernity* when in the beginning of the last chapter of *Vers une architecture* he wrote an aphoristic sentence that might seem trivial, even crude in its simplicity, but which is never submitted to a critical scrutiny. He wrote: '*It is a primal instinct of every living being to ensure a shelter*'. This dictum would bring Le Corbusier in proximity to Robespierre, unwittingly, as I suggested above. In this respect it is appropriate to recall what Heinrich Heine memorably wrote:

> Life is neither end nor means; life is a right. Life wants to enforce its right against the cold hand of death, against the past, and this enforcement is revolution. The elegiac indifference of historians and poets shall not paralyse our energies as we go about our business; and the rhapsodies of starry-eyed prophets shall not seduce us into jeopardizing the interests of the present and of the first human right the needs to be defended—the right to live. 'Bread is people's first right', said Saint-Just, and that is the greatest declaration made in the entire French Revolution.[31]

From 'life is a right' it is a short distance to 'shelter is a right'. Unbeknownst to himself, Le Corbusier said something that would be consistent with the 'greatest declaration made in the entire French Revolution'—never mind that 'revolution can be avoided'. But, at the same time, it is Le Corbusier's failure, or his intellectual deficit, or his obsessive industrial-managerial ideology, that prevented him from following up his dictum. He forgot to add that in a civil society 'every living being', on the face of it, must have a *right* to shelter. He was not a reader of Hegel, nor Marx, nor a student of political economy, for that matter. Nor was he a reader of Freud to qualify the 'biological' slant in his dictum. If he was not the reader of these thinkers, we must not forget that he was nevertheless an avid reader. We know that his favorite writers included Nietzsche (*Thus Spoke Zarathustra*), Eduard Shuré (*The Great Initiates*), George Bataille (*La Part maudite*), and of course Homer (*Iliad*), among others. Interestingly enough, while he was in São Paulo in 1920s, the novelist Oswald de Andrade told him this: 'We study you, along with Freud and Marx. You're on the same level and just as indispensable to the study of the present social movement and to the establishment of a new community organization, etc.'.[32] Equally interesting is the report that in Bogotá, on the first page of an important magazine, he was named along with Marx, Freud, Einstein, and Picasso.[33] He was, of course, much appreciated in Latin America.

To his declaration on 'shelter', Le Corbusier further added the following: '*The various working classes of society* no longer have suitable homes, *neither laborers nor intellectuals*'. This sentence appears before the last cited previously that the '*question of building*' is the '*key to the equilibrium upset today*: *architecture or revolution*'. For Le Corbusier, society is a harmonic corporate entity *free from class antagonism* in which the parts must be kept in a state of 'equilibrium'. In his mind, 'building' is the agency by which this equilibrium can be achieved. I will come back to the word 'equilibrium', a key word for John Maynard Keynes, in the next chapter. Here we should take the declaration above *seriously* and look into 'the various working classes of society'—classified into

Critical pedagogy

two categories of 'laborers' and 'intellectuals'—deprived of 'a suitable home' and examine their status a hundred years after Le Corbusier. He would be anguished to find out that neither 'laborers' nor 'intellectuals' are the beneficiaries of his 'revolution'.

One year after the financial meltdown of 2008, Slavoj Žižek published his *First as Tragedy, Then as Farce*. In the second part of the book he takes up 'The Communist Hypothesis' and writes that it is not enough to remain faithful to the 'communist Idea' but rather one has to locate antagonism in the historical reality which would give the Idea an urgency. He goes on to list four fundamental antagonisms in global capitalism today that would prevent its 'indefinite reproduction', the last of which is directly connected to our concern here: 'and last but not least, the creation of *new forms of apartheid*, new Walls and slums'.[34] A qualitative difference distinguishes this last one, Žižek is quick to point out, which basically consists of 'the gap that separates the Excluded from the Included'.[35] The latter has particular relevance to my purpose at hand. Towards the end Žižek notes that in today's developed society there are not precisely three classes but rather 'three fractions of working class: intellectual laborers, the old manual working class, and the outcasts (the unemployed, those living in slums and other interstices of public space)'.[36] The 'working class' now expanded to include three large fractions, each with its 'way of life' and ideology, Žižek notes. In his Hegelian term, this triad, as he explains, 'is clearly the triad of the universal (intellectual workers), the particular (manual workers) and singular (outcasts)'.[37]

Le Corbusier would be annoyed by our terms 'capitalism' and 'communist Idea', as is apparent in his exasperation when he wrote in his *Urbanisme* in 1925 that 'since the Russian

Revolution it has become the charming prerogative of both our own and the Bolshevist revolutionaries to keep the title of revolutionary to themselves alone', and that 'Everything which has not chosen ostensibly to adopt their label they call bourgeois and capitalist and stupid'.[38] He would be dismayed if we told him that the time of 'progressive-revolutionary' bourgeoisie has been long over and that only an urgent revolutionary *rupture* faithful to the 'communist Idea' would be able to fulfill his own unfinished project. As an intellectual-architect he would be appalled to see how the line of separation between 'working classes' and 'intellectuals' is blurred, no longer recognizable, and that 'building' can never fulfill the lost 'equilibrium' he sought.

But perhaps we should refrain from anguishing our Architect by reminding him that he was naïve and illusionary in thinking that industrial capitalism could restore and bring back the purported 'equilibrium' to society through the act of 'building'. Yet, we must bring ourselves to disturb his tranquility and dare deploying the radical Left critique against him to shatter his illusion. I am afraid, though, by doing this we would be guilty of pushing him to take his leave, once again, from the Metropolis, the city of Paris where he lived all his life, to go on a long trip to his solitary *cabanon* in the bucolic South of France on the shore of Mediterranean Sea, at *Roquebrune-Camp-Martin*, a cosy primitive 'shelter' where he would spend his time in yet another round of paintings on the theme of 'Poem of the Right Angle', in the same heroic style that he took up to illustrate his copy of Homer's *Iliad*. While there, we will see the 'old Saint' plunging again into the Mediterranean water for a swim—he was a great swimmer against his doctor's recommendation to not swim too far, for too long—that would lead to his glorious 'second' death, while recalling what he said on several occasions: 'How nice it would be to die swimming toward the sun'.[39] Indeed. In the meanwhile, we will tell him that we are determined to submit his statement, '*It is a primal instinct of every living being to ensure a shelter*'—an *egalitarian* statement in essence not uttered before in the annals of twentieth-century architectural thought—to the critical but sympathetic analysis it deserves. We will scrutinize his categories of 'living being' and 'primal instinct', that must be submitted to Freudian–Lacanian psychoanalytical theory to transpose them from the domain of *nature* to the discourse of *culture.*

At the same time, we must *reconfigure* this 'living being' in the term 'species being' used by young Marx in his *Economic and Philosophic Manuscripts of 1844* that he later took up again in *Grundrisse*, the same notion that Alain Badiou has differently termed as '*generic humanity*', paying his respects to Marx.[40] After accomplishing this analysis, it still remains to ground what I will call 'philosophy of shelter' in the notion of the 'Communist Hypothesis'. Le Corbusier's maxim on shelter must still be grounded in *ethics*. We will argue that the Idea of Shelter will have to be severed from 'empirical reality' so that it can attain the dignity of its Notion, in the Hegelian system. Based on Hegel's *Philosophy of Right*, we have to liberate the notion of Shelter from Le Corbusier's naturalistic-biological meaning and bring it to the discourse of right, civil society and State, taking into account Marxian critique by advancing the central thesis that the Universality of 'shelter' is immanent in the Universality of 'proletariat'. We must remind Le Corbusier that in his discourse of the *necessity* of shelter he forgot to think of *freedom*. We will tell him that 'Freedom in essence is the *freedom of necessity*'. For all of this, I will implore Le Corbusier to bear with us until we get to the finishing line in this work.

Notes

1. Le Corbusier, 'Architecture ou révolution', [1922], B2(15)153, FLC, cited in Jean-Louis Cohen's extensive 'Introduction' to Le Corbusier, *Toward An Architecture* (Los Angeles: Getty Research Institute, 2007), 67. It should be mentioned here that the chapters composing *Vers une architecture* had previously been published in different issues of *L'Esprit nouveau* except for the last chapter 'Architecture or Revolution' that was added to the book when it was published in 1923.
2. Le Corbusier, *Toward An Architecture*, 292.
3. Le Corbusier, *Toward An Architecture*, 290.
4. See Cohen, 'Introduction'. The document in French reads: 'la crise des logements aménera à la révolution, Préoccupez-vous de l'habitation', 67 [translation modified].
5. Cohen, 'Introduction', 25.
6. Quoted in Geoff Mann, *In the Long Run We Are All Dead: Keynesianism, Political Economy and Revolution* (London and New York: Verso, 2017), 50. Also see Maximilian Robespierre, *Virtue and Terror*, Introduced by Slavoj Žižek (London and New York: Verso, 2007), 'Extracts from "Answer to Louvet's Accusation", 5 November 1792': 'Citizens, did you want a revolution without a revolution?', 43.
7. Geoff Mann, *In the Long Run We Are All Dead*, 50. In the chapter that I have devoted to the relationship between Le Corbusier and Keynes I will transpose the brilliant argument that Mann has developed about Keynesianism and revolution to my discussion of 'Corbusianism and revolution'.
8. Le Corbusier, *Toward an Architecture*, 292.
9. Le Corbusier, *Toward an Architecture*, 292.
10. Le Corbusier, *Toward an Architecture*, 292.
11. George Wilhelm Freidrich Hegel, *The Philosophy of History*, intro. C.J. Friedrich (New York: Dover, 1956), 25.
12. Hegel, *The Philosophy of History*, 26.
13. In this I am following Michael Löwy in his *The Theory of Revolution in the Young Marx* (Chicago: Haymarket Books, 2005). As he argues in capitalist economy there is this 'myth of the savior from on high', which is an 'incarnation of the public virtue contrasted with the competition and particularism of individuals; a demiurge of history to break the chain of fatalism; a superhuman hero who liberates mankind and "constitutes" the new state'. He further argues that this this is the political doctrine of the bourgeoisie in its ascent, as

for 'Machiavelli, he is "the prince," for Hobbes, "the absolute Sovereign," for Voltaire, "the Enlightened Despot," for Rousseau, "the Lawgiver," for Carlyle, "the Hero"', 14. Following this list, I would add that for the 'industrial liberal-capitalism of the twentieth century', it was 'Le Corbusier the Savior'.

14 Following Löwy, on the one hand, the 'Kingdom of Necessity' belongs to bourgeois revolution when the bourgeoisie becomes the 'ruling class', and on the other, the 'Kingdom of Freedom' belongs to the proletarian revolution which is the 'first *conscious* historical transformation of society', a historical moment in which 'individuals who have hitherto been objects and products of history come forward as subjects and producers', in Michael Löwy, *The Theory of Revolution in the Young Marx*, 18.
15 See Eric Hobsbawm, *How to Change the World: Reflections on Marx and Marxism* (New Haven and London: Yale University Press, 2011), 28.
16 Eric Hobsbawm, *How to Change the World*, 29.
17 Sigfried Giedion, *Building in France, Building in Iron, Building in Ferro-Concrete*, intro. Sokratis Georgiadis, trans. J. Duncan Berry (Santa Monica: The Getty Center for the History of art and Humanities, 1995), 88.
18 Sigfried Giedion, *Building in France*, 88.
19 Sigfried Giedion, *Building in France*, 88.
20 Sigfried Giedion, *Building in France*, 89.
21 Sigfried Giedion, *Building in France*, 89.
22 Quoted in Eric Hobsbawm, *How to Change the World*, 28.
23 Eric Hobsbawm, *How to Change the World*, 29.
24 Eric Hobsbawm, *How to Change the World*, 29.
25 Eric Hobsbawm, *How to Change the World*, 28.
26 See my 'The Gift of the Open Hand: Le Corbusier Reading Georges Bataille's *La Part Maudite*', in *Journal of Architectural. Education*, September 1996.
27 See Jean-Louis Cohen, *Le Corbusier and the Mystique of the USSR: Theories and Projects for Moscow, 1928–1936* (Princeton: Princeton University Press, 1992).
28 See John Willett, 'Art and Revolution', in *New Left Review* 112 (July/August 2018), 68. As the editor notes, Willett's essay was first published in Italian translation in Eric Hobsbawm, George Haupt, et al., eds. *Storia del marxismo*, Vol. 111, Turin 1980.
29 See Walter Benjamin, *The Arcades Project* (Cambridge: The Belknap Press of Harvard University Press, 1999), in Convolute N, 'On the Theory of Knowledge, Theory of Progress', N1a, 5, 459.

Critical pedagogy

30 See Walter Benjamin, 'Experience and Poverty' in *Walter Benjamin: Selected Writings, Volume 2, 1927–1934* (Cambridge: The Belknap Press of Harvard University Press, 1999). Benjamin wrote this essay upon his departure from Germany on the eve of the rise of the Nazis to power. For an excellent analysis of this essay and the conditions of the time see John McCole, *Walter Benjamin and the Antinomies of Tradition* (Ithaca and London: Cornell University Press, 1993), especially Chapter 4: 'Owning up to the Poverty of Experience: Benjamin and Weimar Modernism'.

31 Quoted in Stathis Kouvelakis, *Philosophy and Revolution, from Kant to Marx*, Preface by Fredric Jameson, trans. G.M. Goshgarian (London and New York: Verso, 2003), 67.

32 See Nicholas Fox Weber, *Le Corbusier: A Life* (New York: Alfred A. Knopf, 2008), 307. Weber notes that he reported what the novelist told him to his mother to remind her of the 'significance and potential ramifications of his lectures to important audience', 307–308.

33 Weber, *Le Corbusier : A Life*, 507. According to Weber, he quoted the piece to his mother and brother saying ' "T he old Master" has entered his final stages, a youth which adds up to over two hundred years', 507.

34 Slavoj Žižek, *First as Tragedy, Then as Farce* (London and New York: Verso, 2009), 91. Žižek lists the first three as the following: 'the looming threat of an *ecological* catastrophe; the inappropriateness of the notion of *private property* in relation to so-called "intellectual property"; the socio-economic implications of *new techno-scientific development* (especially in biogenetics)', 91.

35 Slavoj Žižek, *First as Tragedy, Then as Farce*, 91.

36 Slavoj Žižek, *First as Tragedy, Then as Farce*, 147.

37 Slavoj Žižek, *First as Tragedy, Then as Farce*, 147.

38 See Le Corbusier, *The City of To-Morrow and its Planning* (New York: Dover, 1987), 300–301.

39 See Nicholas Fox Weber, *Le Corbusier: A Life* (New York: Alfred A. Knopf, 2008), 8

40 See Alain Badiou and Jean-Luc Nancy, *German Philosophy: A Dialogue*, ed. and afterword by Jan Volker (Cambridge: The MIT Press, 2018).

Part I

Chapter 1

The Blank Wall: Architecture and the French Revolution

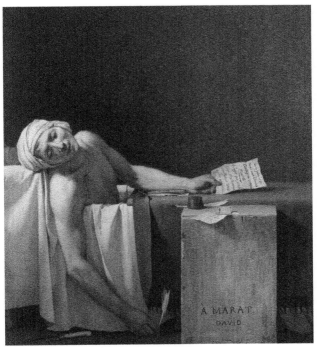

Figure 1.1 Jacques Louis David, *The Death of Marat*. Description: French neoclassical school. The death of Marat (1743–1793), journalist, French revolutionary politician. *La muerte de Marat*. Brussels, Fine Art Museum. Credit: Album / Art Resource, NY

Part I

> It has been said, that the *French Revolution* resulted from Philosophy, and it is not without reason that Philosophy has been called 'Weltweisheit' [World Wisdom].
>
> Hegel, *The Philosophy of History*[1]

Architecture and bourgeoisie

Only one thinker, Walter Benjamin, took a Marxian step to delineate architecture as an instrument of the bourgeois power linking it to the *event* of the French Revolution. He is the thinker of the *irruption* of politics into architecture at the inaugural moment of modernity, which also entails the irruption of *democracy* insofar as 'democracy' is synonymous with 'politics'. This constitutes the cornerstone of *emancipatory* critique in architecture. Benjamin traced the failed revolutionary sequence that ended with the Paris Commune. This would establish a conception of architecture in the era of liberal capitalist modernity that must be understood in the dialectical relation with Revolution. Benjamin's investigation into the failed revolutionary sequence does not leave any doubt as to the relation between 'proletariat' and 'bourgeoisie', a point of contention debated for long that continues to this moment in the twenty-first century. Benjamin did not show any sign of ambivalence about the nature of 'bourgeois revolution'—as opposed to 'proletariat' revolution—the concept of which goes back to Marx when he used the term in his *The Poverty of Philosophy* in 1847. It was the failure of 'progressive' bourgeoisie giving its place to 'reactionary' bourgeoisie with Napoleon Bonaparte's *coup d'état* on 9 November 1799, better known in the revolutionary calendar as 18 Brumaire, year VIII, that would lead to Louis Napoleon's *coup d'état* and the Second Empire in 1851 after the defeat of revolutions of 1830 and 1848. The question that has been asked is the same as the title of Neil Davidson's massive work: *How Revolutionary Were the Bourgeoise Revolutions?*[2] If the 'revolution' in architecture in the moment of modernity is a bourgeois product, I analogically pose this question: *How revolutionary was the revolutionary architecture in the time of the Bourgeoisie?*

Benjamin, implicating architecture in the emergence of the bourgeoisie and its transition to dictatorship in the Second Empire, had a clear vision when he wrote the following passage in his 1935 Exposé:

> The barricade is resurrected during the Commune. It is stronger and better secured than ever. It stretches across the great boulevards, often reaching a height of two stories, and shields the trenches behind it. Just as the *Communist Manifesto* ends the age of professional conspirators, so the Commune puts an end to the phantasmagoria holding sway over early years of the proletariat. *It dispels the illusion that the task of the proletariat revolution is to complete the work of 1789 hand in hand with the bourgeoisie* [emphasis mine]. This illusion dominates the period 1831–1871, from Lyons uprising to the Commune. The Bourgeoisie never shared in this error. Its battle against the social rights of the proletariat dates back to the great Revolution, and converges with the philanthropic movement that gives it cover and that is in the heyday under Napoleon III. Under his reign this movement's monumental work appears: Le Play's *Ouvriers européens* [European Workers]. ... Rimbaud and Corbet declare their support for the Commune. The burning of Paris is the worthy conclusion to Haussmann's work of destruction.[3]

It is not accidental that the moment of the French Revolution also contained the *germ* of an *egalitarian* theory of architecture.

Part I

A revolutionary architect and theoretician emerged who later became a famous teacher at the newly established institution that was founded in 1794 named École Centrale des Travaux Publics, later to be renamed École Polytechnique. This École takes its rightful place as one of the first *écoles spéciales* created by the National Convention. The name of this architect is well known: Jean-Nicholas-Louis Durand. It is unfortunate that Benjamin did not directly address Durand in *The Arcades Project* given the fact that he took a special interest in the École Polytechnique to which he devoted an entire Convolute: 'r [École Polytechnique]'.[4] He was quite familiar with the history of the École as he cited numerous times the work of G. Pinet entitled *Histre de l'École polytechnique* published in 1887. As evidenced in Convolute r, we learn that Benjamin had in fact come across the name Durand and his famous work, if only in passing, when he quoted the architectural historian Emil Kaufmann, the author of *Von Ledoux bis Le Corbusier*, which was published in 1933. Benjamin cites the following passage from Kaufmann's book:

> Shortly after 1800, things were already so far along that the ideas which appear in Ledoux and Boullée—elemental outbursts of passionate natures—were being propounded as official doctrine ... Only three decades separates the late work of Blondel, which still ... embodies the teachings of French classicism, from the *Précis des leçons d'architecture* of Durand, whose thinking had a decisive influence during the Empire and in the period following. They are the three decades of Ledoux's career. Durand, who announced the norm from his chair at the École Royale Polytechnique in Paris ... diverges from Blondel on all essential points. His primer begins ... with violent attacks on famous works of classic Baroque art. St.

Peter's in Rome, along with its square, and the Paris Pantheon are invoked as counterexamples ... Whereas Blondel warns of 'monotonous planimetry' and would not be unmindful of the function of perspective, Durand sees in the elementary schemata of the plan the only correct solution.[5]

Beyond this we cannot find any other reference to Durand in *The Arcades Project*. Alas! Benjamin of course had directed all of his attention to Le Corbusier, making references to his *Urbanisme*, but not to *Vers une architecture*. We can count seven citations of Le Corbusier, mainly in relation to Baron Haussmann, with one noteworthy exception to André Breton. As a reader of Marx's *The Eighteenth Brumaire of Bonaparte* and *The Communist Manifesto*, Benjamin spent his time in the reading room of the *Bibliothèque Nationale* investigating the Second Empire and Napoleon III and his architects.

Durand belonged to the circle around the *Idéologues*. He shared the moral and political outlook of the *Idéologues*. The latter term is the derogatory name that years after its formation the First Napoleon gave to the intellectual circle who gathered around the Société d'Auteuil with a link to the culture of *lumières*.[6] We can recognize the more familiar figures associated with this circle that includes Pierre-Jean-Georges Cabanis, Antoine-Louis-Claude Destutt de Tracy (who coined the term 'Ideology'), Abbé Emmanuel-Joseph Sieyès, Madame de Staël, Benjamin Constant and Volney (the author of *The Ruins*, 1791), some of whom were involved in drafting the final French Declaration of the Rights of Man and Citizen. They would attend the meetings that Madame Helvétius hosted in her villa at Auteuil. There, as Sergio Villari informs us, 'in memory of the deceased author of L'Esprit, the Idéologues continued their work: liberation from ignorance and prejudice, and the dissemination of the scientific truth of *philosophes*'.[7] The Idéologues group had its headquarters at the Institut de France in Paris—inaugurated on 14 April 1796—and was associated with its 'second class', that is moral and political sciences. They reconstituted the 'Radical Enlightenment' in its post-Thermidorian phase. The member of the Idéologues 'were the men who chiefly gave expression to the philosophique standpoint underpinning the Revolution's values, aims, and ideology'.[8] For Durand it was necessary to make sense of the Revolution that had already occurred. It was, moreover, necessary to affirm that the Revolution was 'the product of the high ideals of *philosophie*'.[9] As Villari writes:

> It was important to trace out the meaning of civil engagement, of moral tension, of cultural experience. The inheritance of *philosophie* was understood as the historical consciousness of necessity of guiding great revolutionary events with rational thoughts, as scientific reason illuminating the progress of society, as the necessity of a continuous mediation between *philosophie* and *politique*. Durand's work, in this sense, constituted itself as the extreme and even desperate achievement of that *esprit des lumières* that had so profoundly engaged architects and philosophers of the preceding generation.[10]

The fundamental trait of the emerging revolutionary architecture, with Durand at its center, that must be identified and recognized, was the 'reverential' and 'austere' *void*, the *emptiness*, about which Johann Joachim Winkelmann said: 'aversion to empty spaces thus makes the walls fill in; and pictures empty of thought cover the emptiness'.[11] There is an *elective affinity* between Goethe's Altar of Good Luck, the Cube and Sphere, and Durand's experiment of *emptiness* in elemental geometry.[12] Durand, an student of Etienne-Louis Boullée and Julien-David Leroy (the author of *Les Ruines des plus beaux monuments de la Grèce*), 'matured in the vital climate of the Revolution'.[13] In linguistic terms, this emptiness is the *degree zero*.[14]

At this point an excursus is in order to explicate the revolutionary *event* that led to the space of *emptiness* before it actually could be *enacted* in architecture by Durand.

Invention of the Blank Wall

It is rarely acknowledged that the inaugural *moment* of modernity in painting began with a *crime scene*. The revolutionary Jean-Paul Marat was murdered on 13 July 1793. Jacques-Louis David, the painter of *Marat à son dernier soupir*, hastily finished his painting on 25 *vendémiaire An Dex* on the revolutionary calendar (16 October 1793), in two-and-a-half months. With David's painting, an extraordinary thing was born: The Blank Wall. This is the *degree zero* of modernity that architecture later would adopt, *avant la lettre*. We can declare that modern architecture took off after a *crime was committed* in the midst of the French Revolution. It has a precise date. It was born on 16 October 1793—the date David finished his painting of Marat. This moment in architecture has certain *philosophical* sources. They are the same sources that brought the Revolution to our historical consciousness. We came to it through Kant and Hegel. As we will see later, in their innermost drives, Kant's and Hegel's philosophies are the philosophies of the Revolution. As such, they stand behind the *philosophy* of the Blank Wall, *ex post facto*, after its advent.

Part I

In every sense, *The Death of Marat* is a political painting. According to T.J. Clark, the 'detail of politics is what David's Marat is made out of'. Politics, he claims, is the 'form par excellence of that contingency which makes modernism what it is'.[15] For Clark, 'Modernism is about the impossibility of transcendence'. It is about 'dreamworlds' and 'disenchantment' of the world. He perceptively argues that David's Marat 'turns on the impossibility of transcendence', which shows us 'politics as the form of a world'.[16] 'The cult of Marat', he remarks, 'exists at the intersection between short term political contingency and long term disenchantment of the world'.[17] The revolutionary David himself said that with this painting he wanted to incite the patriotic sentiments of the French people to move to action. Many years after, in 1846, the painting moved Charles Baudelaire so much so that it prompted the poet to memorably depict the scene with the following astonishing words:

> The *divine* Marat, one arm hanging out of the bath, its hand still loosely holding on to its last quill, and his chest pierced by the *sacrilegious* wound, has just breathed his last. On the green desk in front of him, his other hand still holds the treacherous letter: 'Citizen, it is enough that I am really miserable to have a right to your benevolence'. The bath water is red with blood, the paper is blood-stained; on the ground lies a large kitchen knife soaked in blood; on a wretched packing case, which constituted the working furniture for the tireless journalist we read: 'À Marat, David'. All the details are historical and real, as in a novel by Balzac; the drama is there, alive in all its pitiful horror, and by a strange stoke of brilliance, which makes this David's masterpiece one of the great treasures of modern art, there is nothing trivial or ignoble about it. What

is most astonishing in this exceptional poem is the fact that it is painted extremely quickly, and when one considers the beauty of its design, it is all the more bewildering. It is the bread of the strong and the triumph of the spiritual; as cruel as nature, this picture has the heady scent of idealism. What has become of that ugliness that Death has so swiftly erased with the tip of its wings? Marat can henceforth challenge Apollo; Death has kissed him with loving lips and he rests in the peace of his transformation. There is in this work something both tender and poignant, a soul hovers in the chilled air of this room, on these cold walls, around the cold and funereal bath. May we have your permission, politicians of all parties, even you, ferocious liberals of 1845, to give way to emotion before David's masterpiece? This painting was a gift to a tearful nation, and our own tears are not dangerous.[18]

I come back to this famous passage below. Here I want to depict the scene of murder. Jean-Paul Marat was a deputy of the radical faction Montagnards in the Constituent Assembly. The members of this faction were called Montagnards, 'men of the Mountain', the nickname for Robespierre's Jacobin faction, because they sat on the high benches of the auditorium and on the left side of the Convention. They came to power in 10 August 1792 after the collapse of the monarchy. On 13 July 1793 Marat was murdered by Madame Charlotte Corday, a member of the Girondins circle in Caen, who accused Marat to be responsible for the 'September Massacre' of 1792.[19] Marat was not involved in it. She did not escape the scene of the crime. She was arrested and was later tried and executed for her crime. The Girondins, named after Gironde department, was a political faction originally on the left of politics but which then became a 'right wing' of the National Convention by late 1792 to be later taken over by radical Jacobins with the help of *sans-culottes*.[20] By late 1793, the Parisian radicals referred to themselves as *sans-culottes,* literally 'without knee-breeches', who wore the long trousers of the working man and 'went away feeling satisfied that their message has been put across'.[21] They were plebeian revolutionaries but not the modern 'working class' of wage-earners. Corday had prepared a speech about her motivation to kill Marat, to destroy 'the savage beast fattened on the blood of Frenchmen'.[22] This is only one historical slander among all others that have covered the name Marat in the annals of the French Revolution, 'a miasma of falsification about his alleged bloodthirsty desire for mass murder'.[23] Marat was an erudite man of his society. He was trained as a physician and was a scientific authority on optics and electricity. He practiced medicine in London and in 1773 published in English his *Philosophical Essay on Man* which 'shows a wonderful knowledge of English, French, German, Italian and Spanish philosophy'. He became one of the 'prominent scientific men in France—before the Revolution transformed him and everyone else'.[24] The National Convention that came into existence in September 1792—after the September Massacre—witnessed the regular anti-Marat 'lynching' by the Girondins. Robespierre knew that Marat was a target of the Girondins.

Marat suffered from a skin disease which forced him to sit in the bathtub with a vinegar-soaked cloth round his head like a turban to write his provocative journalistic pieces for his newspaper, *L'Ami du people.* The title of his newspaper became his nickname, 'the friend of people'. On 12 July, a day before Marat's assassination, David, who was a prominent member of the Jacobins and for a short time the president of its club in summer of 1793,and also a powerful member of the Committee of Public Instruction, had visited his friend Marat and found him writing in his bathtub. This is what he wrote after his visit:

> The day before Marat's death, the Jacobins sent Maure and me to get news of him; I found him in a state which stunned me. Besides him was a wooden box on which there was an inkwell and paper, and with his hand out of the bath, he was writing his final thoughts for the deliverance of his people.[25]

The day after the assassination when the news of Marat's death reached the Convention, the members from his Paris Section turned to David and told him: 'there is yet one more painting for you to do', and 'return Marat to us whole again'.[26] For David and many others the name of his newspaper was synonymous with Marat himself. He was elected as a Paris deputy to the National Convention on 9 September 1792, sitting with Danton, Robespierre, and David. He was constantly attacked for his newspaper and falsely accused of having a hand in the September Massacre. In April 1793 he was brought to the court by Girondins who attempted to kill him 'legally' on the charges of being, as he put it 'a factionalist, an anarchist, a bloodthirsty and ambitious man who aimed to get supreme power under the title of tribune, triumvir, dictator...'.[27] He successfully defended himself against the charges. It was a fanatical error by Girondins to bring him to trial. He was constantly accused of being a 'dictator'. He would put things as strong, as openly, and starkly as he could. Against the accusation he famously said: 'It is by violence, that liberty ought to be established, and the moment has come to organize temporarily the despotism of liberty in order to wipe out the despotism of kings'.[28]

Part I

Clark pays proper attention to the Blank Wall in Marat's painting that it deserves, perspicuously conceptualizing its meaning in the Real context of political events in the Revolution. He writes:

> And yet, the single most extraordinary feature of the picture, I should say, is its whole upper half's being empty. Or rather (here is what is unprecedented) not being empty, exactly, not being a satisfactory representation of nothing or nothing much—of an absence in which whatever the subject is has become present—but something more like a representation *of* painting, of painting as pure activity. Painting as material, therefore. Aimless. Ultimately detached from any one representational task. Bodily.[29]

He continues, 'it is open to the viewer, that is to say, *to see the upper half of the Marat as satisfactorily empty, or sufficiently like a wall*' ... What we see is 'scumbling'[30] [emphasis mine].

It is a 'scumbling' wall. Clark tries to offer a 'plausible account' of David's intentions, 'of what would have led him to leave the upper half of his picture empty in the first place'.[31] This is what he suggests:

> The emptiness is of a room, perhaps a wall. (No hats and cloaks hung on this one.) It signifies Marat's austerity and self-denial. It makes him one of the People—it and the orange box and the patch on the sheet. As the eye moves right, the emptiness gradually becomes less dark and absolute. We know that David was a great believer in the light of history. The difficulty is not in suggesting the kinds of metaphorical work the upper half was meant to do, but deciding why it

ended up doing them this way. And whether doing them this way was doing them all... We are at the heart of David's belief and purpose, and of the Revolution's.[32]

This is the *effect* of modernism, of its deepest causes, as Clark says. The upper half of the painting, the Blank Wall, is, therefore, an instantiation of the 'People', Clark surmises. There is nothing to 'represent' here. Only 'A wall, or a void or an absence of light'.[33] Other art historians would suggest that David's painting

> represents a single moment of suspense. It makes no attempt to tell the story or describe the scene of Marat's assassination [...] David's is a laconic transparent work, a history painting and an icon whose power to fascinate has hardly diminished since the day of its exhibition.[34]

It has been suggested that the *shock* of David's painting is comparable to the shocking moments in twentieth-century films, namely the nurse in *Battleship Potemkin*, or the razor in *Un Chien Andalou*.[35] For my purposes, there is one single *shocking* element in David's *Marat*, the one that Baudelaire touched on in the last paragraph in one long sentence cited above: 'There is in this work something both tender and poignant, a soul hovers in the chilled air of this room, on these *cold walls*, around the cold and funereal bath' [my emphasis]. The walls in Marat's apartment were covered with paper with illusionistic columns on it. It is significant that David *chose* to depict *none* of them. These 'cold walls', are actually one single *stark* wall that we see in this depthless painting that is hovering over Marat's head dominating the scene. This Blank Wall is one single *gift* of the French Revolution to *modernity* and *architecture*. It exemplifies the *void*. If for nothing else, the French Revolution must be credited and appreciated for the singular depiction of this 'unadorned wall'! The massive oppressive walls of the Bastille, this 'monument to *despotisme*', were brought down by the revolutionaries so that the revolutionary *blank wall* could come into existence. It must be said, therefore, that our *modernity* begins with a *spectacle*: *The Death of Marat* is a *theatrical* scene, playing the *spectacle* of the *blank wall* watching over the martyr Marat. It holds a ghostly secret, the eerie presence of the absence of Charlotte Corday, the assassin. The 'blank wall', the 'cold wall', or the 'silent wall' is a witness to the crime committed. Its words are 'spoken in the void', as Adolf Loos would have said. This Blank Wall is a *testimony* that we are not *done* with the legacy of the French Revolution. It has nevertheless been defamed many times and by many 'criminals'. Those of our contemporaries have *tattooed* the Blank Wall. They are, in the words of Loos, either 'criminals' or 'degenerates'. And I have heard of none going to the guillotine!—of course, metaphorically speaking.

Interestingly, in the 1989 bicentennial anniversary of the storming of Bastille, the same year the Berlin Wall came down, London's *Daily Telegraph* published an editorial cartoon reproducing David's painting. Instead of that piece of paper that Marat is holding in his left hand, we see the same hand holding a book entitled *Yet Another Book About the French Revolution*. As Geoff Mann notes, it tries to suggest that we are 'done' with the Revolution.[36] Why do we keep returning to it then? *The Death of Marat* terrifies, still, the liberal capitalist democracy. It cannot get rid of its *menace* and makes every attempt to exorcise its specters. Here I want to invoke Baudelaire's sentence in the last paragraph of the passage quoted above where it reads: 'May we have your permission, politicians of all parties, even you, ferocious liberals of 1845, to give way to emotion before David's masterpiece?' Here I paraphrase Baudelaire's remarks: 'May we have your permission, you reactionary bourgeois authoritarian politicians, even you arrogant conservative-liberal and left-liberal of the 2020s, to give way to the emotion of the *modernity* of the Blank Wall before David's masterpiece?'

Here I end this excursus and turn to the exposition of the *theses* on the Idea of the Blank Wall I want to advance.

Theses on the Blank Wall

We can confidently declare that the French Revolution brought into being *modernity as spectacle.* Its birth coincides with *justice* and *democracy,* but also *law* and *rights.* This *void*, this *blank wall*, in Hegelian terms, is the moment of *absolute negativity*. Under the emancipatory law of 'contradiction' in Hegel,[37] the 'blank wall' is a 'wall' and its negation. The Blank Wall is the *sublation* of the idea of 'wall'. Another way to say it: 'This Is Not A Wall', drawing analogically on René Magritte's painting of a Pipe with its caption, *ceci n'est pas une pipe*. Any thought not versed in Hegel's dialectical thought of contradiction, and its extension in Marx, suffers from the malaise of 'affirmation' dominant in Western thought. If, in the same line of argument, we could be legitimately thinking of the 'absolute knowledge' in architecture, it would be the 'knowledge' of the *negativity* of the Blank Wall. In the consciousness of the Blank Wall, architecture arrives at its *universal spirit*. It would come to its 'absolute spirit'. The philosophy of the *blank wall*, as *absolute spirit*, is the highest expression of humanity. As it is said, 'all human activities are, in a way, failed attempts to provide what can only be accomplished through

Absolute Spirit'.[38] In this system of thought, architecture is closer to philosophy than to art or religion. They both are activities grounded in the 'architectonic reason', to put it in Kantian terms. In Hegelian terms, architecture can come to its own 'self-awareness', to its own self-knowing only in the Blank Wall as the *absolute*. As such, architecture *and* Hegelian philosophy are embedded in modernity coming into existence only with the Revolution. Without the French Revolution as the moment of our modernity, the *event* of the 'Blank Wall' as inauguration of modernity in architecture would not have entered the historical consciousness.

On the other hand, we must think of the Blank Wall as the embodiment of a *lack*—it is *the* lack itself. As such, it is the birthplace of psychoanalysis *avant la lettre*. The *void* is the Freudian 'partial object', or what Jacques Lacan called '*objet petit a*', along with the 'gaze'. I wished that Lacan had shown David's painting to the members of his Seminars when talking about the void! He went to Rome and saw a lot of Baroque paintings there, but I suspect that he missed going to Belgium to see the original *The Death of Marat*! Or perhaps he did. But in any case, we *must* say that the *unconscious,* before its actual discovery by Freud, was already born with the French Revolution in the 'blank wall', first in the act of painting and second in its architectural *construction*. The void of the Blank Wall is *also* the moment of *ethical* construction, from Kantian ethics to the 'ethics of psychanalysis' in Lacanian theory. It may be called the 'Categorical Imperative' of architecture. It is with Kant that 'The Void Called Subject' came into being. In Žižek's estimation, Kant comes before Descartes, or his 'transcendental subject of apperception' is corrective of the Cartesian *cogito*.[39] But if I told you, analogically, that you are a 'blank wall', you would take it as an insult, if not react violently! So let me put it a 'polite' way to tell you 'who you are'—without offending you—by deploying an algorithm—*à la* Badiou and Lacan—that can be rendered in the following algebraic 'formula', in which $ is signifier for the 'divided subject' or the 'subject of signifier':

$$[\text{void} \cap \text{blank wall} \in \text{lack} \leftrightarrow \$]$$

This can be a definition for the 'Subject of Desire' when confronting the 'Blank Wall'. The 'blank wall' is the *object cause* of your desire as a 'revolutionary subject'. Before the subject became a capitalist desiring subject desiring consumer objects it was a 'revolutionary subject' desiring the 'blank wall', seeing himself in the 'blank wall'. Kant would tell you that there is a *unity* in the 'experiences of the subject' called the 'transcendental subject of apperception'. As Lacan reminded us, without Kant the discovery of psychoanalysis would have been impossible. More importantly, without Kant the French Revolution would not have entered the revolutionary consciousness. As the great poet Heinrich Heine, a friend of Marx, once said, 'Kant is our Robespierre'. In Hegelian terms, the 'blank wall' is its own *negation*, it is a 'self-relating' *negativity*. The Notion of the 'blank wall', therefore, requires philosophical *and* psychoanalytical construction before its *empirical* experiences. In this specific sense, the 'blank wall' is a *transcendental* construction.

The architect Le Corbusier, after David (the painter) and Durand (the architect), reconfigured and reenacted the Blank Wall. In this reenactment, he brought the wall to *light*. I might point out here that Mies van der Rohe—the *enfant terrible* of architecture as Manfredo Tafuri called him—did away with the notion of the 'wall' altogether. The utopia of the 'glass house', the antithesis of 'security' and 'domesticity', is still with us. It only belonged once to a bourgeois client. But I am more concerned here to *reconstruct* a genealogy that stretches from Durand to Le Corbusier in conjunction with the French Revolution and its construction of the Blank Wall. We have not exhausted the *subjectivity* behind the *blank wall*. This assertion must yet be supported by the *philosophical* theory of Revolution and the *psychoanalytical* construction of the Subject.[40] I will come back to it later. Here I want to mention in passing that Benjamin in 1933, on the eve of his unfortunate forced departure from Nazi Germany, penned an important essay entitled 'Experience and Poverty'. There he eulogized Paul Scheerbart's utopia of glass, the phenomenal absolute of the *absence* of the wall.[41] But Benjamin's *optimistic* hope in this seminal essay was put on Le Corbusier. For Benjamin it came to a simple equation: Le Corbusier = transparency. He learned about it through Siegfried Giedion whose book he enthusiastically and appreciatively read as soon as he received it as a gift from the famous historian of modern architecture.[42]

The 'revolutionary' architecture owes its formation to the event of the French Revolution when the *void* as *absolute negativity* was constituted. The Second Empire violated it. Napoleon III put an end to its thought. Benjamin indicted the architects of the Second Empire for their ignorance and memorably wrote:

> Just as Napoleon failed to understand the functional nature of the state as an instrument of domination by the bourgeois class, so architects of his time failed to understand the functional nature of iron, with which the constructive principle begins its domination of architecture. These architects design

supports resembling Pompeian columns, and factories that imitate residential houses, just as later the first railroad stations, will be modeled on chalets. 'Construction plays the role of subconscious.' Nevertheless, the concept of engineer, which dates from the revolutionary wars, starts to gain ground, and the rivalry began between builder and decorator, École Polytechnique and École des Beaux-arts.[43]

Susan Buck-Morss in her *The Dialectics of Seeing* masterfully discusses this institutional division, technology vs. art, in the context of *The Arcades Project*.[44] Against this division, again, I wished that Benjamin had taken up Durand directly for discussion.

In this work, I link Durand's revolutionary architecture to the determinate ideas coming out of the French Revolution that was betrayed by Bonapartism. I name its re-emergence in our own twenty-first century as Neo-Bonapartism, a Thermidorean onslaught by the 1980s on the 'red years' of the 1960s and in destruction of the twentieth century's 'Passion of the Real', invoking Alain Badiou's term.[45] Here I only say that the fundamental feature of contemporary architecture is the betrayal of the *negativity* of the *void,* the *degree zero* of the Blank Wall. It is no longer honored. Thermidorians of the 1980s put an end to it. Its destruction is an act of pure counter-revolution against the radical Enlightenment and the French Revolution.

As it is said, 'Only with the French Revolution did the concept "revolution" take on its modern meaning'.[46] The French Revolution is thus the defining moment of our modernity. The French Revolution, as Eric Hobsbawm writes, 'was indeed a set of events sufficiently powerful and sufficiently universal in its impact, to have transformed the world *permanently* in important respects; and to introduce, or at least to give names to forces that continue to transform it'.[47] Whose property is the French Revolution? It belongs not only to the French and not only to the West. Apart from Haiti's revolution around 1800, it also belongs to the major revolutions in the late twentieth century, and the Iranian Revolution of 1978–1979 that shows some remarkable structural parallels with the French Revolution in spite of noticeable contrasts and differences.[48] Hobsbawm who takes note of this fact comments that 'Countries as remote from 1789 as Islamic fundamentalist Iran are basically national territorial states structured on the model carried into the world by the Revolution, together with so much of our modern political vocabulary'.[49] It was the commitment of Michel Foucault to 'what are we to make of the will to revolution' and, therefore, to Enlightenment, that prompted his enthusiasm for the Iranian Revolution, since 'the revolution plainly continues and completes the basic process of the Enlightenment'.[50] Significantly, Foucault's turn to Kant in his later career helped him to correct his positions of 1977–1979 on the Iranian Revolution, evidenced by the open letter he wrote to the then Iranian prime minister, published in *Le Nouvel Observateur* in 1979.[51] This is the case that, as Stathis Souvelakis perceptively remarks, 'Being modern means facing up to the question opened by the Enlightenment and the Revolution; but it means doing so at an irreducible distance from the action, as a spectator who, albeit sympathetic, is also forever separated from the event'.[52] The French Revolution is the property of every people who engage in revolutionary struggle that fails when the bourgeoisie—progressive then, reactionary now—assumes the hegemony in the class struggle with the proletariat and when it violates the Rights of Man and Citizen, and aborts the ideals of *equality, liberty, fraternity* leaving intact the hegemony of liberal capitalist democracy.

Virtue and Terror

The French Revolution is the moment that an *egalitarian theory* of society was born. It is also the moment of the birth of the philosophical Critique. Born in its wake is a specter seen by liberal capitalism as a *menace* that has to be conjured away. A thesis would follow: the emancipatory act of the French Revolution must be *repeated*—in the Freudian sense of the word. No other time than ours proves the truth of the dictum, Slavoj Žižek tells us, that 'Every history is the history of the present'.[53] The fall of the Berlin Wall in 1989, the bicentennial year of the French Revolution, and the eventual collapse of Communism in 1990, brought back the historical significance of the French Revolution debated heatedly for long and that has flared up again in contemporary political discourse. In his presentation of Maximilian Robespierre's 'Virtue and Terror', Žižek provocatively invokes Benjamin's notion of 'Divine Violence'. He writes that the liberal revisionists tried to impose the notion that the 'demise of Communism in 1989 occurred at exactly the right moment: it marked the end of the era which began in 1789, the final failure of the statist-revolutionary model which first entered the scene with the Jacobins'.[54] The French Revolution is rejected on the grounds that it was a 'catastrophe from its very beginning, the product of the godless mind; it is to be interpreted as God's punishment of the humanity's wicked ways, so its traces should be undone as thoroughly as possible'.[55] In this, the choice of 'sensitive liberals', is a 'differentiated one', Žižek notes. Its formula is: '1789 without 1793'. What they want, as Žižek put it sarcastically, 'is a *decaffeinated revolution*, a revolution that doesn't smell of revolution'[56] [emphasis mine]. The revisionist-reactionary historians, the likes of the French François Furet, go a step further to deny the French Revolution as the founding event of modernity and democracy.[57] According to Žižek, what the liberal Furet aimed to do was to 'de-eventalize the French Revolution', to deprive it as the defining moment of modernity that stems from the tradition in philosophy from Kant to Hegel (as I will discuss later), treating it as a 'local accident with no global significance, one conditioned by the specifically French tradition of absolute monarchy'.[58]

One cannot understand the French Revolution without understanding Robespierre, the 'Incorruptible'. In her *Fatal Purity*, Ruth Scurr helps us better than any other to understand the man.[59] We have to be his 'friends', as Scurr says, in order to understand him, knowing also that friends sometimes treacherously are capable of betraying you. Robespierre claimed that he represents the 'pure republic of virtue' and an enemy said that Robespierre 'would have paid someone to offer him gold, so as to be able to say that he had refused it', hence the apt nickname, the 'Incorruptible'.[60] The French *vertu* has larger connotations than the English 'virtue'. 'Righteousness' and 'public good' are among its wider meanings. For both Saint-Just and Robespierre *vertu* was key to the *patriotic* conviction in republic and democratic government. For Robespierre it would be 'the triumph of the general good over private interest or personal relationship'. Furthermore, as Scurr quotes Robespierre: 'A man of high principle will be ready to sacrifice to the State his wealth, his life, his very nature—everything, indeed, except his honor'.[61] These aspects of *vertu* came to Robespierre through his readings of Montesquieu and his favorite, Rousseau. Saint-Just put it in a larger historical perspective:

The early Romans, Greeks, and Egyptian were Christians because they were good and kind, and that is Christianity. Most of those called Christians since the time of Constantine have been nothing but savages and madmen. Fanaticism is the work of European priest craft. A people that has suppressed superstition has made a great step toward liberty. But it must take great care not to alter its moral principles, for they are the basic law of *vertu*.[62]

We must now get to the conjunction of virtue and terror. Is Terror to be interpreted against all liberal-conservative revisionists of the French Revolution? In her daring book entitled *In Defence of the Terror*, Sophie Wahnich brings up the notions of 'emotion', 'dread' and 'vengeance' and sets the stage by portraying the scene of Marat's funeral in Summer of 1793. She writes: 'Around Marat's corpse, which represented the injured people and the Declaration of the Rights of Man and of the Citizen, feelings of affliction and grief were transformed into enthusiasm'.[63] Declaring that 'Marat is not dead' and proclaiming that the 'revolution has not been destroyed', it became possible to 'demand vengeance, and put terror on the agenda'.[64] Wahnich reads into this an 'aesthetic of politics' that has to do with 'the circulation of emotions and sentiments' and the fact that the body of Marat was considered to be 'sacred' and had been profaned. But the Revolution also had to do with 'law' and the '*patrie*' (homeland). Wahnich writes:

> To demand that terror be placed on the agenda meant demanding a politics aimed at constantly renewing this sacred character of the laws, permanently reaffirming the normative value of the Declaration of Rights, demanding vengeance and punishment

for the enemies of the *patrie*. The slogan '*patrie en danger*' and watchword 'terror; were launched by the people.[65]

As to the question of 'revolutionary violence', Wahnich at one point puts the interpretation of the September Massacres in the Revolution under the notion of 'sovereign scene' in accord with Walter Benjamin. She cites Benjamin's *Critique of Violence* in which he wrote:

> all mythic lawmaking violence, which we may call 'executive', is pernicious. Pernicious, too, is the law-preserving, 'administrative' violence that serves it. Divine violence, which is the sign and seal but never the means of sacred dispatch, may be called 'sovereign' violence.[66]

Wahnich notes that this 'divine violence' is the violence of '*vox populi, vox dei*' ['voice of people, voice of god'].[67] The interpretations of the events of September 1792 led in 1793 to the notion of 'popular sovereignty'. Then what we know by the name Terror is now better understood as 'the employment of sovereign vengeance by the people'.[68] On a higher level, a 'human sensibility' was born out of the Terror that was translated into 'political sensibility', still an operative notion until now. The politics of conflict, nevertheless, would render impossible the politics of sensibility. Confirming that the 'abyss of terror' would swallow all the actors in the *journées* of 1792–1793, Wahnich notes that 'After Thermidor, politics would no longer be the place of a division of sensibilities; it rather became the place of professional distribution of knowledge of the social art'.[69]

Further, there must be a relation between politics and morality in terror. The exercise of terror cannot be separated from 'morality'. Wahnich notes that 'The dynamic of the Terror does not invoke politics against morality; the politics that it practices is indissociable from the morality to be introduced'. It is here that virtue comes to Terror. She cites Robespierre's declaration to the Convention as the following:

> Since the soul of the Republic is virtue, equality, and since your aim is to found and consolidate the Republic, it follows that the first rule of your political conduct must be to relate all your operations to the maintenance of equality and the development of virtue. With virtue and equality, therefore, you have a compass that can guide you in the midst of the storms of all passions and the whirlpool of intrigues that surround you.[70]

Wahnich ends her extraordinary explorations into the time of the Terror by commenting that 'terrorism' and 'terrorists' are the words that originated with Thermidor:

> Those who sought to found a new and egalitarian political space were defeated by history. The terrorists meant Robespierre and Saint-Just, but also all who fought for 'liberty or death'—the Jacobins whose club was closed, the citizens reduced to political passivity by the establishment of a property-based suffrage and the abolition of the right of resistance to an oppression which refused them any active citizenship ... The Terror would be the name given by history to this period of 'terrorism'. The view of The Republic as a period of terror and dread is essentially Thermidorian.[71]

Wahnich invokes Walter Benjamin's *Critique of Violence* to further illuminate her point.[72] She notes that Benjamin criticized a 'theorem' that was put forward by a certain Kurt Hiller who argued,

> the sanctity of life, which they either apply to all animal and even vegetable life, or limit to human life. Their argument, exemplified in an extreme case by the revolutionary killing of the oppressor, runs as follows: 'if I do not kill, I shall never establish the world domination of justice ... that is the argument of the intelligent terrorist ... We, however, profess that higher even than the happiness and justice of existence stands existence itself'.[73]

For Benjamin, however, as Wahnich quotes him,

> the proposition that existence stands higher than a just existence is false and ignominious, if existence is to mean nothing other than mere life ... Man cannot, at any price, be said to coincide with the mere life in him, any more than it can be said to coincide with any other of his conditions and qualities, including even the uniqueness of his bodily person.[74]

Wahnich incisively concludes that 'The political project of the French year II aimed at a universal justice that still continues to remain a hope: that of equality among men as a reciprocity of liberty, of equality among peoples as a reciprocity of sovereignty'.[75]

What are the resonances of Robespierre and the French Revolution for the radical Left today? After the historical rupture that took place in 1990, Žižek in his *In Defense of Lost Causes* writes, the current *doxa* is that the Left must abandon the Jacobin 'revolutionary Terror'. Whose proclaimed goal, Žižek asks, is 'to return the destiny of liberty into the hand of the truth'? Robespierre's 'politics of Truth' can 'only be enforced in a terrorist manner' he argues and cites Robespierre for its affirmation:

> If the mainspring of popular government in peacetime is virtue, amid revolution it is at the same time virtue and terror: virtue, without which terror is fatal; terror, without which virtue is impotent. Terror is nothing but prompt, severe, inflexible justice; it is therefore an emanation of virtue. It is less a special principle than a consequence of the general principle of democracy applied to our country's most pressing need.[76]

Faithful to the legacy of the radical Left, and remembering the May '68 as a unique event that paralyzed the structure of state power, as a 'moment of unification of students' contestation with the workers' protests', Žižek argues that we have to *own* the legacy of the past terror. Not giving the terrain up to the liberal or rightist opponents we must fearlessly admit as *ours* the 'rational kernel' of, as Žižek paraphrases Marx's critique of Hegel's dialectic, the Jacobin Terror. In its affirmation, he cites Alain Badiou who in his *Logics of Worlds* wrote:

> Materialist Dialectics assumes, without particular joy, that, till now, no political subject was able to arrive at the eternity of the truth it was deploying without moments of terror. For, as Saint-Just asked: 'what do those who want neither Virtue nor Terror want?' His answer is well known: they want corruption—another name for the subject's defeat.[77]

Returning to Benjamin's *Critique of Violence,* Žižek says that the revolutionary Terror of 1792–1794 was not a case of 'state-founding violence', but rather a case of 'divine violence'. He notes that the interpreters of Benjamin have rightly been wondering what exactly this 'divine violence' means. To illustrate it, Žižek cites Friedrich Engels's comment on the Paris Commune as an example of the 'dictatorship of the proletariat', where Engels at the end of his Introduction to Marx's *Civil War in France* wrote:

> Of late, the social-Democratic philistines have once more been filled with wholesome terror at the words: Dictatorship of the Proletariat. Well and good, gentlemen, do you want to know what this otedictatorship looks like? Look at the Paris Commune. That was the Dictatorship of the Proletariat.[78]

Žižek's response to the 'philistines', *mutatis mutandis*, is: 'Well and good, gentlemen of critical theorists, do you want to know what this divine violence looks like? Look at the revolutionary Terror of 1792–94, That was Divine Violence'.[79] To avoid 'obscurantist mystification', Žižek argues that one has to fiercely identify 'divine violence' with the concrete cases of historical phenomena. He writes: 'When those outside the structured social field strike "blindly," demanding *and* enacting immediate justice/vengeance, this is "divine violence"'.[80] The 'dictatorship of proletariat', Žižek further adds, is thus another name for Benjaminian 'divine violence', which is 'outside the law, a violence exerted as brutal revenge/justice' and then asks, 'but why divine?'. He explains that 'Divine' points in the direction of a dimension that can be called 'inhuman'. He suggests a 'double equation: divine violence = inhuman terror = dictatorship of proletariat'.[81] He explains this formula by invoking the same Latin phrase that Wahnich also employed as we have seen above: 'Benjaminian "divine violence" should be conceived as divine in the precise sense of the old Latin motto *vox populi, vox dei*: not in the perverse sense of "we are doing it as mere instruments of the People's Will," but as the heroic assumption of the solitude of a sovereign decision'.[82] He further clarifies it:

> It is a decision (to kill, to risk or lose one's own life) made in absolute solitude, with no cover from the big Other. If it is extra-moral, it is not 'immoral,' it does not give the agent license just to kill with some kind of angelic innocence. The motto of divine violence is *fiat iustita, pereat mundus* ['let justice be done, though the world perish']: it is through *justice,* the point of non-distinction between justice and vengeance, that the 'people' (the anonymous part of no-part) imposes its terror and makes other parts pay the price—Judgment Day for the long history of oppression, exploitation, suffering—or, as Robespierre himself put it in a poignant way,

quoting him directly:

> What do you want, you who would like truth to be powerless on the lips of representatives of the French people? Truth undoubtedly has its power, it has its anger, its own despotism: it has touching accents and terrible ones, that sound with force in pure hearts as in guilty consciences, and that untruth can no more imitate than Salome can imitate the thunderbolts of heaven; but accuse nature of it, accuse the people, which wants it and loves it.[83]

Žižek says this is what Robespierre was targeting when in his speech to the Convention of 1792 he famously said 'Citizens, did you want a revolution without revolution?' Žižek's take on it is that:

they want a revolution deprived of the excess in which democracy and terror coincide, a revolution respecting social rules, subordinated to preexisting norms, a revolution in which violence is deprived of the 'divine' dimension and thus reduced to a strategic intervention serving precise and limited goals.[84]

Here I want to paraphrase Robespierre and say that the 'blank wall' amid revolutionary time compounds virtue *and* terror: *terror of the blank wall*, without which the virtue of the 'wall' is impotent, *virtue of the blank wall*, without which terror is fatal! Architecture must hold together the terror and virtue of the blank wall if it is to be revolutionary. Only then can it enter into the dialectic of freedom and necessity, and the problematic of poverty, to which I come in later chapters. In the next section I examine the constitution of the Blank Wall in the philosophical foundation of the Revolution.

The Blank Wall and the philosophy of revolution

There must be a *philosophy* attributed to the revolution of the 'Blank Wall'. It is the same philosophy that is inseparable from the French Revolution. As far as I know, neither Kant, nor Hegel, nor Marx ever referred to David's *La Mort de Marat*—or *Marat Assassiné*. This absence is conspicuous only because of the fact that the French Revolution 'resulted from philosophy'. Our conception of the French Revolution is impossible without Kant and Hegel, along with the young Marx in 1834–1844 with his forceful critique of Hegel's *Philosophy of Right*. In *The Philosophy of History* Hegel wrote:

> It has been said, that the *French Revolution* resulted from Philosophy, and it is not without reason that Philosophy has been called 'Weltweisheit' [World Wisdom]; for it is not only

Truth in and for itself, as the pure essence of things, but also Truth in its living form as exhibited in the affairs of the world. We should not, therefore, contradict the assertion that the Revolution received its first impulse from Philosophy.[85]

He went as far as to call the Revolution 'a glorious mental dawn'.[86] And we must recall that by philosophy, Hegel meant a 'movement of modern thought that goes under the name of Enlightenment'.[87] As Stathis Kouvelakis, in his remarkable *Philosophy and Revolution: From Kant to Marx,* discussing the enthusiasm of the Germans about the event of freedom happening in Paris and spreading to the whole of Europe, notes:

> This provides some indication of the depth of the enthusiasm that the revolutionary event called up in the most militant wing of the German Enlightenment, particularly in Kant and Fichte, to mention no one else. Yet the concerns of the thinkers who were then at the center of the philosophical stage was not merely to defend this event, but even more, to *theorize* it—so much so that it hardly seems an exaggeration to say that German philosophy as such became the philosophy of the revolution *par excellence*.[88]

It is worth mentioning that Kouvelakis puts the young Marx's relation to the 'revolutionary democracy' and Hegel in this specific way: 'Marx turned Hegel against himself; he elaborated a Hegelian critique of Hegel. That, needless to add, is the only way to radicalize the process of Hegelian thought, and blaze a path to a Hegel beyond Hegel.'[89]

At this point I pose this question: Is the revolutionary essence of the Blank Wall of a 'bourgeois' kind or something else? Insofar as the Blank Wall must be linked to the Terror, the answer is bound to be a complicated one. To make it even more complicated, it should be asked if the revolution of the Blank Wall is to be attributed to the 'proletariat revolution' *avant la lettre*, and even go so far as to say that the image of the Blank Wall is an image that the 'dictatorship of the proletariat' must claim as its own. The problematic behind these questions is tied to the whole debate that has raged for two hundred years and keeps flaring up in our own time, when the reactionary revisionists argue that the cycle of 1789 events ended in 1989, noted by Žižek as I cited above. One thing is certain: the Blank Wall is Jacobin, no matter how a hundred years later a 'bourgeois' architect, like Le Corbusier, would appropriate it. Even the Russian revolutionary architects adopted and appropriated the same Blank Wall from Le Corbusier, in spite of the latter's derogatory comments about them. It suffices to mention here that the bourgeois revolution and its theory is the process by which capitalism came into being and dominates the world, and for that matter, architecture.[90] It was the industrial capitalism and technological images that would prompt Le Corbusier's theoretical 'blank wall', as much as it was the result of his observation in his youth of the vernacular architecture of Asia Minor obtained by his 'Voyage to the East' *à la* Rousseau.[91] No matter who would appropriate the Blank Wall, it remains a 'right', a people's right, so to speak, like food, indispensable to 'life'. Here I cite the poet Heinrich Heine who said the following in the spirit of the French Revolution:

> Life is neither end nor means; life is a right. Life wants to enforce its right against the cold hand of death, against the past, and this enforcement is revolution. The elegiac indifference of historians and poets shall not paralyse our energies as

we go about our business; and the rhapsodies of starry-eyed prophets shall not seduce us into jeopardizing the interests of the present and of the first human right that needs to be defended—the right to live. 'Bread is people's first right', said Saint-Just, and that is the greatest declaration made in the entire French Revolution.[92]

If to declare life to be a 'right', amounts to 'to identify it with the irreducible necessity of taking sides in a struggle',[93] as Kouvelakis asserts, I say that declaring a 'right' to the Blank Wall, is *also* an 'irreducible necessity' in taking sides in the same struggle. The *right* to the *blank wall* as a 'human right', on the ground of its *necessity* to the *spiritual* life after the 'first right' to bread is satisfied, must be granted. Not just in the moment of 1789, not in the Jacobins' moment of 1793, but here and now, in the conjuncture of the twenty-first century, we must claim a right to its ownership. We are the inheritors of this 'right'. The *categorical imperative* of this 'right' has never expired but has been questioned. Later in this work I will link the right of the Blank Wall to a more fundamental right: the right to 'shelter'. Here, still, we need to delve a bit more into the relationship between philosophy (here strictly German Idealism) and Revolution (here strictly the French Revolution) before we decipher the *secret* behind the Blank Wall. And we must first venture a *philosophical theory* of the Blank Wall, coupled by the psychoanalytical theory I advanced above, before it can take its rightful place in *architectural theory*. If there is a *center* in modern architecture, by definition an *absent center* in its political ontology, a *voided* center, it must belong to the *void* of the Blank Wall. To put it in *ethical* terms, the Blank Wall is the Categorical Imperative of architecture.

Between German Theory and the French Revolution, I let our great poet, Heine, a German in permanent exile in Paris until he died in 1856, intervene. 'Avaunt, ye specters! I am speaking of one whose very name possesses an exorcising power: I speak of Immanuel Kant', Heine wrote in his *Religion and Philosophy in Germany*.[94] 'How, then, must they stand aghast', he continues, 'when confronted with Kant's *Critique of Pure Reason*! This book is the sword with which, in Germany, theism was decapitated'.[95] Heine takes on the French:

> To be candid, you French are tame and moderate compared with us German. At the most, you have slain a king; and he had already lost his head before he was beheaded … It is really rewarding Maximilian Robespierre too much honour to compare him with Immanuel Kant.[96]

'But', Heine continues:

> If Immanuel Kant, that arch-destroyer in the realms of thought, far surpassed Maximilian Robespierre in terrorism, yet he had certain points of resemblances to the latter that invite a comparison of the two men. In both we find the same inflexible, rigid, prosaic integrity. Then we find in both the same instinct of distrust—only that the one exercises it against ideas, and names it a critique, while the other applies it to men, and calls it republican virtue. In both, however, the narrow-minded shopkeeper type is markedly manifest.[97]

And when it comes specifically to the question of the relationship between philosophy and revolution, Heine's reflections are astonishing:

> We shall not be so foolish as to attempt seriously to refute these malcontents. German philosophy is a matter of great weight and importance, and concerns the whole human race. Only our most remote descendants will be able to decide where we deserve blame or praise for completing first our philosophy and afterward our revolution. To me it seems that a methodical people, such as Germans are, must necessarily have commenced with the Reformation, could only after that proceed to occupy ourselves with philosophy, and not until the completion of the latter could we pass on to the political revolution. This order I find quite sensible. *The heads which philosophy has used for thinking, the revolution can afterwards, for its purposes, cut off. But philosophy would never have been able to use the heads which had been decapitated by the revolution, if the latter had preceded.*[98] [Emphasis mine.]

As Kouvelakis nicely puts it,

> For Hegel's disciple Heine, the same year, 1830, was one of those dates that marked the beginning of a new period; the first reports of the July events woke him—this time for good—from German reveries and meditations of which he was all too fond. A herald of the new spirit of the day, Heine could no longer live (or die) anywhere but in its epicenter, Paris—the 'chief city', as he put it, not 'just France, but the whole civilized world'; 'the capital of the nineteenth century', as Walter Benjamin would say, in a time closer to our own.[99]

'For Hegel', as Joachim Ritter in his *Hegel and the French Philosophy* writes, 'the French Revolution is that event around which all the determinations of philosophy in relation to its time are clustered, with philosophy marking out the problem through attacks on and defenses of the Revolution'.[100] 'Conversely', Ritter notes, 'there is no other philosophy that is a philosophy of revolution to such a degree and so profoundly, in its innermost drive, as that of Hegel'.[101] Ritter positively observes that 'neither the experience of the Terror nor the critical insight into the Revolution's inability to come to any positive and stable political solutions were able to turn Hegel into its opponent'.[102] Hegel affirmatively accepted the French Revolution, Ritter points out. Hegel 'Makes philosophy the theory of the age', Ritter writes, 'it is given the task of conceiving the political freedom of the Revolution in its essences, the foundation upon which the Revolution "bases all" shall be philosophical determination'.[103] Hegel's philosophy, therefore, remains a philosophy of revolution from the beginning that determines its end. The chief objective of Revolution was the construction of a Republic of Virtue. As Hegel depicts it, Smith notes, 'the reign of Terror was nothing more than the working out on the public stage of this obsessive concern with inner purity'.[104] Hegel in *Philosophy of History* wrote:

> Virtue is here a simple abstract principle and distinguishes the citizens into two classes only—those who are favorably disposed and those who are not. But disposition can only be recognized and judged of by disposition. Suspicion therefore is in the ascendant; but virtue, as soon as it becomes liable to suspicion, is already condemned. […] Robespierre set up the principle of virtue as supreme, and it may be said that with this man virtue was an earnest matter. Virtue and Terror are the order of the day; for Subjective Virtue, whose sway is based on disposition only, brings with it the most fearful tyranny. It exercises its power without legal formalities, and the punishment it inflicts is equally simple—Death.[105]

At the end, there is a paradox in Hegel's treatment of the French Revolution as Smith points out. 'While Revolution caused reprehensible terror and violence, it was still regarded by Hegel as a "progressive" force in history', moving humanity closer to a certain desirable goal, namely, freedom'.[106] This is why he praised the revolutionary heroes and this on the assumption of the doctrine of 'cunning of Reason' whereby 'whatever individuals may have subjectively intended, the actual import of their deeds was and could not but be unknown to them'.[107] Much of Hegel's reflections on revolution in his *Philosophy of Right* is related to the systems of 'freedom' and 'necessity', state and civil society, to which I will come back later in this work.

As for Kant's theory of legality and morality in relation to revolution, Kouvelakis writes that 'the revolution, is by the same token, objectionable from the standpoint of individual morality, which dictates obedience to existing laws in order to preserve the foundations of the community'.[108] Yet, he points out,

> once he has established this, Kant at no point rejects the revolutionary regime on moral ground; on the contrary, he defends both its legality and its internal link to the imperatives of 'moral politics', even in the case of the Jacobin Terror. Indeed, he would appear to criticize the Jacobins less for resorting to force than for the plebeian social dimension of their policy—in other words, for raising broad egalitarian demands. In this sense, he is a Thermidorian *avant la latter* who anticipated the closure of the debate on equality opened by the Revolution of 10 August 1792.[109]

For Hegel, the Revolution was a radical new beginning. In him, and in other German Idealists, we find the 'core of

Jacobin conception of the Revolution, especially in the central importance he [Hegel] ascribes to the moment of Terror as a key to understanding the revolutionary process'.[110] Kouvelakis importantly notes that 'Like the standpoint of subjective morality, the freedom created by the French Revolution must be grasped in its internal limits, in the movement of self-transcendence triggered again and again by the very spectacle of its defeat. The Revolution is by no means finished; it is not a shore that has been left behind and can now be safely contemplated from afar. It dominates the whole of the historical period that followed it'.[111] He further offers the following perceptive observations which may serve as a summary of the arguments I have presented so far:

> At the moment when consciousness turns back upon itself, it retroactively grasps its own progression by confronting the void, the constitutive lack formed by the absolute negativity at its core. It recognizes its own becoming in the Revolution. It is in this sense that even the moment of the Terror—the moment, precisely, in which absolute freedom changes into its opposite and is identified with death and nothingness—enters into the process by which freedom become necessity; that is to say, it is in this sense that the Terror is always-already there, behind us and within us. In other words, it is at the moment when, under the impact of this retroactive performativity, consciousness recognizes that its own freedom is realized in the state's, that it posits the necessity of Terror, and assigns it its significance: that of an internal precondition for emancipation process.[112]

On the one hand, Kouvelakis remarks, 'from a theoretical point of view, Kant is plainly contemporaneous with the French Revolution. But a typically Hegelian reversal shows us how to state the same thing the other way round: the French Revolution is Kantian. A critique of the one that applies to the other as well'.[113] It is after all these reflections on the confrontation of German Idealism—Kant and Hegel in particular—with the French Revolution, albeit treated briefly, that we can now come to Marx. Marx went into exile in Paris in the Fall of 1843, as Heine did after the July Revolution. It was in the crisis year of 1843 that Marx went over to the revolutionary camp. In a letter some years later to Ferdinand Freiligrath Marx wrote, 'whereas you are a *poet*, I am a *critic* and for me the experiences of 1849 to 1852 are quite enough'.[114] If his friend Heine was a poet, Marx was a critic and theoretician. A political break underlies Marx's theoretical break, a transition from the radical 'reformism' known as 'Rhenish liberalism' to a revolutionary camp. The young Marx in exile took allegiance with the *communist* position and by the time The Communist Manifesto was drafted in 1847, Marx (with Engels) had already formulated the *class analysis* of the 'Bourgeois Revolution'. Marx's 'political break', in Kouvelakis's evaluation, puts him in a precise relationship with Hegel against the usual interpretation dissolving him in the 'Young Hegelian' movement. An important aspect of this relation is, to recall, that 'Marx turned Hegel against himself; he elaborated a Hegelian critique of Hegel. That, needless to add, is the only way to radicalize the process of Hegelian thought, and blaze a path to a Hegel beyond Hegel'.[115] Furthermore, the emancipatory core of the French Revolution had to be repeated in order to put an end to 'Germany's *ancient régime*—how, that is, with the "German *misère*" as one's starting point, to take up a position on the trajectory of this founding event, and accede to the universality of the new world-historical moment'.[116] In Marx's conception, the 'man' of the French Declaration of Rights, names 'the most radical of the perspectives held out by the French Revolution'. [117] Significantly, 'Marx places himself in the tradition of the French Revolution and the project of a "popular political economy" defended by the Robespierrians, the urban *sans-culottes*, and the most radical wing of peasant movement: a project centered on subordinating property rights to the right of existence'.[118]

At this point I want to return to the line I highlighted in bloc quotation cited in the beginning by Benjamin where he wrote: '*It dispels the illusion that the task of the proletariat revolution is to complete the work of 1789 hand in hand with the bourgeoisie*'. Benjamin had specifically referred to *The Communist Manifesto* in the cited passage, which alludes to the necessity of 'class struggle' in the analysis of the French Revolution that Marx took up. It is in this relation that I want to bring up, again, the notion of the 'Blank Wall'. But this time I want to attribute a 'class character' to it and ask this question: *Who must lay claim to its ownership?*—Bourgeoisie or the Proletariat? Implicit in this question is the notion that the 'blank wall' must be conceived as a phenomenon manifesting '*social antagonism*', for which the 'proletariat' is the name that Marx gave it in 1844. In the context of the French Revolution it had been called the 'Third Estate', 'people', '*sans-culotterie*', etc. It must be pointed out that the *emancipatory critique* is immanent in this social antagonism. The question posed above, moreover, leads to the complexity of the 'class analysis' of the French Revolution, a complex subject debated by Marxist scholars into which we cannot enter here.[119]

Here I want to resume confronting the liberal reactions against the French Revolution I touched upon before. Is the Revolution over? It is said that the French Revolution is *unfinished*. Its *relevance* to the present persists, notwithstanding the spectacle of its *failure*. This failure is immanent in the revolutionary sequence following 1789: 'The revolution of 10 August 1792 and those of 31 May and June 1793, which opened the way to Jacobins' rise to power, the Terror, Thermidor, and Napoleon's *coup d'état*, all turned on this question of the "end" of the Revolution, an end that was as ardently desired as it was stubbornly resisted.'[120] If not 'ended', then liberal capitalism feels its *menace* and tries to conjure away its specters by all means. The year 1989 is said to mark the end of the cycle that had begun in 1789. In the same year the 'end of history' was proclaimed. On the other hand, the postmodern 'end of the grand narrative' was also proclaimed by Jean-François Lyotard only to make room for a 'grand narrative' favorable to triumphant liberalism and its utopia driving out all other rival narratives from the political scene, thus denying the *moment* of our modernity in the French Revolution. We are told there is no alternative to capitalism. The revisionist historian of the French Revolution, François Furet, delegitimized the Revolution by titling the first part of his book as: 'The French Revolution is over'.[121] But does Furet succeed, like his other predecessors in conjuring away the specters of Revolution, Kouvelakis aptly asks:

> It is an attempt, which, as such, can only offer additional testimony to the stubborn presence (in, precisely, a spectral mode, the mode of that which returns to haunt the present) both of what it is charged with exorcising and also of the fundamental ambivalence (fascination/repulsion) that it continues to inspire.[122]

The French Revolution anticipates all other *unfinished* and *failed* revolutions. It is a *defeated* Revolution. But the

Part I

> '*constitutive tension*' at its founding moment persists and the questions it poses linger in any revolutionary movement: 'property right versus the right to existence; the relationship between liberty and equality; the question of revolutionary war and "terror", of the nation and cosmopolitanism'.[123]
>
> And furthermore, revolutionary time presents itself as the becoming-necessary of emancipation—on the expressed condition that we understand this necessity not as the manifestation of an a priori meaning or goal, but as the retroactive effect of an event, irreducibly contingent and undecidable in itself, that poses its own presuppositions, thus defining them as the conditions for its realization.[124]

By the same token, I would like to claim that the revolutionary Blank Wall in *The Death of Marat* also persists. It is *unfinished* if not *defeated*. It must therefore be repeated. It has a right to existence. The liberal academy pretends it never existed and conjures away its *menace*. In conclusion I say this: architecture discourse, today, suffers from a *theoretical* liberalism. This liberalism manifests reactionary traits. It has abandoned the *blank wall*. Architecture thus suffers from an ideological *malaise* it has contracted from the *reactionary bourgeois ideology* with no sign of 'spiritual' cure on the horizon. Here I ask again: Is the Blank Wall in David's *The Death of Marat* 'bourgeois' or 'proletariat'? Of the two, who is entitled to claim its ownership? In the last part of this book I will try to provide some answers to these questions.

Notes
1 G.W.F. Hegel, *The Philosophy of History*, intro. C.J. Friedrich (New York: Dover, 1956), 446.

2 See Neil Davidson, *How Revolutionary Were the Bourgeoise Revolutions?* (Chicago: Haymarket Books, 2012).
3 Walter Benjamin, 'Paris, the Capital of the Nineteenth Century, Exposé of 1935', in *The Arcades Project* (Cambridge: The Belknap Press of Harvard University Press, 1999), 12–13. Also see 'Exposé 1939'. Benjamin's prescient insight in 1935 concerning the relation between bourgeoisie and proletariat (that he adopted from Marx) in the aftermath of the French Revolution with the victory of the bourgeoise in 1830 in France anticipates the more comprehensive historical analysis that appeared later in the twentieth century by Marxist historians, and which continues to our time. For the best example, see Eric J. Hobsbawm's *Echoes of the Marseillaise: Two Centuries Look Back on the French Revolution* (London and New York: Verso, 1990).
4 See Walter Benjamin, *The Arcades Project*, 'r [École Polytechnique]'. In this convolute Benjamin writes: 'From the time of Napoleon I, the École Polytechnique was subject to continual reproach for providing practical training with an overly broad theoretical foundation. These criticisms led, in 1858, to proposals for reform, against which Arago took a most determined stand. At the same time, he dismissed the charge that the school had become a breeding ground of revolutionary animus'. Here Benjamin quotes Francçois Arago from his *Sure l'ancienne École Polytechnique* (Paris, 1853) as having said: 'I have been told of a reproach directed against polytechnical instruction, and according to which the mathematical disciplines—the study of differential calculus and of integral calculus, for example—would have effect of transforming their students into socialists of the worst stamp … How has it escaped the author of such a reproach that its immediate consequences is nothing less than to range the likes of a Huygens, a Newton, a Leibniz, a Euler, a Lagrange, a Laplace among the most hot-headed of demagogues?', 821. Also, Benjamin quotes Marx on the June Insurrection: 'In order to dispel the people's last illusion, in order to enable a complex break with the past, it was necessary for the customary poetic accompaniment of a French uprising. The enthusiastic youth of the bourgeoisie, the students of École Polytechnique, the three-cornered hats—all to take the side of the oppressors', 823.
5 Walter Benjamin, *The Arcades Project*, 'r [École Polytechnique], 823–824.
6 See Sergio Villari, *J.N.L. Durand (1760–1834), Art and Science of Architecture* (New York: Rizzoli, 1990).
7 See Sergio Villari, *J.N.L. Durand (1760–1834)*, 31.

Part I

8 Jonathan Israel, *Revolutionary Ideas, An Intellectual History of the French Revolution from The Rights of Man to Robespierre* (Oxford and Princeton: Princeton University Press, 2014), 622. Israel further remarks that 'Crypto-royalists viewed the Idéologues d'Holbachian refusal to conceive morality as something divinely installed in the human heart to be deeply damaging to the social order. But this endemic strife lingered mostly below the surface until after the triumph of Bonaparte's authoritarianism in 1799–1800, a development that encouraged expression of more forthrightly antimaterialist and Christian position. La Révelliere-Lépeaux [a member of the Idéologues] though also promoting a new public morality, found himself in a category of his own as a militant Rousseauist, anti-Robespierriste, an ardent enthusiast for organized cult of deism. For his part, Mercier [a veteran republican] agreed with Idéologues that Robespierre had declared war on both the Enlightenment and the Revolution, and that the Institut's task was to obliterate every vestige of Montagnard thinking and ideology, and restore the (nonreligious) Enlightenment to its proper place as the veritable guide of a humanity bolstered by democracy, human rights, and the world revolution', 624.
9 Sergio Villari, *J.N.L. Durand (1760–1834)*, 32.
10 Sergio Villari, *J.N.L. Durand (1760–1834)*, 32. Villari informatively writes that there was an intellectual affinity between Durand and the members of the Comité d'instruction publique during 1793–1794. 'Constituted by the legislative assembly, the Comité d'instruction publique was the institutional stronghold of the Idéologues. Their commitment to the elaboration of a new system of national public education was rooted in one of the issues most permeated with moral tensions of all those opened up by the *philosophie*: "ignorance," wrote Diderot , "is the heritage of slavery … education gives man dignity, and the slave soon realizes that he was born to be other than slave." In the political thought of the Idéologues, the widening of education to include all social classes became the indispensable condition of moral and civil progress. As an instrument of personal emancipation from prejudice and intellectual dependency, education assures "a real content of the formal political principle of equality"', 33.
11 Quoted in Sergio Villari, *J.N.L. Durand (1760–1834)*, 12–13.
12 For this comparison see Sergio Villari, *J.N.L. Durand (1760–1834)*. Villari writes that 'Neoclassical architects believed they saw in the sphere, an ancient symbol of eternity and perfection, the ineffable presence of the

sublime. It was a presence that served potently to celebrate the earth, immortality, equality, and Newton—or more precisely, reason itself', 41.
13 Sergio Villari, *J.N.L. Durand (1760–1834)*, 22.
14 I am here following the fine reflections by Villari in *J.N.L. Durand (1760–1834)*. He writes: 'Such unadorned walls, constituted as absence, have in the paradigmatic order of discourse a semantic *imprint* that is equally as strong as the continuous fugal variations of plan and the infinite, sensuous suspensions and gradated repetitions of the articulated volumes of the baroque spatial continuum. In broad terms, this is what Gerard Genette would define as *zero degree*'. He cites the following paragraph by Genette: 'that is to say, a sign defined by the absence of the sign, the value of which is perfectly recognized. Absolute sobriety of expression is a mark of an extreme elevation of thought ... Old Horace says, quite simply: "would that he had died!" Medea says: "I!" Genesis says: "And there was light." Nothing is more *marked* than this simplicity: it is the very figure, indeed the perfectly obligatory figure, of the sublime', 13.
15 See T.J. Clark, 'Painting in the Year Two', in *Representations* 47, Summer 1994, 20. Clark mentions that it is same politics that goes to Gericault's *Raft* and Delacroix *Liberty* and many other cases in the nineteenth and the twentieth centuries that he lists. He says only a fool would deny that 'politics provided the occasion for art in some or all of these cases', 21.
16 T.J. Clark, 'Painting in the Year Two', 22.
17 T.J. Clark, 'Painting in the Year Two', 31.
18 Quoted in *David's The Death of Marat*, eds. William Vaughan and Helen Weston (Cambridge: Cambridge University Press, 2000), 1–2.. For the original French, see Charles Baudelaire, 'Le Musée Classique du Bazar Bonne-Nouvelle, *Le Corsaire-Satan*, 21 January 1846; reprinted in *Oeuvres complètes* (Paris: Gallimard, Pléiade edition, 1976), 2: 410.
19 For more details of Corday's preparations and conditions of her arrival in Marat's apartment to carry out her assassination plan see *David's The Death of Marat*.
20 I do not have space in this work to go through a detailed account of the French Revolution and discuss controversies and misconceptions surrounding the Terror, 1792–1794, in association with the figure of Robespierre and his faction in the National Convention mentioned above. Here I want to cite razor sharp comments by Geoff Mann in his *In the Long Run We are All Dead, Keynesianism, Political Economy and Revolution* (London and New York: Verso, 2017) which concisely renders a correct judgment with

which I concur. He writes: 'Only when he [Robespierre] no longer believed the bourgeoise order capable of accommodating an honorable poverty did Robespierre abandon this position and commit himself to the necessarily violent construction of a new society founded on a more radical equality, one in which poverty would not exist and hence would have no meaning', 90. And further, 'To those who think Jacobinism as irrational proto-communist radicalism driven by uncompromising ideological purity, Robespierre's answer might come as something of a historical surprise. Jacobin politics was neither so rigid nor so unsubtle as is often thought, nor was the Jacobin Club static or homogeneous. From the beginning of the Revolution, Jacobins shared a commitment to property rights with the provincial elites who dominated the Convention at the time and who later came to be known as Girondins, after the region around Bordeaux from which many of their leaders hailed. (Indeed, the idea that the two groups were always clearly distinct is a convenient simplification; the line between them was often blurrier than canned histories make it seem.) If the Revolution undoubtedly "inaugurated a liberal commercial order," the Jacobins played their role. In the months that followed Robespierre's speech, the two factions united, if uneasily, in defense of private property as central to the revolutionary cause and in condemnation of calls for radical redistribution from *les Enragé's*, 92. [*Les Enragés* were a loose group of radicals at the far Left of the Revolutionary movement (beyond even Robespierre's *Montagnards*). Led by the radical cleric Jacques Roux, they were involved in the termination of the Girondins and the beginning of the Terror in Fall [1793], 92. Here I must state that I do not share Mann's criticism of Slavoj Žižek's invocation of Walter Benjamin's notion of 'Divine Violence' for his affirmative view of the Terror. In this regard, see Slavoj Žižek's 'Introduction' to *Robespierre, Virtue and Terror* (London and New York: Verso, 2007), entitled 'Robespierre, or, the "Divine Violence" of Terror'. Among many recent books written on the French Revolution see especially Eric Hazan, *A People's History of the French Revolution* (London and New York, 2017); also see David Andress, *The Terror: Civil War in the French Revolution* (London: Abacus, 2005).

21 See David Andress, *The Terror: Civil War in the French Revolution*, 76.
22 Quoted in William Vaughan and Helen Weston, eds. *David's The Death of Marat*, 4.
23 In Hal Draper, *Karl Marx's Theory of Revolution: The "Dictatorship of the Proletariat"*, volume III (New York: Monthly Review Press, 1986), 22.
24 Hal Draper, *Karl Marx's Theory of Revolution*, 22.

25 Quoted in Vaughan and Weston, *David's The Death of Marat*, 4.
26 Quoted in William Vaughan and Helen Weston, eds. *David's The Death of Marat*, 6.
27 In Hal Draper, *Karl Marx's Theory of Revolution*, 24; also see Vaughan and Weston, *David's The Death of Marat*.
28 In Hal Draper, *Karl Marx's Theory of Revolution*, 25. Draper discusses the meaning of 'dictatorship' in a broader context with a historical perspective going back to the etymology of the Romans' word *dictatura*.
29 T.J. Clark, 'Painting in the Year Two', 48.
30 T.J. Clark, 'Painting in the Year Two', 48.
31 T.J. Clark, 'Painting in the Year Two', 49.
32 T.J. Clark, 'Painting in the Year Two', 49.
33 T.J. Clark, 'Painting in the Year Two', 51. Clarks says that 'This produces, I think, a kind of representational deadlock, which is the true source of the Marat's continuing hold on us. No painting ever believed in illusionism more fiercely. No objects were ever offered the viewer more beguilingly than Corday's and Marat's letters', 51.
34 This is a good example by William Vaughan and Helen Weston in their 'Introduction' to *David's The Death of Marat*, 7–8.
35 By William Vaughan and Helen Weston in their 'Introduction' to *David's The Death of Marat*, 2.
36 I came across this information in Geoff Mann's *In the Long Run We Are All Dead, Keynesianism, Political Economy and Revolution* (London and New York: Verso, 2017), chapter 8. For reproduction of the painting, see William Doyle, *The French Revolution: A Very Short Introduction* (Oxford: Oxford University Press, 2001), 104. I will come back to Mann's important book in later chapters.
37 See the impressive exploration by Todd McGowan in his recent *Emancipation After Hegel: Achieving a Contradictory Revolution* (New York: Columbia University Press, 2019).
38 Glenn Alexandre Magee, *The Hegel Dictionary* (London: Continuum, 2010), 28.
39 For an excellent exposition of this point see Slavoj Žižek, *Tarrying With Negative, Kant, Hegel, and the Critique of Ideology* (Durham: Duke University Press, 1993), see especially chapter 1 'Cogito: The Void Called Subject'.
40 See Stathis Kouvelakis, *Philosophy and Revolution, From Kant to Marx*, preface by Fredric Jameson, trans. G.M. Goshgarian (London and New York: Verso, 2003).

41 See Walter Benjamin, 'Experience and Poverty', in *Walter Benjamin, Selected Writings, Volume 2, 1927–1934* (Cambridge: The Belknap Press of Harvard University Press, 1999).

42 The book in question is Siegfried Giedion's *Building in France, Building in Iron, Building in Ferro-Concrete*, intro. Sokratis Georgiadis, trans. J. Duncan Berry (Santa Monica: The Getty Center for the History of Art and Humanities, 1995). Giedion sent a copy of it to Benjamin when it came out in German entitled *Bauen in Frankreich, Bauen in Eisenbeton*, in 1928. Benjamin wrote a cordial response. For more see Georgiadis's 'Introduction'.

43 Walter Benjamin, 'Paris, the Capital of the Nineteenth Century, Exposé of 1935', 4. Also see the 1939 Exposé.

44 See Susan Buck-Morss, *The Dialectics of Seeing, Walter Benjamin and the Arcades Project* (Cambridge: The MIT Press, 1989).

45 For the specific meaning of 'Thermidorean' used here see Alain Badiou, *Metapolitics* (London and New York: Verso, 2005), especially chapter 9 entitled 'What is Thermidorean?'. For the phrase 'Passion of the Real' see Alain Badiou's *The Century* (Cambridge: Polity, 2007).

46 Theda Skocpol and Meyer Kestnbaum, 'Mars Unshackled: The French Revolution in World-Historical Perspective', in *The French Revolution and the Birth of Modernity*, ed. Ference Fehér (Berkeley: University of California Press, 1990), 13.

47 E.J. Hobsbawm, *Echoes of Marseillaise, Two Centuries Looking Back on the French Revolution* (London and New York: Verso, 1990), 111.

48 See Theda Skocpol and Meyer Kestnbaum, 'Mars Unshackled: The French Revolution in World-Historical Perspective'. In terms of similarities and differences, the authors explain that 'French revolutionaries' political culture was a secularist alternative to divine-right monarchy, because the French revolutionaries fought the prerogatives and symbols of Catholicism as well as monarchy and aristocratic privilege. The Iranian Revolution, by contrast, has opposed a secularist, "modernizing" absolutist monarchy in the name of Islamic theocratic regime … Old-Regime France was a Great Power in which monarchy and bureaucratic Catholic church were allied, thus encouraging critics of the Old Regime to elaborate secularist Ideals. In contrast, Old-regime Iran was a minor power facing cultural and economic penetration from the secular west.' They continue by tracing the similarities: 'Despite the obvious cultural and structural contrasts between France and Iran, however, notice the remarkable similarities in the overall political and geopolitical dynamics of these revolutions. Just as the French Revolution

did, the Iranian Revolution brought to power an ideological leadership more obsessed with virtue and national regeneration than with economic struggles or modernizing efficiency. Similarly, the Iranian Revolution mobilized masses of formerly excluded people into national politics and excelled at motivating the new citizens, through ideology and exemplary leadership, to participate in protracted and humanly costly international warfare', 26.

49 E.J. Hobsbawm, *Echoes of Marseillaise, Two Centuries Looking Back on the French Revolution*, 111.

50 Quoted in Stathis Kouvelakis, *Philosophy and Revolution*, 2. Kouvelakis insightfully evaluates the Iranian revolution and Foucault's commitment to it by saying: 'A revolution against the Enlightenment—in the sense of which Gramsci called October 1917 a "revolution against *Capital*"—and, above all, against a version of the Enlightenment associated with Marxism, the Iranian revolution is posed as a possible alternative, for the space of an instant or an illusion, to the trajectory of the revolution that turned into state enterprise as the realization of a promise and a desire leading straight to the Gulag', 3.

51 See Janet Afray and Kevin B. Anderson, *Foucault and the Iranian Revolution: Gender and the Seductions of Islamism* (Chicago: The University of Chicago Press, 2005), in Appendix, 'Open Letter to Prime Minister Mehdi Bazargan, first published in *Le Nouvel Observateur*, April 24, 1979'. In this letter Foucault protested the killing of the opposition members and reminded the Prime Minister of his obligations to protect the result of the revolution. Also see Stathis Kouvelakis, *Philosophy and Revolution*.

52 Stathis Kouvelakis, *Philosophy and Revolution*, 3. Below I will come back to Kouvelakis's insights on the philosophical foundation of the French Revolution.

53 See Slavoj Žižek's 'Robespierre, Or, the "Divine Violence" of Terror', Introduction to *Robespierre, Virtue and Terror* (London and New York: 2007), vii.

54 Slavoj Žižek's 'Robespierre, Or, the "Divine Violence" of Terror', vii.

55 Slavoj Žižek's 'Robespierre, Or, the "Divine Violence" of Terror', vii.

56 Slavoj Žižek's 'Robespierre, Or, the "Divine Violence" of Terror', vii.

57 See François Furet, *Interpreting the French Revolution* (Cambridge: Cambridge University Press, and Paris: Editions de la Maison des Sciences de l'Homme, 1981). For a discussion of the revisionist historiography see George C. Comninel, *Rethinking the French Revolution, Marxism and the Revisionist Challenge* (London and New York: Verso, 1987).

58 See Slavoj Žižek's foreword to Sophie Wahnich's ground-breaking book entitled *In Defence of the Terror* (London and New York: Verso, 2012), xii. Žižek further writes: 'there seems to be a shared perception that 1989 marks the end of the epoch which began in 1789—the end of a certain "paradigm", as we like to put it today: the paradigm of a revolutionary process that is focused on taking over state power and then using this power as a lever to accomplish global social transformation. Even the "postmodern" Left (from Antonio Negri to John Holloway) emphasizes that a new revolution should break with this fetishization of state power as ultimate prize and focus on the much deeper "molecular" level of transformation of daily practice', xiii–xiv. I discuss Wahnich's book above.

59 See Ruth Scurr, *Fatal Purity, Robespierre and the French Revolution* (New York: Henry Holt, 2006). Also see the equally balanced study by David Andress in *The Terror: Civil War in the French Revolution* (London: Abacus, 2005).

60 Narrated in Ruth Scurr, *Fatal Purity*, 8.

61 Ibid., *Fatal Purity*, 46.

62 Quoted in Ruth Scurr, *Fatal Purity*, 246.

63 Sophie Wahnich, *In Defence of the Terror*, 21.

64 Sophie Wahnich *In Defence of the Terror*, 21.

65 Sophie Wahnich, *In Defence of the Terror*, 27.

66 Quoted in Sophie Wahnich, *In Defence of the Terror*, 45. For information about the 'September Massacres' see, for example, David Andress in *The Terror: Civil War in the French Revolution*.

67 Wahnich also brings up Giorgio Agamben in this regard and writes: 'For Giorgio Agamben, "the sovereign sphere is the sphere in which it is permitted to kill without committing homicide and without celebrating a sacrifice"; as for the lives of those massacred, they are the "sacred lives" of homo sacer, exposed to murder and unsacrificable, captured in the "first properly political space of the West distinct from both the religious and the profane sphere, from both the natural order and regular juridical order". These theoretical illuminations help us understand how everyone has found the September massacres intolerable, despite the great majority of spectators finding them legitimate at the time', 46.

68 Sophie Wahnich, *In Defence of the Terror*, 49.

69 Sophie Wahnich, *In Defence of the Terror*, 55. Wahnich further notes that contrary to common interpretations, 'the Terror was thus aimed at establishing limits to the sovereign exception, putting a brake on the legitimate

violence of the people and giving a public and institutionalized form to vengeance. Terror as justice was thus a desperate and despairing attempt to constrain both political crime and the legitimate popular vengeance that could result from it. As a form of exercise of power, it did not amount to a condemnation of the vengeance wreaked in September 1792, but rather of the form that this assumed as a result of the impunity in which the elites had left the counter-revolutionaries', 65.

70 Quoted in Sophie Wahnich, *In Defence of the Terror*, 73.
71 Sophie Wahnich, *In Defence of the Terror*, 99.
72 See Walter Benjamin, 'Critique of Violence', in *Walter Benjamin, Selected Writings, Volume 1, 1913–1926* (Cambridge: The Belknap Press of Harvard University Press, 1996).
73 Quoted in Sophie Wahnich, *In Defence of the Terror*, 101.
74 Quoted in Sophie Wahnich, *In Defence of the Terror*, 102.
75 Sophie Wahnich, *In Defence of the Terror*, 108. Wahnich makes her final statement in connection with her discussion of the 11 September 2001 event in New York City, picking up the notion of 'terrorism' in the political jargon of the American political project that came after the event. She notes, 'After 11 September 2001, New York experienced a "state of dread". Disturbance and discouragement came in the wake of the large number of dead and this mass death's effect of de-subjectification. As the target of these attacks, the "sacred body" of the United States had been assassinated. The question was how to rediscover courage after the misfortune', and further, 'The American sacred body is of course the center of commerce, the fetish of capitalism, the government in Washington, the presidential and military power, but above all—one might say, before all else—the bodies of the dead', 104.
76 Quoted in Slavoj Žižek, *In Defense of Lost Causes* (London and New York: Verso, 2008), 159. This is part of the speech Robespierre delivered on 5 February 1794/18 Pluviose Year II; for the entire speech see Slavoj Žižek, *Robespierre, Virtue and Terror.*
77 Slavoj Žižek, *In Defense of Lost Causes,* 160. Žižek renders his own translation from the French *Logiques des monde*, which is slightly different from the English edition. It reads as follows: 'Without any particular joy, the materialist dialectic will work under the assumption that no political subject has yet attained the eternity of the truth which holds without moments of terror. For, as Saint-Just asked: "what do those who want neither Virtue nor terror want"" His answer is well known: they want corruption—another

name for the failure of the subject', in *Logics of Worlds* (London: Continuum, 2009), 88.
78 Slavoj Žižek, *In Defense of Lost Causes,* 161. See also, *Karl Marx and V.I. Lenin, Civil War in France: The Paris Commune,* with essay by Nikita Fedorovsky (New York: International Publishers, 1940), 22.
79 Slavoj Žižek, *In Defense of Lost Causes,* 162.
80 Slavoj Žižek, *In Defense of Lost Causes,* 162.
81 Slavoj Žižek, *In Defense of Lost Causes,* 162.
82 Slavoj Žižek, *In Defense of Lost Causes,* 162.
83 Slavoj Žižek, *In Defense of Lost Causes,* 163.
84 Slavoj Žižek, *In Defense of Lost Causes,* 163. Žižek quotes the whole relevant passage in Robespierre's speech to the same convention: 'Citizens, did you want a revolution without revolution? What is this spirit of persecution that has come to revise, so to speak, the one that broke ou chains? But what sure judgment can one make of the effects that can follow these great commotions? Who can mark, after the event, the exact point at which the waves of popular instruction should break? At that price, what people could ever have shaken off the yoke of despotism? For while it is true that a great nation cannot rise in a simultaneous movement, and that tyranny can only be hit by the portion of citizens that is closest to it, how would these ever dare to attack it if, after the victory, delegates from remote parts could hold them responsible for the duration or violence of the political torment that had saved the homeland? They ought to be regarded as justified by tacit proxy for the whole of society. The French, friends of liberty, meeting in Paris last August, acted in that role, in the name of all the departments. They should either be approved or repudiated entirely. To make them criminally responsible for a few apparent or real disorders, inseparable from so great a shock, would be to punish them for their devotion', 163. Žižek comments that 'it is this radical revolutionary stance which also enables Robespierre to denounce the "humanitarian" concern with victims of revolutionary "divine violence"' quoting Robespierre as having said: 'a sensibility that wails almost exclusively over the enemies of liberty seems suspect to me. Stop shaking the tyrant's bloody robe in my face, or I will believe that you wish to put Rome in chains', 164.
85 G.W.F. Hegel, *The Philosophy of History,* intro. C.J. Friedrich (New York, Dover, 1956), 446.
86 G.W.F. Hegel, *The Philosophy of History,* 447.

87 See Steven B. Smith, 'Hegel and the French Revolution: An Epitaph for Republicanism', in *The French Revolution and the Birth of Modernity*, ed. Ference Fehér (Berkeley: University of California Press, 1990). Smith writes that 'The Enlightenment set itself the ambitious task of liberating thought from the "kingdom of darkness" in order to make men into the masters and possessors of the world', 221.

88 Stathis Kouvelakis, *Philosophy and Revolution*, 9. For my reflections in this section I am entirely indebted to Kouvelakis's extensive explorations in his book on this subject.

89 Stathis Kouvelakis, *Philosophy and Revolution*, 236.

90 See Neil Davidson, *How Revolutionary Were the Bourgeois Revolutions?*

91 I am referring to amazing writings of Le Corbusier (Charles-Eduard Jeanneret) in his youth traveling to the East, see Le Corbusier, *Journey to the East*, trans. and ed. Ivan Žaknić, in collaboration with Nicole Pertuiset (Cambridge: The MIT Press, 1987). Also see Adolf Max Vogt, *Le Corbusier, the Nobel Savage: Toward an Archaeology of Modernism*, trans. Radka Donnell (Cambridge: The MIT Press, 1998).

92 Quoted in Stathis Kouvelakis, *Philosophy and Revolution*, 67.

93 Stathis Kouvelakis, *Philosophy and Revolution*, 67.

94 Heinrich Heine, 'Religion and Philosophy in Germany' in *The Prose Writings of Heinrich Heine* (Newton Stewart: Anodos Books, 2019), 92. Also see Heine Heinrich, *On the History of Religion and Philosophy in Germany and Other Writings*, ed. Terry Pinkard, trans. Howard Pollack-Milgate (Cambridge: Cambridge University Press, 2007).

95 Heinrich Heine, 'Religion and Philosophy in Germany', 92.

96 Heinrich Heine, 'Religion and Philosophy in Germany', 92.

97 Heinrich Heine, 'Religion and Philosophy in Germany', 93.

98 Heinrich Heine, 'Religion and Philosophy in Germany', 93–94.

99 Stathis Kouvelakis's *Philosophy and Revolution*, in 'Chapter 2: Specters of Revolution: On a Few Themes in Heine', 45. For a complex analysis of the position of Kant and Hegel on the 'theory of revolution', that is, the Kantian and Hegelian 'Theory of the French Revolution', and for the discussion of *ambivalence* in both, I refer readers to Kouvelakis's text.

100 See Joachim Ritter, *Hegel and the French Revolution, Essays on The Philosophy of Right*, trans. Ricard Dien Winfield (Cambridge: The MIT Press, 1984), 43.

101 Joachim Ritter, *Hegel and the French Revolution*, 43.

102 Joachim Ritter, *Hegel and the French Revolution*, 46.

Part I

103 Joachim Ritter, *Hegel and the French Revolution*, 48.
104 See Steven B. Smith, 'Hegel and the French Revolution: An Epitaph for Republicanism', 230.
105 Hegel, *Philosophy of History*, 450–451. Also see Steven B. Smith, 'Hegel and the French Revolution: An Epitaph for Republicanism', 230.
106 Steven B. Smith, 'Hegel and the French Revolution: An Epitaph for Republicanism', 232.
107 As put by Steven B. Smith, 'Hegel and the French Revolution: An Epitaph for Republicanism', 232.
108 Stathis Kouvelakis, *Philosophy and Revolution*, 21.
109 Stathis Kouvelakis's *Philosophy and Revolution*, 21–22.
110 Stathis Kouvelakis's *Philosophy and Revolution*, 25.
111 Stathis Kouvelakis's *Philosophy and Revolution*, 25. Here Kouvelakis refers to the 'astounding' section of Hegel's *Phenomenology* devoted to 'absolute freedom and terror' on which his subsequent remarks are based.
112 Stathis Kouvelakis's, *Philosophy and Revolution*, 25–26.
113 Stathis Kouvelakis's *Philosophy and Revolution*, 26. He further notes that 'None the less, from the standpoint of the concrete historical totality, the German situation has not progressed beyond "tranquil theory". It is therefore *not* contemporaneous—except in the one-sidedness of theory—with the revolutionary event; from this point of view, Kant falls behind his historical moment. This shows up two sets of questions. What part is theory—that is, philosophy—to play in this historical period? How can Germany not only catch up with the French Revolution, but even overtake it, in order to become contemporaneous with its own times?—and what, ultimately, would it mean to "overtake" the French revolution?', 26–27.
114 Cited in Stathis Kouvelakis, *Philosophy and Revolution*, 403, n.5.
115 See Stathis Kouvelakis, *Philosophy and Revolution*, 236. This is the contribution of Kouvelakis in his novel reading of Hegel in relation to Marx. He further explains: '*Pace* the interpretations which set out to reduce the specificity of the young Marx's trajectory to dissolving it into the collective trajectory of the Young Hegelian movement—whether with an eye to applauding Marx's early views or, on the contrary, in order to contrast them with the direction his thought took after *The German Ideology*—it is, in my view, the *substantial* nature of Marx's relationship to Hegel which sharply differentiates him from the rest of the Young Hegelian movement, and functions as a veritable *conceptual operator* of the break. It is true that when Marx became Hegelian, in around 1837, the Hegelian school

was already officially in crisis, riven, since the 1835 publication of Strauβ's *The Life of Jesus*, by internal division charged with political significance (a "right", a "left" and a "center"). In a certain sense, it was already too late, by then, to appeal to anything that could claim the mantle of Hegelian orthodoxy, so that Marx's—or any other contemporary thinker's—relationship to Hegelian was necessarily problematic, stemming as it did from appropriation of the system as mediated by others. But the fact remains that the distinctive character of the early Marx's approach was palpable from the moment he made his entry on to this fragmented scene: with, that is, his 1841 doctoral dissertation', 236.

116 See Stathis Kouvelakis, *Philosophy and Revolution*, 235.
117 Stathis Kouvelakis, *Philosophy and Revolution*, 247.
118 Stathis Kouvelakis, *Philosophy and Revolution*, 270.
119 Among them see Hal Draper, *Karl Marx's Theory of Revolution, The Politics of Social Classes, Volume* II (New York and London: Monthly Review Press, 1978); Neil Davidson, *How Revolutionary Were the Bourgeoise Revolutions?* (Chicago: Haymarket Books, 2012); George C. Comninel, *Rethinking the French Revolution, Marxism and the Revisionist Challenges* (London and New York: Verso, 1987); and Michael Löwy, *The Theory of Revolution in the Young Marx* (Chicago: Haymarket Books, 2003).
120 In Stathis Kouvelakis, *Philosophy and Revolution*, 337–338. For my reflections here I am closely following the insightful comments by Kouvelakis in the concluding chapter of his book.
121 See François Furet, *Interpreting the French Revolution*.
122 Stathis Kouvelakis, *Philosophy and Revolution*, 340.
123 Stathis Kouvelakis, *Philosophy and Revolution*, 340.
124 Stathis Kouvelakis, *Philosophy and Revolution*, 341.

Chapter 2

The architecture of (Neo)Bonapartism

Corbusianism and Bonapartism

The proper name 'Le Corbusier' belongs to the twentieth century. But 'Corbusianism' is the name of a genealogy that goes back to the nineteenth century with a historical trajectory into the twentieth century and continuing into our own twenty-first century. In this sense, Le Corbusier is the figure standing behind Corbusianism *avant la lettre*. We can say that Le Corbusier himself was *not the first* Corbusian. Corbusianism, therefore, must be taken to be the *ontology* of architecture in the era of liberal capitalist modernity, of which 'Corbu' is only an historical instance.

Hegel in his *Philosophy of Right* described philosophy as 'apprehending its own time in thought'.

Analogically, I want to say, Corbusianism is 'apprehending the time of liberal capitalist modernity in *architectural thought*'. Two distinct lines can be discerned in this genealogy. One line goes back to the political-architectural system known as *Bonapartism* in the second half of the nineteenth century in the Second Empire under Louis Napoleon III. In this line, Le Corbusier's name can be linked to the (in)famous Prefect of Paris, Baron Haussmann. This is rather a 'regressive' line. Then there is the second line which goes back to the time of the *philosophes* and the *lumières* intellectual circles to which J.N.L. Durand belonged, as we have seen. In this line, Le Corbusier must be associated with Durand. This is the 'progressive' line. Here, *Bonapartism* is taken to be an attributive term referring to a political system in bourgeois capitalist modernity that is associated with authoritarianism containing the germ of the later Fascism in the twentieth century; Antonio Gramsci called it Caesarism, a western political thought that can be associated with its various cognates such as 'tyranny' or 'dictatorship' with a contradictory history.[1] This is a political system that remains dormant in bourgeois liberal democracy. When this political system fails it potentially leads to fascism, as Walter Benjamin incisively recognized. Based on this, we can define our present political moment as 'Neo-Bonapartism' that would stand for political *absolutism* in the global liberal capitalism under the rule of what Kojin Karatani calls the 'absolute monarchy of capital'. Badiou recently called it '*democratic fascism*'. I come back to this below.

The genealogy of this system must only be understood in the background of the political legacy of modernity founded by the French Revolution and other failed revolutions in its wake, up to our present time, including the failed 'Riots and Uprisings'—to adopt Alain Badiou's characterization in his *The Rebirth of History*—against postmodern capitalism and political authoritarianism.[2] It is within this inherited genealogy that I attempt to link Corbusianism to the cluster of ideas attributed to John Maynard Keynes and the concept of Keynesianism—explored by Geoff Mann,[3] to which I attend in the next section. The central idea in this association is that 'revolution' was deemed *unnecessary*—by both Le Corbusier and Keynes, as mentioned previously. In general terms, the most famous economist of the century and the most famous architect of the same century wanted to save the capitalist industrial 'civilization'. But this quest for 'civilization' in our times under the guise of 'modernization' has become a 'furious campaign' as Badiou remarks in his aforementioned book. Curiously, the origin of this furious campaign goes back to the Second Empire during which an equally *furious* activity of building was taken up with the purpose, among others, of preventing revolution and discouraging building barricades in the streets of Paris. Badiou, with his special orientation in Marxism—opting for Marx as the political activist and the journalist rather than the 'intellectual' Marx who resumed his economic studies after 1850 by working on his masterpiece the *Capital*[4]—summarizes what must go against the current frenzy of 'modernization', which I quote here in part:

1. Under the interchangeable rubrics of 'modernization', 'reform', 'democracy', 'the West', 'the international community', 'human rights', 'secularism', 'globalization' and various others, we find nothing but an historical attempt at an unprecedented regression, intent upon creating a situation in which the development of globalized capitalism, and the action of its political servants, conforms to the norms of their birth: a dyed-in-the wool liberalism of mid-nineteenth-century vintage, the ultimate power of a financial and imperial oligarchy, and a window-dressing of parliamentary government composed (as Marx put it) of 'Capital's executives'. To that end, everything which the existence of the organized forms of the workers' movement, communism and genuine socialism had invented between 1960 and 1980, and imposed on a world scale, thereby putting liberal capitalism on the defensive, must be ruthlessly destroyed, and

the value system of imperialism—the celebrated 'values'—recreated. Such is the sole content of the 'modernization' underway.

2. The present moment is in fact that of the first stirrings of a global popular uprising against this recession. As yet blind, naïve, scattered and lacking a powerful concept or durable organization, it naturally resembles the first working-class insurrections of the nineteenth century. I therefore, propose to say that we find ourselves in a *time of riots* wherein a rebirth of History, as opposed to the pure and simple repetition of the worst, is signaled and takes shape. Our masters know this better than us: they are secretly trembling and building up their weaponry, in the form of both of their judicial arsenal and the armed taskforces charged with planetary order. There is an urgent need to reconstruct or create our own.[5]

Later, in 2019, Badiou published a book simply entitled *Trump*.[6] There he states that since 1980, for 40 years, we have witnessed the victory of global capitalism and the disappearance of socialist states, which extends to the disappearance of 'theory and philosophy'. Today, he writes, Marxism is regarded as a thing of the past, as 'a relic of thoughts and conflicts that are no longer ours' and that 'The time is very distant from a time in which Sartre could still declare that Marxism was "the untranscendable horizon of our time"'.[7] Badiou further points out that from the French *philosophes* in the eighteenth century to the movements of the 1960s and 1970s, 'public opinion' was divided between 'two opposite ways of thinking about the destiny of humanity', at first, the 'opposition between the republican vision of the state and monarchical despotism'.[8] That later turned into the opposition between 'the liberal doctrine of the free market on the one hand and the different variety of socialism and communism on the other'.[9] The 'consensus' of global capitalism under Trump that produces a 'spurious effect of novelty', Badiou remarks, is that everywhere in the world 'we witness this *democratic fascism*, which is internal to the parliamentary practice of modern capitalist "democracy"'[10] [emphasis mine]. Badiou's term, 'democratic fascism', is apt. It is in fact a full expression of the political essence of the contemporary liberal-authoritarian capitalism that, for my purposes here, I call Neo-Bonapartism. As to Badiou's remarks on the 'disappearance of philosophy' and the urgent need to look into our predicament today *philosophically*, I want to invoke Hegel's famous statement in the 'Preface' to his *Philosophy of Right*, a statement much discussed by contemporary thinkers: 'when philosophy paints grey in grey, a shape of life has grown old, and it cannot be rejuvenated, but only recognized, by the grey in grey of philosophy; the owl of Minerva begins its flight only with the onset of dark'.[11] Simply put, philosophy always comes *too* late, after the fact, it cannot be the cause of politics.

Based on this argument and from the vantage point of the present we can retroactively delineate the inception of Corbusianism that has its roots in Bonapartism in the Second Empire. Let us recall here Le Corbusier's sympathy for Haussmann and the massive reconstruction of Paris after the destruction of its historic fabric, about which Le Corbusier with an approving tone said that it was achieved by a bunch of primitive tools. In his *Urbanisme,* originally published in 1925 and translated into English as *The City of To-Morrow and its Planning*, Le Corbusier wrote:

The vital thing is to have an idea, a conception, and a programme.
And the means?

The architecture of (Neo)Bonapartism

Do we not possess the means?

Haussmann cut immense gaps right through Paris, and carried out the most startling operations. It seemed as if Paris would never endure his surgical experiments.

And yet to-day does it not *exist* merely as a consequence of his daring and courage?

His equipment was meager; the shovel, the pick, the wagon, the trowel, the wheel barrow, the simple tools of every race and […] before the mechanical age.

His achievement was truly admirable. And in destroying chaos he built up the Emperor's finances!

In those days the French Chambers of Deputies attacked this dangerous man in stormy scenes. One day, in an excess of terror, they accused him of having created a *desert* in the very center of Paris! That desert was Boulevard Sébastopol which is now so congested that every expedient is being tried to relieve it: the policemen's white truncheon, the whistle, mounted police and electric signals, both visual and aural! Such is life![12]

Walter Benjamin in *The Arcades Project* quotes the above passage and registers the following:

> The mighty seek to secure their potion with blood (police), with cunning (fashion), with magic (pomp). [E5a, 7]. The widening of streets, it was said, was necessitated by the crinoline [E5a, 8].[13]

Le Corbusier further wrote:

> The avenues he [Hausmann] cut were entirely arbitrary: they were not based on strict deductions of the science of town

planning. The measures he took were of a financial and military character (*surgery*).[14]

What did Haussmann do that prompted Le Corbusier's admiration? Benjamin quotes a certain J.J. Hongger who wrote:

> Having, as they do, the appearance of walling-in a massive eternity, Haussmann's urban works are a wholly appropriate representation of the absolute principles of the Empire: repression of every individual formation, every organic self-development, 'fundamental hatred of all individuality'.[15]

The name of Baron George-Eugène, the admired and hated Prefect of Paris, is connected to every liberal *and* authoritarian regime in capitalist modernity, from the Second Empire and Napoleon III, from which we have inherited the term Bonapartism, to our own new 'Empire', or Neo-Bonapartism. He is the *revenant* of every big city in this same era. The more his name is conjured away, the more his ghost is exorcised, the more we are haunted by its specters. This primarily means that both camps, the one that loathes him and the one that admires him, have got his name wrong. His name, rather, represents an *antagonism* that is 'sublated' in class struggle, both in the bourgeois order of the Second Empire *and* in the contemporary new Empire of global capitalism. The big city is the arena where this antagonism is staged. This *mutatis mutandis* applies to the term Corbusianism. Underlying both is a theory of state linked to Bonapartism to which I come back.

Monsieur Haussmann had a nickname: 'Pasha Osman'! For he wanted to provide the city with spring water: 'I must build myself an aqueduct', he said.[16] He also bragged, 'I have been named artist-demolitionist'.[17] He achieved it with the same 'meager' tools Le Corbusier mentioned. Friedrich Engels in 'On the Housing Question' of 1872 puts it aptly when he defines the term 'Haussmann':

> By the term 'Haussmann,' I do not mean merely the specifically Bonapartist manner of the Parisian Haussmann—cutting long, straight, broad streets right through closely built working-class neighborhoods and lining them on both sides with luxurious buildings, the intention having been, apart from the strategic aim of making barricade fighting more difficult, to develop a specifically Bonapartist building-trade proletariat dependent on the government, and turn the city into a luxury city pure and simple. By 'Haussmann' I mean the practice, which has now become general, of making breaches in the working-class neighborhood of our big city, particularly in those which are centrally situated ... The result is everywhere the same: the most scandalous alleys ... disappear to the accompaniment of lavish self-glorification by the bourgeoisie.[18]

Benjamin cites Gisela Freund as having said:

> Louis-Napoléon Bonaparte felt his vocation to be the securing of the 'bourgeois order' ... Industry and trade, the affair of the bourgeoisie, were to prosper. An immense number of concessions were given out to railroads; public subventions were granted; credits were organized. The wealth and luxury of the bourgeois world increased.[19]

For Benjamin, Haussmann championed a 'phantasmagoria of civilization', which manifested itself in the transformation of

Paris: 'With the Haussmannization of Paris, the phantasmagoria was rendered in stone'.[20]

In his 1935 Exposé Benjamin wrote:

> Empire is the style of revolutionary terrorism, for which the state is an end in itself. Just as Napoleon failed to understand the functional nature of the state as an instrument of domination by the bourgeois class, so the architects of his time failed to understand the functional nature of iron, with which the constructive principle begins its domination in architecture.[21]

As I noted before, Benjamin adopted Sigfried Giedion's thesis that 'Construction plays the role of the subconscious' and observed that with engineering starting to gain ground, the 'rivalry begins between builder and decorator, École Polytechnique and École des Beaux-Arts'. [22] This nineteenth-century 'rivalry' was in fact 'sublated' when Le Corbusier appeared on the scene in the twentieth century. But the instrumental role of the architectural *agency* for the State still remains undertheorized. For the purposes at hand, I want to attend to Benjamin's statement above that 'Napoleon failed to understand the functional nature of the state as an instrument of domination by the bourgeois class'. This is, of course, the well-known Marxian definition of state on which Benjamin relies that only partially explains the political essence of Bonapartism to which other terms are associated, including Caesarism, Imperialism, Dictatorship, in relation to the democracy and the theory of state,[23] and of course the much abused term 'totalitarianism'.[24] Before I discuss the theory of Bonapartism, I must point out here that it is in the nexus of Haussmann–Le Corbusier/Hausmannization–Corbusianism that we must frame the function of architecture *agency* in Bonapartism and Neo-Bonapartism.

Louis Bonaparte, Napoleon III, came to power through a *coup d'état* on 2 December 1851 and established the Second Empire that lasted until 1870. The humiliating defeat of the French in the Franco-Prussian war in 1870 put an end to it, followed by the insurrection of the nationalists. Before he became Napoleon III, Louis Bonaparte had democratically been elected President of the Second Republic, 1848–1851. His uncle, Napoleon Bonaparte, on 18 Brumaire, year VIII on the revolutionary calendar (or 9 November 1799) dissolved the Directory and put an end to the revolutionary upheaval and reaction, called himself Emperor and established a bourgeois dictatorship. Marx called the General Napoleon Bonaparte's *coup d'état* a 'tragedy' and the second *coup d'état* by his nephew a 'farce'. Any deep understanding of Bonapartism must first begin with a close reading of Marx's *The Eighteenth Brumaire of Louis Napoleon*, not only for the understanding of the Second Empire but also the lessons needed to understand our own contemporary Neo-Bonapartism.[25] Famously, Marx starts his text by citing Hegel as having observed 'somewhere' that 'all the great events and characters of world history occur twice, so to speak',[26] only to take him to task: 'He forgot to add: the first time as high tragedy, the second time as low farce'.[27] Marx then takes a sarcastic tone:

> The eighteenth Brumaire of the fool after the eighteenth Brumaire of the genius! And there is the same cartoon-quality in the circumstances surrounding the second imprint of the eighteenth Brumaire. The first time France was on the verge of bankruptcy, this time Bonaparte is on the brink of debtor's prison.[28]

And then the following much cited passage:

> Men make their history, but they do not make it just as they please in circumstances, given and inherited. Tradition from all the dead generations weighs like a nightmare on the brain of the living. And just when they appear to be revolutionizing themselves and their circumstances, in creating something unprecedented, in just epochs of revolutionary crisis, that is when they nervously summon up the spirit of the past, borrowing from them their names, marching orders, uniform, in order to enact new scenes in world history, but in this time-honoured guise and with this borrowed language.[29]

Analyzing perceptively Marx's *The Eighteenth Brumaire*, Terrell Carver writes, 'Marx's theory of dictatorship does not depend on a dictator, his theory of Bonapartism does not depend on a Bonaparte, and his theory of Caesarism is one of resurrection and parody'.[30] He further notes that 'In the *Eighteenth Brumaire*, it is class politics of representative democracy that delivers a deadly dictatorship to the living republic and a mock empire to the farcical Bonaparte'.[31] Marx discusses how the 'party of order' paved the way for Louis Bonaparte's *coup*. 'The irony of history', Carver argues, 'is more in evidence in this text than the working of any dialectic', but more pertinently, 'Marx identified a dynamic within "free market" liberal democracy that is ever-present'.[32] Marx's text already reveals Bonapartism *qua* proto-fascism, as Kojin Karatani informs us, and 'how it came into existence out of the complex coexisting advanced industrial capitalism and conventional relations of production and class structure—by way of analyzing the very mechanism of the representation [*Darstellung*] and representative system [*Vertretung*]'.[33] Karatani importantly notes that, 'Thus the idea that the advent of Fascism in 1930 brought something novel—against which Marx's analysis was obsolete—was finally wrong. The idea only proves that Marx had not been read closely enough'.[34] The rise of Neo-Bonapartism, as I would argue, requires even a closer reading of Marx's text today. Marx attempted a highly complex political narrative and class analysis in the *Eighteenth Brumaire*, as Carver reminds us. He was concerned with the 'interaction of economic interest with political tradition', and equally with the interaction of both with 'individual psychology, strategic maneuver, and collective decision-making'.[35] Marx in the new preface to *The Eighteenth Brumaire*, written in 1869, emphasized that only under Louis Bonaparte 'does the state *seem* to have achieved independence with respect to society and to have brought it into submission'.[36] What is important to learn from Marx's analysis is that, as Carver shows,

> Marx locates dictatorship and ever-present possibility within representative ('Bourgeois') democracy, precisely because of the way that he separates out the complex class-relation *within* the bourgeoisie, and precisely because of the way that he traces the interaction of personal and collective 'spin' within mass electoral politics most particularly in hallucinatory politics of delusion.[37]

In the Second Republic, thus, 'democratization was undone *in and through democratic institutions*, and the state was handed over to Louis Bonaparte as democracy collapsed'.[38] We need not go further into in-depth explications of Marx's complex text that have been done by various commentators.[39] The last comments suffice to return us to Haussmannization once the dictatorial role of the state in Bonapartism was handed down to Louis Bonaparte that opened the opportunity for the collaborative work that the emperor himself assumed with his Prefect of Paris, Baron Haussmann, to brutally reshape the city. The restructuring of Paris and the resulting 'image' is a historical case study in capitalist modernity as to how the 'class struggle' manifests itself at the level of 'superstructure' and wins. Paris was *reconstructed* by the winning *bourgeoisie*, coming to power through undemocratic measures.

It has been pointed out that, on economic grounds, the emperor wanted to bring 'prosperity' by his 'bold' development projects. He apparently believed in the Saint-Simonian idea that economic progress would bring about 'an improvement in the condition of the largest and poorest class', and 'thus the satisfaction of the masses'.[40] This required a 'modernization' of the nation that would prompt the emperor to launch an 'industrial revolution' to bring France up to the standards already reached in England. By 1851 the urban population of France reached 9,130,000. The narrow confines of the overpopulated capital were extended to the fortifications built in 1841–1845. Paris was divided into its current 20 *arrondissements*. The tightly knitted old fabric of Paris was recklessly opened by wholesale demolitions.

It was noted by Saccard in Émile Zola's *La Curée* (*The Kill*) who observed the developments from the top of Montmartre:

> Down there, in the [les] Halles square, they have cut Paris in four. Yes, the great crossroads of Paris, as they say. They're clearing the area around the Louvre and Hôtel de Ville. When the first network is finished, then the great dance will begin. The second network will pierce the city everywhere and so connect *faubourgs* to the first network. The city's truncated sections will suffer the pangs of death in plaster ... one cut

here, one cut there, cuts everywhere. Paris slashed by sabre-cuts, with its veins open.[41]

All was done under the impulses of Napoleon III and Monsieur Haussmann. The emperor envisioned the vast boulevards and it is reported that he showed Haussmann 'a map of Paris on which he had personally traced—in blue, red, yellow and green, in order of priority—the various new avenues that he wanted to build'.[42] Napoleon III thought that Baltard's drawn plan for the Les Halles was 'too massive' and advised him, perhaps at 'Viollet-le-Duc's instigation' to use only iron and glass. He handed the Prefect a sketch: 'What I need is wide umbrella, nothing more'.[43] Hausmann stationed at Hôtel de Ville from 1853 to 1870, 'almost as a minster of the capital' and got to work when the term *urbanisme* had not yet existed. The motives for both Napoleon III and his Prefect were the same: 'they were guided by a concern to maintain order when they destroyed alleys propitious to barricades and built impressive barracks from which there radiated a series of rectilinear avenues apparently suitable for artillery fire or cavalry charges'.[44] The emperor was, of course, concerned to avoid unemployment through a gigantic building project.

Haussmann was called a 'ripper' and a 'vandal', guilty of 'irreparable destruction'. His actions prompted Charles Baudelaire to write:

Le vieux Paris n'est plus, la forme d'une ville
Change plus vite, helas! que le coeur d'un mortel
(Old Paris is no more; a city's shape
Changes faster, alas, than a mortal's heart)[45]

But the most memorable of all analyses is still by Walter Benjamin, without a slightest touch of melancholy as in

Baudelaire's. He puts the whole affair of Hausmannization of Paris in the context of Revolution and the bourgeoise conspiracy. The 1935 Exposé, in this respect must be read in complement to Marx's *The Eighteenth Brumaire*. In the section 'VI: Haussmann, or the Barricades' of the Exposé Benjamin wrote:

> Hausmann's ideal in city planning consisted of long perspective down broad straight thoroughfares. Such an ideal corresponds to the tendency—common in the nineteenth century—to ennoble technological necessities through artistic ends. The institutions of the bourgeoisie's worldly and spiritual dominance were to find their apotheosis within the framework of the boulevards. Before their completion, boulevards were draped with canvas and unveiled like monuments—Hausmann's activity is linked to Napoleonic imperialism. Louis Napoleon promotes investment capital, and Paris experiences a rash of speculation. Trading on stock exchange displaces the forms of gambling handed down from feudal society. The phantasmagoria of space to which the flaneur devotes himself finds a counterpart in the phantasmagorias of time to which the gambler is addicted. Gambling converts time into a narcotic. <Paul> Lafargue explains gambling as an imitation in miniature of the mysteries of economic fluctuation. The expropriations carried out under Haussmann call forth a wave of fraudulent speculation. The rulings of the Court of Cassation, which are inspired by the bourgeois and Orleanist opposition, increase the financial risks of Haussmannization.
>
> Haussmann tries to shore up his dictatorship by placing Paris under an emergency plan. In 1864, in a speech before the National Assembly, he vents his hatred of the rootless urban

population, which keeps increasing as a result of his projects. Rising rents drive the proletariat into the suburbs. The *quartiers* of Paris in this way lose their distinctive physiognomy. The 'red belt' forms. Haussmann gave himself the title of 'demolition artist,' *artiste démolisseur*...

The true goal of Haussmann's projects was to secure the city against civil war. He wanted to make the erection of barricades in Paris impossible for all time. With the same end in mind, Louis Philippehad already introduced wooden paving. Nonetheless, barricades played a role in the February Revolution. Engels studies the tactic fighting. Haussmann seeks to neutralize these tactics on two fronts. Widening the streets is designed to make the erection of barricades impossible, and new streets are to furnish the shortest route between the barracks and the workers' district. Contemporaries christen the operation 'strategic embellishment.'...

The Barricade is resurrected during the Commune. It is stronger and better secured than ever. It stretches across the great boulevards, often reaching a height of two stories, and shields the trenches behind it. Just as the *Communist Manifesto* ends the age of professional conspirators, so the Commune puts an end to the phantasmagoria holding sway over the early years of the proletariat. It dispels the illusion that the task of the proletariat revolution is to complete the work of 1789 hand in hand with the bourgeoisie. This illusion dominates the period 1831–1871, from the Lyons uprising to the Commune. The bourgeoisie never shared in this error. Its battle against the social rights of the proletariat dates back to the great Revolution, and converges with the philanthropic movement that gives it cover and that is in its heyday under Napoleon III.[46]

Back to Le Corbusier. Which Le Corbusier did Benjamin admire? He would not want to admire Le Corbusier admiring Haussmann. Rather, he wanted to admire Le Corbusier the avant-garde and the champion of 'transparency' against 'Louis Phillippe, or the cult of the 'Interior'.

Keynesianism and Corbusianism

By 1930 Western capitalism was already deep into crisis. Coinciding with it was the international crisis of modern architecture.[47] The architect of the century, Le Corbusier, and the economist of the century, John Maynard Keynes, both came to a tacit agreement—although I suspect that they never knew of each other—that architecture *and* economy must be revolutionized in order to prevent revolution—Revolution is *unnecessary*. But I am sure that Le Corbusier would be sympathetic to what Keynes is reported to have once said: '[W]e have reached a condition where there is no shortage of houses, but where nevertheless no one can afford to live in the houses that there are'.[48] 'In other words', as Geoff Mann puts it, 'an "excess of riches" cannot prevent an "excess of poverty"'.[49] Or, to put it another way, the bourgeois capitalist society that produces wealth *also* produces poverty. Keynesians, but not Corbusians, always pose this question, to which they then try to provide an answer: 'What causes "poverty" in the midst of plenty"?' Further, Keynesians, but not Corbusians, constantly pose this question: 'Why, "despite an *excess of wealth*," is civil society *"not wealthy enough"*?'[50] Le Corbusier might find himself to be in agreement with the 'left-Keynesian' Joan Robinson, who in her essay entitled 'Latter Day Capitalism' wrote: '*The foundation of a comfortable standard of life is a decent house*'[51] [emphasis mine].

The architecture of (Neo)Bonapartism

Apart from Le Corbusier himself, all other Corbusians failed to pose the questions that Keynesians posed.

Keynesianism, to which I am associating 'Corbusianism', in a certain sense, is 'liberalism's most significant theoretical and political development in the face of revolutionary menace'.[52] We have yet to know exactly what 'Keynesianism' means, and to which I come back below. Here I want to cite Eric Hobsbawm who in 1999, shortly after the fall of the Berlin Wall and the Communist bloc, wrote that 'Keynes himself made no bones about the fact that his aim was to save liberal capitalism'.[53] Le Corbusier would not make such an explicit claim. Well before the crisis point in 1929, Le Corbusier had published his *Vers une architecture* in 1923 and Keynes his *The General Theory* in 1936; the two important manifestos in the twentieth century, which seemingly having nothing to do with each other. Le Corbusier, for his part, would revolutionize architecture; aligning it with the most 'advanced tasks of economic and technological reality', as Manfredo Tafuri puts it, is 'still incapable of assuming coherent and organic form', which makes it surprising that what is known as 'realism' in Le Corbusier's hypotheses 'was regarded as utopian'.[54] Following Tafuri, we must grant that, in general, the 'failure' of Le Corbusier is a symptom of a larger ideological crisis surrounding the *failed* economic-political program of liberal capitalism around the same time.

In advancing their respective theses, it is no accident that both Keynes and Le Corbusier employed the same word, 'equilibrium'—the architect sparingly, and the economist profusely. To recall, Le Corbusier in *Toward an Architecture* wrote: 'It is a question of building that is key to the *equilibrium* upset today: architecture or revolution'[55] [emphasis mine]. And it is no accident also that during the same time the word

119

'plan' and the French term '*planisme*' became ubiquitous and were used in architecture and economics. According to Hobsbawm, conservatives and liberals, but also the Left, who went to the Soviet Union—including Le Corbusier—learned about 'plan' which was a buzz-word at the time related to the first 'Soviet-Five-Year Plan'. We must remember that in the France of the 1930s, the term *planisme* was extensively in use, which, it is worth mentioning here, was probably the connecting idea that would bring Georges Bataille to take an interest in Le Corbusier.[56] In relation to the idea of 'plan', Tafuri complains that the initial blame for the 1930 crisis is attributed to the rise of European Fascism and Stalinism and what is ignored is the appearance, after the crisis of 1929, of a 'decisive new protagonist: the international reorganization of capital, the affirmation of systems of anticyclical planning, and the realization of the First Soviet Five-Year Plan'.[57] This prompts Tafuri to brings up Keynes and say that 'It is significant that almost all the objectives formulated in the economic field by Keynes's [*The*] *General Theory* can be found as pure ideology in modern architecture'.[58] For his scanty discussion of Keynes, Tafuri solely relies on an essay written by Antonio Negri—still very influential—in 1968 entitled 'Keynes and the Capitalist Theory of the State post-1929'. This essay is much discussed by the Left. Tafuri cites Negri's leading statement: 'Free oneself from the fear of the future by fixing the future as the present'.[59] Tafuri argues that this is at the base of Keynesian intervention, which, in a 'political sense', is also at the 'base of Le Corbusier's theories of urbanism'.[60] Tafuri further notes that 'Keynes reckons with the "party of catastrophe" and tries to control its menace by absorbing it at an always new level'.[61] He then situates Le Corbusier at this 'level' and writes:

> Le Corbusier takes account of the reality of class in the modern city and transposes the conflicts to a higher level, giving life to the most elevated proposal for the integration of the public, involved as operators and active consumers in the urban mechanism of development, now rendered organically 'human'.[62]

Tafuri claims that his 'initial hypothesis' is confirmed: 'architecture as ideology of the plan is swept away by the *reality of the plan* when, the level of utopia having been superseded, the plan becomes an operative mechanism'.[63] In further affirmation he asserts:

> The crisis of modern architecture begins in the very movement in which its natural consignee—large industrial capital—goes beyond the fundamental ideology, putting aside the superstructure. From that moment on architectural ideology no longer has any purpose. The obstinate insistence on seeing its own hypothesis realized becomes either a surpassing of outdated realities or an importunate disturbance.[64]

And further, 'The ideology of form seems to abandon its dedication to a realistic outlook and fall back on the alternative position inherent in the dialectic of bourgeois culture'.[65] It is worth pointing out here that Tafuri conducts his critique without engaging fully with Negri's thesis on Keynesianism and without advancing any discussion on 'political economy' when discussing architecture in relation to Keynesianism, as his argument was focused on his 'critique of ideology' rather than on 'critique of political economy'. Since Tafuri wrote in 1973, scholarship on Keynesianism, and especially its criticism on the Left, have substantially advanced and this should be taken into account. In general, the name 'Keynes', as Hobsbawm would say, is synonymous with 'saving capitalism from itself' by 'revolutionizing' the bourgeois concept of economics. And as Mann puts it, 'Keynes is a key to understanding the politics of modern capitalism and liberal democracy'.[66] In this respect, I would argue that the crisis of architecture did not in fact begin in the 1930s, as Tafuri claims, but rather goes back to the Second Empire and Bonapartism. In this genealogy, again, the name Le Corbusier represents both an *interruption* and a *continuation*.

The hallmark of Negri's powerful analysis is the way he sees Keynes and the rise of Keynesianism as a reaction against the victory of the 'working class' with the October Revolution, in the background of which is the crisis of 1929 in the capitalist world. He initially notes:

> It was the extraordinary strength of the working class, backed by the revolutionary experience it had undergone, that made its mark and imposed those disequilibria that constantly required intervention at all levels of the system. Capitalist science had to register this fact. The extent to which it did so is the measure, so to speak, of its grasp and understanding of the new situation. To follow this complex process, unmasking it and distinguishing its scientific and ideological components, is the task of working class critique.[67]

He continues by explicitly stating his thesis:

> I trace the development of Keynes' thought and reflection on the overall crisis of the capitalist system from the October Revolution to the depression years. For it was he who showed the greatest awareness and the most refined political intuition

in confronting the new situation facing capital at this crucial turning point. It was Keynes whose disenchanted diagnosis indicated for the international capitalist class the therapy to be applied. Keynes was perhaps the most penetrating theorist of capitalist reconstruction, of the new form of the capitalist state that emerged in reaction to the revolutionary working-class impact of 1917.[68]

In a passage directly relating to our concerns, Negri brings up the notion of 'equilibrium' and the idea of 'plan', that would shed light on what I previously brought up in Le Corbusier's use of the word 'equilibrium', and Tafuri's point about the 'ideology of plan'. Negri writes:

Paradoxically, capital turned to Marx, or at least learned to read *Das Kapital* (from its own viewpoint, naturally, which, however mystified, is nonetheless efficacious). Once the antagonism was recognized, the problem was to make it function in such a way as to prevent one pole of the antagonism breaking free into independent destructive action. Working-class political revolution could only be avoided by recognizing and accepting the new relation of class forces, while making the working class function within an overall mechanism that would 'sublimate' its continuous struggle for power into a dynamic element within the system. The working class was to be controlled functionally within a series of mechanisms of equilibrium that would be dynamically readjusted from time to time by a regulated phasing of the 'incomes revolution'. The state was now prepared, as it were, to descend into civil society, to continuously recreate the source of its legitimacy in a process of permanent readjustment of the conditions of equilibrium. The new 'material basis of the constitution' became the state as planner, or better still, the state as the plan. For soon this mechanism for re-equilibrating incomes between the forces in play was articulated in the form of Revolution Retrieved periodic planning. The model of equilibrium assumed for a plan over a given period meant that every initiative, every readjustment of equilibrium to a new level, opened up a process of revision in the constitutional state itself.[69]

We cannot go through a detailed discussion of Negri's thick and complex essay here. Geoff Mann in his *In the Long Run We Are All Dead*—the title is an allusion to the witty statement Keynes himself once made—extensively discusses Negri's influential essay and perceptively submits it to his sympathetic critique. Mann considers Negri's analysis to be best critical account of Keynesianism. Negri's crucial move, according to Mann, is his reading of *The General Theory* as a 'political manifesto', which has implications for the theory of political economy, which is in fact the bourgeois science of government in liberal capitalism. He notes that according to Negri,

the particular but simultaneous problems *The General Theory* struggles to understand are economic (the Great Depression) and political (the 'full independent expression' of working class politics in the Russian Revolution of 1917), but nonetheless two sides of the same process: the latter effectively triggered the former.[70]

This is because Negri argues that 'capital's response to the Bolshevik victory let to the technological "repression" of the working class and hence to overaccumulation crises associated with unsustainable organic composition of capital'.[71] Nevertheless, Mann believes that Negri 'misconstrues his subject in fundamental ways'. Mann argues that Negri fails to embed the Keynesian critique in a larger liberal tradition that goes back before the Russian Revolution. This is consistent with Mann's argument in his book that, on a longer view of the history, Keynes and Hegel share the same criticism of liberalism and the same idea about poverty in wealthy bourgeois society. He observes that 'For Negri, Keynesianism ultimately represents the always contradictory effort to save capitalism from communism, the means to become a "planner state" (*stato plano*) that keeps the workers happy enough to prevent them from going red'.[72] If the question is 'What did Keynes come to save capitalism from and why?', Negri's answer, according to Mann, is that 'Keynesianism here arrives to rescue capitalism from the proletarian liberation that marches inexorably towards it on all sides'. Negri argues that Keynes offers a more effective solution to the *same problem* to which 'immature ruling classes responded with fascist repression: the "inherent antagonism of the working class"'.[73] Mann asserts that 'this is not true'. He elaborates:

> Insofar as capitalist civil society persistently produces poverty, and thus the immanent potential for the emergence of rabble driven by necessity and unfreedom to undo social order, then as far as Keynes was concerned, it was indeed a possibility that some collective that identified as 'the working class' would be rendered 'inherently' antagonistic to the social relations of liberal capitalism.[74]

Further Mann remarks that 'Keynes feared the radical Left, certainly, but no more (and arguably quite a bit less) than fascism, radical conservatism, authoritarianism, demagoguery, and anything else that smacked of dogmatic "fundamentalism," because he understood all of them as undermining the stability of "civilization"'.[75] Keynes feared the Right as much as the Left, Mann says. He wanted to protect the 'modern bourgeois civilization' from disorder and chaos, and this means to save the capitalist political economic architecture in which, Mann would conclude, '*révolution sans révolution* will always prioritize load-bearing features of status quo'.[76]

We need not go further into Mann's strong responses to Negri's influential critique of Keynes. My intention is mainly to draw attention to Tafuri's summary fashion in his unconditional use of Negri for his insights on Le Corbusier in his *Architecture and Utopia*, which needs to be reconfigured. As I contend throughout this work, it is the '*révolution sans révolution*' which is the key for re-visiting Le Corbusier's 'defensible dilemma' about 'architecture or revolution'. When Tafuri correctly argued that Le Corbusier 'revolutionized architecture' he nevertheless neglected to mention that it was against 'revolution' itself. It is on different terms, therefore, that we must necessarily draw certain links that can be traced between Keynes and Le Corbusier. This requires that, in contrast to Tafuri, we revise the misplaced emphasis on the theory of ideology, with which the discourse of the Left in the architecture academy of the 1960s was obsessed, and instead return to the Marxian *critique of political economy*. In this regard, it is worth mentioning that the word 'ideology' is nowhere to be found in *Capital*. We will come to this in later chapters.

Neo-Bonapartism and specters of Le Corbusier

To paraphrase Jacque Derrida's enunciation of Marx's specters that '*there is more than one of them, there must be more than one of them*', I want to say that 'there is more than one specter of Le Corbusier, there must more than one'. Le

Corbusier's specters will refuse to be conjured away, no matter how much the architects and critics would declare they are done with him. In a sense, we belong to the same historical epoch that produced Keynes and Le Corbusier. The present conjuncture, some call it 'neoliberalism', I call it Neo-Bonapartism, better qualified as the 'absolute monarchy of capital' in Karatani's terms, is in continuation of the 'old' liberalism, the same liberal democracy in the bourgeois capitalist modernity and its parliamentary system that is prone to harbor fascism. Badiou, as we have seen, has already called it 'democratic fascism'. In this sense, the current political system shows certain family resemblances, but also unmistakable differences, with the Second Empire of Napoleon III at political, technological, economic and architectural levels.

In our present conjuncture, can we conjure away the specter of Le Corbusier? Should we attempt to 'resurrect' him? Can he be *repeated*? Is his 'architecture or revolution' a 'defensible dilemma'? Is there any credibility to his alleged changed position later in the 1930s that would prompt us to change the 'or' with an 'and' and say: 'Architecture *and* Revolution'?[77] Before going further, I must reiterate that Le Corbusier's specter*s*, more than one, haunt Corbusiansim. Contemporary architects, as much as they would like to vehemently disavow it, are Corbusians, one way or another, no matter how hard they try to disavow it. The difference between them and Le Corbusier is that they are incapable of 'revolutioniz[ing] architecture', let alone having the courage to utter the slogan '*révolution sans révolution*'. As it was said before, the label Corbusianism should serve as an explanatory term for architecture in the entire epoch of liberal capitalist modernity. I would like to quote what Le Corbusier wrote in the final pages of his *Urbanisme*:

> People tax me very readily with being a revolutionary. It is an effective if somewhat flattering way of putting a distance between a society preoccupied with maintaining its present equilibrium and eager minds which are likely to disturb it. Yet this equilibrium which they try so hard to maintain is for vital reasons purely ephemeral: it is a balance which has to be perpetually re-established.
>
> On the other hand, since the Russian Revolution it has become the charming prerogative of both our own and the Bolshevik revolutionaries alone. Everything which has not chosen ostensibly to adopt their label they call bourgeoise and capitalist and stupid.
>
> Economic and social progress can only be the result of technical problems which have found a proper solution. The aim of this work has been the unfolding of a clear solution; its value depends on its success in that direction. It has no label, it is not dedicated to our existing Bourgeois-Capitalist Society nor to the Third International. It is a technical work.
>
> And I do not propose to bear witness in the highways and byways as though I belonged to the Salvation Army.
>
> *Things are not revolutionized by making revolutions. The real Revolution lies in the solution of existing problems.*[78]

It is not enough to attribute these claims to Saint-Simonian economics or Taylorism-Fordism and then trace them in Le Corbusier, as architecture historians tend to do. For the same reason, Fordism is not the only feature of Keynesianism. If he dismissed the Left while being sympathetic to them, Le Corbusier, like Keynes, was not so much a 'capitalist' as he was a *bourgeoise* 'technician'. Le Corbusier, and Keynes, in the guise of bourgeois-reformists, wanted '*révolution sans révolution*' and had a vulgarized view of Marx, or the Russian

Revolution. Those who read Marx's *Capital*, Volume One, as Fredric Jameson has noted, would know that

> The lesson that capitalism is a total system, however, is designed to demonstrate that it cannot be reformed, and that its repairs, originally intended to prolong its existence, necessarily end up strengthening and enlarging it [...] But it is precisely the power of and the constructional achievement of *Capital* to show that the "injustice and inequalities" are structurally at one with this total system as such, and they can never be reformed.[79]

Corbusianism and Keynesianism are two terms that believe otherwise. They will try but they will fail—They failed then and they fail now. This is an argument to be had, as Jameson points out, against what used to be called social democracy, which today,

> far more openly than ever before in its past history, asserts the possibility of reforming capitalism; or rather, in a kind of negative demonstration, acquiesces in the conviction that no other system is possible and that therefore all that remains is the piecemeal diminution of its injustice and inequalities.[80]

In the last page of *Urbanisme* Le Corbusier reproduced a famous engraving showing Louis XIV commanding the building of Les Invalides and attached a caption to it that reads: '*Homage to a great town planner. This despot conceived immense projects and realized them. Over all the country this noble work still fills us with admiration. He was capable of saying, "We wish it," or "such is our pleasure"*'.[81] A few pages earlier he had written:

> The centers of great cities represent the most important of all land values. Let us call this value A. Haussmann pulled down the crumbling districts of Paris and replaced them by sumptuous quarters. His efforts were really financial operations and he filled the Emperor's coffers with gold.[82]

His admiration for the despots and emperors from the *ancient régime* to Napoleon III with his architects and builders would come into conflict with the image of architect as the 'intellectual', carrying the whole tradition of the twentieth century avant-garde. The failed enthusiasms, or rather his fantasy, in the 1920s frustrated Le Corbusier as he entered the 1930s.

At the end I must invoke Durand's name once again. His specter must come to haunt, not only us but also Le Corbusier who inherited his legacy. Durand directed his theory to the Revolution that had just occurred. Le Corbusier, in contrast, wished to conjure away that same Revolution. In relation to Durand we must remember two things. First: 'Either society is made for architecture and architects, or architecture and architects for society. Is there anyone worthy of the name of architect who can remain in doubt even for an instant about the answer to such a question?' And second: 'Durand was politically and morally opposed to both the Napoleonic regime and the Restoration, and he paid for this with silence and isolation'.[83] Politically and ethically, the architect, today, has learned nothing from Durand.

Notes

1 For more see Benedetto Fontana, 'The Concept of Caesarism in Gramsci', in *Dictatorship in History and Theory, Bonapartism, Caesarism, and Totalitarianism*, eds. Peter Baehr and Melvin Richter (Cambridge: Cambridge University Press, 2004).

2. See Alain Badiou, *The Birth of History, Times of Riots and Uprisings* (London and New York: Verso, 2012).
3. I will extensively discuss Geoff Mann's *In the Long Run We Are All Dead, Keynesianism, Political Economy and Revolution* (London and New York: Verso, 2017). For my drawing of an analogy between Corbusianism and Keynesianism I am mainly indebted to this fine book.
4. See Bruno Bosteels, 'The Fate of Generic: Marx and Badiou', in *(Mis) Reading of Marx in Continental Philosophy*, eds. J. Habjan and J. Whyte (Palgrave: New York, 2014).
5. Alain Badiou, *The Rebirth of History*, 4–6.
6. Alain Badiou, *Trump* (Cambridge: Polity, 2019). The book consists of the two lectures that Badiou delivered at the University of California, Los Angeles, and Tufts University, Boston, both in 2016.
7. Alain Badiou, *Trump*, 4.
8. Alain Badiou, *Trump*, 4.
9. Alain Badiou, *Trump*, 4–5.
10. Alain Badiou, *Trump*, 14.
11. See Hegel, *Elements of the Philosophy of Right*, ed. Allen W. Wood (Cambridge: Cambridge University Press, 1991), 23.
12. Le Corbusier, *The City of To-Morrow and its Planning, with 215 Illustrations* (New York: Dover, 1987), 156.
13. See Walter Benjamin, *The Arcades Project* (The Belknap Press of Harvard University Press, 1999), 133.
14. Le Corbusier, *The City of To-Marrow and its Planning*, 261.
15. See Walter Benjamin, *The Arcades Project*, 'Convolute E [Haussmannization, Barricade Fighting]', (E1a, 1], 122.
16. In Walter Benjamin, *The Arcades Project*, 127–128. In this and what follows, I am freely drawing on a section of my co-authored book, *The Architecture of Phantasmagoria, Specters of the City* (New York: Routledge, 2017).
17. Walter Benjamin, *The Arcades Project*, 219.
18. Quoted in Walter Benjamin, *The Arcades Project*, [E12, 1] 145.
19. In Walter Benjamin, *The Arcades Project*, 133.
20. Walter Benjamin, 'Paris, Capital of the Nineteenth Century, Exposé 1939', in *The Arcades Project*, 24.
21. Walter Benjamin, 'Paris, Capital of the Nineteenth Century, Exposé 1935', in *The Arcades Project*, 4.
22. Walter Benjamin, 'Paris, Capital of the Nineteenth Century, Exposé 1935', in *The Arcades Project*, 4. See also, Sigfried Giedion, *Building in France,*

Building in Iron, Building in Ferro-Concrete, intro. Sokratis Georgiadis, trans. J. Duncan Berry (Santa Monica: The Getty Center for the History of art and Humanities, 1995). Giedion sent a copy of his book to Benjamin when it came out in German, *Bauen in Frankreich, Bauen in Eisenbeton*, in 1928, as a gift, to which Benjamin wrote a cordial response; for more see Georgiadis's 'Introduction'. Giedion writes that: 'Construction in the nineteenth century plays the role of the subconscious. Outwardly, construction still boasts the old pathos; underneath, concealed behind facades, the basis of our present existence is taking place', 87.

23 See the fine collection of essays in *Dictatorship in History and Theory, Bonapartism, Caesarism, and Totalitarianism*, eds. Peter Baehr and Melvin Richter (Cambridge: Cambridge University Press, 2004).

24 For its abuse see Slavoj Žižek, *Did Somebody Say Totalitarianism? Five Interventions in the (Mis)Use of a Notion* (London and New York: Verso, 2001).

25 See Karl Marx *The Eighteenth Brumaire of Louis Bonaparte*, in *Marx, Later Political Writings*, ed. Terrell Carver (Cambridge: Cambridge University Press, 1996). As Carver points out the understanding of the complexity of Marx's text has been exasperated by bad translations. He himself has presented a new translation of it and has written an illuminating essay about it that I cite below and discuss in the text. It is useful to read Marx's 'The Eighteenth Brumaire' in conjunction with his *The Civil War in France* to which it is the sequel.

26 Marx 'The Eighteenth Brumaire of Louis Bonaparte', 31.

27 Marx 'The Eighteenth Brumaire of Louis Bonaparte', 31.

28 Marx 'The Eighteenth Brumaire of Louis Bonaparte', 32.

29 Marx 'The Eighteenth Brumaire of Louis Bonaparte', 32.

30 Terrell Carver, 'Marx's Eighteenth Brumaire of Louis Bonaparte: Democracy, Dictatorship, and the Politics of Class Struggle', in Peter Baehr and Melvin Richter, eds. *Dictatorship in History and Theory, Bonapartism, Caesarism, and Totalitarianism* (Cambridge: Cambridge University Press, 2004). This is by far the best explication of the complex argument in Marx's landmark piece. For my discussion I heavily rely on his analysis.

31 Terrell Carver, 'The Eighteenth Brumaire of Louis Bonaparte' in *Marx, Later Political Writings*, 105.

32 Terrell Carver, 'The Eighteenth Brumaire of Louis Bonaparte' in *Marx, Later Political Writings*, 105.

33 See Kojin Karatani, *Transcritique, On Kant and Marx*, trans. Sabu Kohso (Cambridge: The MIT Press, 2005), 256.

34 See Kojin Karatani, *Transcritique, On Kant and Marx*, 256.
35 Terrell Carver, 'The Eighteenth Brumaire of Louis Bonaparte', 108.
36 Quoted in Terrell Carver, 'The Eighteenth Brumaire of Louis Bonaparte', 110.
37 Terrell Carver, 'The Eighteenth Brumaire of Louis Bonaparte', 114.
38 Terrell Carver, 'The Eighteenth Brumaire of Louis Bonaparte', 115–116.
39 Readers should consult Terrell Carver's fine reading cited above.
40 See Alain Plessis, *The Rise and Fall of the Second Empire, 1852–1871* (Cambridge: Cambridge University Press and Paris: Editions de la Maison des Sciences de l'Homme, 1985), 62.
41 Quoted in Alain Plessis, *The Rise and Fall of the Second Empire, 1852–1871*, 119.
42 Alain Plessis, *The Rise and Fall of the Second Empire, 1852-1871*, 120.
43 Quoted in Alain Plessis, *The Rise and Fall of the Second Empire, 1852–1871*, 120. I am mainly following Plessis' narrative here.
44 Alain Plessis, *The Rise and Fall of the Second Empire, 1852–1871*, 121.
45 Quoted in Alain Plessis, *The Rise and Fall of the Second Empire, 1852–1871*, 123.
46 Walter Benjamin, 'Paris, the Capital of the Nineteenth Century, 'Exposé of 1935', in *The Arcades Project*, 11–13.
47 See Manfredo Tafuri, *Architecture and Utopia, Design and Capitalist Devolvement* (Cambridge and London: The MIT Press, 1979), esp. Chapter 6: 'The Crisis of Utopia: Le Corbusier at Algiers'.
48 Quoted in Geoff Mann's *In the Long Run We Are All Dead, Keynesianism, Political Economy and Revolution* (London and New York: Verso, 2017), 208.
49 Geoff Mann's *In the Long Run We Are All Dead*, 208.
50 Geoff Mann's *In the Long Run We Are All Dead*, 275.
51 See Joan Robinson, 'Latter Day Capitalism', in *New Left Review* (1:16, 1962), 46. Also see Mann's *In the Long Run We Are All Dead*, 275.
52 This formulation belongs to Geoff Mann in his *In the Long Run We Are All Dead*, 206. I rely heavily on Mann's text for my argument in this section.
53 See Eric Hobsbawm, 'Goodbye To All That', in *Marxism Today* (October 1999). This is one of the best essays in evaluating the events of 1989 putting it in a larger context of the twentieth century.
54 Manfredo Tafuri, *Architecture and Utopia*, 134.
55 Le Corbusier, *Toward an Architecture*, intro. Jean-Louis Cohen, trans. John Goodman (Los Angeles: Getty Research Institute, 2007), 292.
56 See my 'The Gift of the Open Hand: Le Corbusier Reading Georges Bataille's *La Part Maudite*', in *Journal of Architectural Education* (September 1996).

Part I

57 Manfredo Tafuri, *Architecture and Utopia*, 134–135.
58 Manfredo Tafuri, *Architecture and Utopia*, 135.
59 See Antonio Negri, 'Keynes and the Capitalist Theory of the State post-1929' [1968], in *Revolution Retrieved: Writing on Marx, Keynes, Capitalist Crisis and New Social Subjects* (London: Red Notes, 1988).
60 Manfredo Tafuri, *Architecture and Utopia*, 135.
61 Manfredo Tafuri, *Architecture and Utopia*, 135.
62 Manfredo Tafuri, *Architecture and Utopia*, 135.
63 Manfredo Tafuri, *Architecture and Utopia*, 135.
64 Manfredo Tafuri, *Architecture and Utopia*, 136.
65 Manfredo Tafuri, *Architecture and Utopia*, 136.
66 Geoff Mann's *In the Long Run We Are All Dead*, 36.
67 Antonio Negri, 'Keynes and the Capitalist Theory of the State post-1929', 7.
68 Antonio Negri, 'Keynes and the Capitalist Theory of the State post-1929', 8.
69 Antonio Negri, 'Keynes and the Capitalist Theory of the State post-1929', 7.
70 Geoff Mann, *In the Long Run We Are All Dead*, 377–378.
71 Geoff Mann, *In the Long Run We Are All Dead*, 378.
72 Geoff Mann, *In the Long Run We Are All Dead*, 379.
73 Geoff Mann, *In the Long Run We Are All Dead*, 379–380.
74 Geoff Mann, *In the Long Run We Are All Dead*, 380.
75 Geoff Mann, *In the Long Run We Are All Dead*, 380–381.
76 Geoff Mann's *In the Long Run We Are All Dead*, 381.
77 More on this see Mary McLeod's '"Architecture or Revolution": Taylorism, Technocracy, and Social Change', in *Art Journal*, Vol. 43, No. 2 (Summer 1983).
78 Le Corbusier, *The City of To-Marrow and its Planning*, 300–301
79 See Frederic Jameson, *Representing Capital, A Reading of Volume One* (London and New York: Verso, 2011), 146–147.
80 Frederic Jameson, *Representing Capital, A Reading of Volume One*, 147.
81 Le Corbusier, *The City of To-Marrow and its Planning*, no pagination.
82 Le Corbusier, *The City of To-Marrow and its Planning*, 294.
83 Sergio Villari, *J.N.L. Durand (1760–1834)*, 37.

Part II

Chapter 3

Marx and Critique

Critique and Enlightenment

Before we lay down the foundation for Marxian *critique*, it is necessary to speak about the Kantian *turn* in Critique. In the most fundamental way, it is conceived as 'a signifier of the fundamental scrutiny of rational human faculties'.[1] This anticipates the theory of critique that will be grounded in the notion of 'transcendental' that Kojin Karatani has conceptually named *Transcritique*. We will come to the explication of this complex term. Here a brief inquiry into the notion of Critique in Kant is in order.

The term Critique only attained a new elevated meaning when *Critique of Pure Reason* appeared—the first edition in 1781, version A, and the second edition in 1787, the revised version B. By elevating it to a philosophical meaning, Kant gave the term an 'epistemological function' and therefore endowed it with a 'theoretical dignity'.[2] Kant by redefining the 'theoretical as genuinely practical' transformed the critique into a 'concept with practical meaning', and this, for Kant, 'meant a concept of political relevance'.[3] The importance of *Critique* precisely lies in the *recognition* that practical and theoretical reason are intertwined. This is related to the notion of 'autonomy' that Kant conceived as 'self-legislation'. Kant's proposition is that 'Critique is only possible on the grounds of self-determination'.[4] Self-determination in a discursive sense is already signified in the title of the *Critique of Pure Reason* with its 'duality of the genitive construction, in its objective and subjective aspects'. The objective mainly points to 'critique *of Pure Reason*', while the subjective to the '*Critique* of pure reason', as Willi Goetschel in his *Constituting Critique* puts it.[5] In this circularity,

> Reflexive two-way thinking is thus already inscribed in the title of Kant's project. An arrow bent back on itself [↺], the double meaning creates a space beyond a mere two-way directionality: the double meaning expands into a surplus of sense […] The title thus enacts the project of critique as the process of self-referential theorizing about its own procedure.[6]

After three decades of 'pre-critical' writings, Kant arrives at critical philosophy. His critical project is not just an 'aesthetic' enterprise but, rather 'a fundamental rethinking of epistemology'. For when Kant suggests, as Goetschel notes, 'eliminating aesthetics as an independent branch of knowledge and giving transcendental aesthetics a fundamental role instead in the process of knowledge formation, he changes the way in which the problem of representation is conceived'.[7] After those three decades, Kant moved towards his epistemological-critical and finally to *Transcendental* philosophy. 'Thus constructed' in this philosophy, the notion of critique 'emerges as a discursive practice that is aware of the fact that it remains always tied to its constitutive moments […] Critique, so to speak, has only become critical since Kant'.[8] In this notion of Critique, by becoming a self-reflective process, 'reason no longer determines truth', but it rather, 'engages in self-reflection, on its own presuppositions. Kant's celebrated phrase speaks of the *conditions for the possibility of knowledge* that critique must determine'.[9] As Goetschel aptly puts it:

> Reason assumes the place of the judge, critique represents the court, and the *Critique of Pure Reason* serves as the record of the trial. It is no accident that legal metaphor plays such a prominent role in Kant's thought. One is reminded sometimes of Immanuel K.'s poor brother, Joseph K., of Kafka's *The Trial*.[10]

In *Critique* Kant wrote: 'Our age is the genuine age of criticism, to which everything must submit'.[11] This age of 'criticism' is the same as the 'age of enlightenment'.[12] Therefore,

> if *enlightenment* signifies both a period and a theoretical agenda, and if only a dual approach leads to an adequate understanding of enlightenment, then the approach to understanding critique should also be dual. Ever since Kant fused the two notions, enlightenment has carried critique deeply inscribed as its determination, and critique has become constitutively connected to enlightenment.[13]

In his famous journalistic article published in 1984 entitled *An Answer to the Question: What is Enlightenment*, Kant defined 'Enlightenment' as '*man's emergence from his self-imposed immaturity*'.[14] This immaturity 'is *self-imposed*', Kant wrote, 'when its cause lies not in the lack of understanding, but in lack of resolve and courage to use it without guidance from another'. Therefore: '*Sapere Aude!* "Have courage to use your own understanding!"—that is the motto of enlightenment'.[15]

He made it clear that we do not presently 'live in an *enlightened* age', but 'we do live in an age of *enlightenment*'.[16] Thus Kant warned us that the *process* of enlightenment is a slow process. 'Thus a public', he wrote, 'can only attain enlightenment slowly', adding: 'Perhaps a revolution can overthrow autocratic despotism and profiting or power-grabbing oppression, but it can never truly reform a manner of thinking'.[17] He of course achieved this revolution in thought with his Copernican turn. The project of Critique belongs to this *unfinished* age of enlightenment. Everything—*everything*—must be submitted to the imperative of this project. In this sense the cornerstone of the *project of critique* as an emancipatory project was laid down that will only culminate in Marx.

In *An Answer to the Question: What is Enlightenment?* Kant brought forward the notion of the 'public use of reason'. With a radical step, Kant forever changed our received understanding of the notion of 'public' as it relates to the question of enlightenment.[18] In the center of this notion of the 'public' is the question of *freedom*. 'Nothing is required for this enlightenment, however, except *freedom*' he wrote. And this freedom, which is 'least harmful of all', is indeed the 'freedom to use reason publicly in all matters'.[19] 'But on all sides', he wrote,

> I hear: '*Do not argue!*' The officer says, 'Do not argue, drill!' The taxman says, 'do not argue, pay!' The Pater says, 'do not argue, believe!' (Only one ruler in the world [Fredric II, (the Great), king of Prussia] says, '*Argue* as much as you want and about what you want, *but obey!*' In this we have [examples of] pervasive restrictions on freedom. But which restriction hinders enlightenment and which does not, but instead actually advances it? I reply: The Public use of one's reason must

always be free, and it alone can bring about enlightenment among mankind.[20]

Kant makes it clear that the *private use* of reason, however narrowly restricted, does not hinder the progress of enlightenment. The 'reason' in the public use is *universal*. The *universal reason* addresses the whole of mankind. For many, Kant's distinction is a paradox. Slavoj Žižek, on the Marxian ground, while acknowledging the paradox in Kant's formula of the 'public use of reason', defends it and brings it into his discussion of the 'Communist Hypothesis'.[21] By defining it as 'singular universality', bypassing particular determination, he writes:

> When Paul says that, from a Christian standpoint. 'there are no men or women, no Jews or Greeks,' he thereby claims that ethnic roots, national identity, etc. are *not a category of truth*. To put it in precise Kantian terms: when we reflect upon our ethnic roots, we engage in a *private use of reason* constrained by contingent dogmatic presuppositions, that is we act as 'immature' individuals, not as free humans who dwell in the dimension of the universality of reason.[22]

Invoking Kant's notion of 'World-civil-society' in his *Idea For a Universal History with a Cosmopolitan Intent*, the piece Kant wrote in the same year as his essay on 'What is Enlightenment?', in 1784, Žižek points out that 'public space' of course exemplifies the 'paradox of universal singularity' of a singular subject who, 'in a kind of short-circuit, bypassing the mediations of the particular, directly participates in the Universal'.[23] Pointing out Kant's paradoxical formula of 'think freely, but obey', Žižek, nevertheless, recognizes and endorses the vision of the 'transnational universality of the exercise of one's reason' and rightly points out that in this vision of 'public space characterized by the unconstrained exercise of Reason', Kant in fact invokes a 'dimension of emancipatory universality *outside* the confines of one's social identity, of one's position within the order of (social) being'.[24]

Going back to the concept of Critique in Kant, I now turn to Karatani who perceptively traces the sources and origin of the term in Kant in a larger picture of his three *Critiques* never discussed before. First, Karatani argues that in his three *Critiques*, Kant posited a distinctive relationship between science, art, and ethics. What is important to note, according to Karatani, is that Kant presented a structure in which the three categories form a ring which corresponds to a 'triadic categorical structure' with three different levels, namely, 'thing-in-itself', 'phenomenon', and 'transcendental illusion', keeping in mind that 'every one of which is indispensable for attaining the structure', which can be compared to the 'Borromenean knot' in Lacanian terms.[25] But, 'it is misleading', Karatani warns us,

> to think that in the third *Critique* he resolved the impasse he had encountered in the previous two. It is not that the Kantian critique—the discovery of the triadic structure—was brought to a completion by Kant's account of art or of the judgment of taste, in the third *Critique*. Instead, it could be said that, from the beginning, the Kantian critique had been derived from the problematic of the artistic experience.[26]

Although the etymological root of the term 'critique' that Kant used goes back to ancient Greece, in the light of its actual historical formation, Karatani links it to the term 'criticism' in the literal sense, that is, 'commercial journalism—an *arena* [*Kampfplatz*]—wherein the classical aesthetics ascribed to Aristotle are no longer relevant, and thus ongoing is the struggle with respect to the assessment of value'.[27] It appears that Kant, as Karatani traces it, must have been awakened by the Scottish critic, Henry Home (1766–1782) who wrote *Elements of Criticism* (1763–1766).[28] According to Hans Vailing whom Karatani cites, the following remark indicates that Kant read Home's book with excitement: 'Home has more correctly called Aesthetic Criticism, because it does not, like Logic, furnish a priori rules'.[29] Karatani suggests that according to this remark, Kant may have indeed derived the term 'critique' from Home. Karatani further explains that Kant first used the term 'critique of reason' in 'An Announcement for the arrangement of the Lectures in the Winter Semester 1765/1766.' In the text, 'the critique of reason [*die Kritik der Vernunft*]' is considered logic in the wide sense, in juxtaposition to the 'critique of taste [*die Kritik des Geschmacks*]'—namely aesthetics—as that which has a very close affinity of material cause. From this, too, one can presume a nexus shared by Kant's 'critique' and Home's book with its eponymous 'criticism'.[30] Karatani concludes that Kant, by taking up Home's term 'criticism', further developed his own concept of 'critique'.

I conclude this section, anticipating my later discussion of *critique* in Marx, by pointing out that we should not forget that *Marx belongs to the tradition of the age of Enlightenment*. As mentioned in the previous chapter, following Fredric Jameson, Marx's *project* is a program of 'proletarian enlightenment' in confrontation with 'bourgeois enlightenment'. It is noteworthy that Marx acknowledged both 'the benefit and costs of progress' in capitalism but, in contrast to Max Weber, he 'jettisoned the teleology while preserving the critical and emancipatory vision of the Enlightenment'.[31] By having departed from the Enlightenment concept of progress, 'only as far as was necessary to break out of its bourgeois ideology, and having replaced teleology with *historical process*', Marx was able to take up 'the Enlightenment programme of human emancipation'.[32] Marx achieved this project by his *Contribution to the Critique of Political Economy*. Before taking it up, I need to discuss the manner in which Marx is read by our contemporary radical thinkers.

Transcritique

Critique moves—'transversally' and 'transcendentally'. Karatani has termed this move as *Transcritique*. He has devoted his impressive *Transcritique: On Kant and Marx* to its elucidation, in which a new reading of Kant and Marx *recovers* the significance of *critique*. In this reading, Critique becomes *scrutiny*, a rather 'elaborate self-scrutiny', as he put it. By this category, Karatani has brought a new intelligence into the theory of Critique and its practice. Marxian *emancipatory critique* has now to take this conception of Transcritique into account. In the light of this category, Marx's '*critique* of political economy' enters the discourse of *ethics*. Transcritique is defined as a space that forms 'transcodings', as Karatani informs us, between *ethics* and *political economy*, that moves between Kantian critique and Marxian critique. From this *transcritical* reading, Kant, according to Karatani, will no longer come across as a 'bourgeois philosopher', but rather as a philosopher of 'German socialism'. Thus it is no longer interesting *not* to read Marx with Kant and Kant with Marx. In capitalism people treat each other as 'a means to and end'. But Kantian 'kingdom of freedom' or 'kingdom of ends', Karatani notes, 'clearly comes to entail another new meaning, that is, communism'.[33] In fact, communism, he notes, never was conceptualized without a moral thinking arising from Kantian ethics. The young Marx, as we recall, invoked Kant's 'categorical imperative' when he wrote: 'The criticism of religion ends with the doctrine that *man is the highest being of man,* hence with the *categorical imperative to overthrow all conditions* in which man is a degraded, enslaved, neglected, contemptible being'.[34] The pairing of Marx and Kant, of course, goes back to the late nineteenth century in the so-called 'Kantian Marxism'. But Karatani's treatment of it is radically novel. The Marxian *turn* is now entangled in the Kantian *turn*. Karatani later extended his *transcritical* project to Kant and Freud in his *Nation and Aesthetics, On Kant and Freud*.[35] In the background of this latter pairing still reside the Marxian *economics*, but not in the mode of 'production' but rather in the mode of 'exchange'. We will see later what this notion of *exchange* entails.

Aside from the Transcritique on Kant and Marx, I will use Karatani's term to characterize another intellectual enterprise in our time by our radical thinkers reading Marx *with* Hegel. This latter pairing is accomplished by Slavoj Žižek. He reads Marx via Hegel and Hegel via Marx, avoiding altogether the old tired mold of so-called 'Hegelian Marxism'. Although the notion of 'Transcritique' is never mentioned, Žižek has nevertheless deployed Karatani's term 'Parallax' in his *The Parallax View*. Karatani adopted the precise term 'pronounce parallax' from Kant but Žižek puts it rather differently in his own terms calling it the 'parallax gap'. In his book Žižek of course acknowledges his debts to Karatani's work, notwithstanding his criticism of the latter for neglecting Hegel.[36] Specifically, Žižek takes Karatani to task for forgetting to discuss the much neglected author Alfred Sohn-Rethel (a friend of Theodor Adorno) and his book entitled *Intellectual and Manual Labour: A Critique of Epistemology*.[37] Significantly, Sohn-Rethel was among the first who, as Žižek's explains, 'directly deployed the parallel between Kant's transcendental critique and Marx's critique of political economy, but in the opposite critical direction: the structure of commodity universe *is* that of the Kantian transcendental space', which basically means that 'Sohn-Rethel's goal was to combine Kantian epistemology with Marx's critique of political economy'.[38] Since the publication of *The Parallax View*, Žižek has extensively elaborated on his reading of Marx via Hegel and Hegel via Marx in his massive *Less Than Nothing* and later in his *Absolute Recoil*.[39]

Still, another intellectual enterprise, I contend, can also be categorized under the term Transcritique: Reading Marx with Lacan. This pairing is, in turn, in close proximity to the pairing of Lacan and Hegel. It seems that it is now a necessity to read Marx through psychoanalysis, long after Jacques Lacan who once said that Marx is the inventor of 'symptom' long before Freud. As Žižek somewhere said, 'To be a Marxist today, one HAS to go through Lacan'.[40] For the achievements gained in reading Lacan with Hegel and Marx with Lacan, it is necessary here to recognize the formation of a formidable intellectual circle that gathered in Ljubljana, Slovenia, beginning in the late 1980s. Among the members of this circle, besides Slavoj Žižek himself, two other notable names must be mentioned, namely Mladen Dolar and Alanka Zupančič who, along with their other colleagues, have effectively inaugurated a radical *turn* in reading Hegel, Lacan, and Marx. One of the most important outcome of their highly complex readings is the reconstruction of the theory of Ideology through psychoanalytical theory which goes beyond the Critical Theory of the Frankfurt School and its so-called Freudo-Marxian enterprise, with an impressive result with which we must reckon.[41] To appreciate the significance of the Slovenian intellectual circle, I would like to point out here that after the famous '*Cercle d'Épistémologie*' at École Normale Superieur (ENS) on rue d'Ulm in Paris under the towering figures of Louis Althusser and Jacques Lacan and its famous journal *Cahiers pour l'Analyse* (1960–1966), no other intellectual circle in Europe and in fact on the international scene has succeeded in contributing more to the new theoretical enterprise of reading Marx with Hegel and Lacan than the Slovenian intellectual circle.[42] In this respect, it is useful to recall the theoretical results of the Circle in Paris collected in *Reading Capital* under Althusser's leadership, which is still influential.[43] But by a renewed reading of Hegel, against Althusser's entrenched anti-Hegelian stance, the intellectual circle in Slovenia has effectively gone beyond the limitations of the *Cercle d'Épistémologie* in Paris.

I will come back in due course to each 'pairing' I have named above. At this point, I want to first discuss how Karatani formulates the term 'Transcritique' and its precise meanings. As we will see, implicit in this term is the notion of 'transcendental' in the specific way Karatani interprets it. In the chapter entitled 'The Kantian Turn' he first analyzes Kant's use of a key phrase, 'pronounced parallax', in an early journalistic and 'self-deprecating' essay Kant wrote in 1766 entitled 'Dreams of a Visionary Explained by Dreams of Metaphysics'. In this article Kant wrote:

> Formerly, I viewed human common sense only from the standpoint of my own; now I put myself into the position of

another's reason outside myself, and observe my judgments, together with their more secret causes, from the point of view of others. It is true that the comparison of both observation results in *pronounced parallaxes*, but it is the only means to prevent the *optical delusion*, and of putting the concept of the power of knowledge in human nature into its true place [emphasis mine].[44]

In this passage Kant is not stating a commonplace, as Karatani reminds us, that one must see things not from one's own point of view only, 'but also, simultaneously, from the point of view of others'. If this were the case, 'it would be run-of-the mill: the history of philosophy is filled with reflections of one seeing oneself as others would see'.[45] The 'pronounced parallax' is not exactly the 'point of view'. To illustrate it, Karatani brings up the new technology of photography not available in Kant's time. Before photography, 'reflection' was thought by the metaphor of seeing one's image in the mirror. The image in the mirror was identified to be seen by the other. But it is still in complicity with one's point of view, it is fixed, let alone that it is right/left inverted or inside out. Whether the reflection of one's image in mirror or water, or a painted portrait, they were too subjective. In contrast, as Karatani reasons, 'photography sustains a different, much more severe, *objectivity*'.[46] He elaborates on this by employing the main Kantian notions:

> Even though there is always a photographer, his or her subjectivity is less influential than the painter's, for there is an ineradicable, mechanical distance in photographic image. Strange as it may be, we cannot see our faces (read the thing-in-itself), except as an image reflected in the mirror

(read phenomenon). And only thanks to the advent of photography, did we learn that fact. But, again, photography is also an image, and of course, people eventually get used to the mechanical images, so much so that they eventually come to feel that the image is themselves.[47]

'But the crux here is', Karatani further explains, the '"pronounced parallax"—that which people presumably experience when they "first" see their photographic image'.[48] Kant is usually understood to have located his 'transcendental critique' from a place between 'rationalism' and 'empiricism'. However, Karatani argues, upon reading the 'Dream of a Visionary', 'one finds it impossible to say that he was simply thinking from a place between these two poles. Instead it is the "parallax" between positions that acts'.[49] Kant confronted rationalism with empiricism and empiricism with rationalism, both dominant in his time. His critique moves between these two poles. Therefore, Karatani asserts, 'The transcendental critique is not some kind of stable third position. It cannot exist without transversal and transitional movement'. It is for this reason that, he further states, 'I have chosen to name the dynamic critiques of Kant and Marx—which are both transcendental and transversal—"transcritique"'.[50]

At this point, a definition of the word 'Parallax' itself is in order. Žižek who acknowledges his debt to Karatani for the title of his *magnum opus*, *The Parallax View*, gives the 'standard definition' of the term putting it in the context of the relation between 'subject' and 'object'. He writes: 'the apparent displacement of an object (the shift of its position against a background), [is] caused by a change in observational position that provides a new line of sight'.[51] Put in philosophical context, he adds, 'the observed difference is not simply "subjective," due to the fact that the same object which exists "out there" is seen from two different stances, or points of view'.[52] In a Hegelian way, Žižek further says, 'subject and object are inherently "mediated," so that an "epistemological" shift in the subject's point of view always reflects an "ontological" shift in the object itself'.[53] For Žižek, 'Parallax' basically means replacing the 'polarity of opposites' with the 'concept of the inherent "tension," gap, noncoincidence, of the One itself'.[54] He explains his project as based on a 'strategic politico-philosophical decision to designate this gap which separates the One from itself with the term *parallax*'.[55] He then goes on to explore this 'parallax gap' in different domains of modern theory and the philosophical-political series in which this 'gap' is an operative factor.

However, in Karatani's terms, we must tie the definition of 'pronounced parallax' to 'transcendental critique'. He first notes that 'parallax' in Kant appears in the form of 'antinomy', which would indicate that thesis and antithesis are nothing more than 'optical illusion'. Interestingly, I must mention in passing that Žižek sees that the '*parallax gap*' (in which no neutral common ground between two perspectives is possible) might in a first approach appear as a kind of 'Kantian revenge over Hegel'. He asks: 'is not "parallax" yet another name for a fundamental *antinomy* which can never be dialectically "mediated/sublated" into a higher synthesis, since there is no common language, no shared ground, between two levels?'[56] His answer is that, far from posing an obstacle to dialectics, the notion of parallax gap 'provides the key which enables us to discern its subversive core', and further, that 'to theorize this parallax gap properly is the necessary first step in the rehabilitation of *dialectical materialism*'.[57]

Following Karatani's argument, a 'simple' definition of 'transcendental' in Kant can be given as follows: 'the transcendental seeks to cast light on the *unconscious* structure that precedes and shapes experience'[58] [emphasis mine]. Bringing up the term 'unconscious' in this definition, Karatani significantly grounds the notion of 'transcendental' in psychoanalytical theory and relates it to the question of the *other* that resides in the notion of 'pronounced parallax' in Kant. This definition must be specifically understood within the so-called 'Copernican turn' in Kant. It begins with the following: in pre-Kantian metaphysics, it was thought that the 'subject copies the external object'. But Kant proposed that 'objects are constituted by the form that subject *projects into* the world'.[59] On the face of it, this might seem to be the opposite of what the 'Copernican turn' is about. But Karatani's explanation clears the misunderstanding. It is in the categories of the 'thing-in-itself' and the 'transcendental object' that Karatani attempts to demonstrate that Kant in fact echoed the very essence of the Copernican turn. But the Copernican proposition itself begs a more precise interpretation. To get to it, we must consider first a key passage in *Critique of Pure Reason* cited by Karatani. Kant wrote:

> The sensible faculty of intuition is really only a receptivity for being affected in a certain way with representation, whose relation to one another is a pure intuition of space and time (pure forms of our sensibility), which, insofar as they are connected and determined in these relations (in space and time) according to laws of the unity of experience, are called object. The non-sensible cause of these representations is entirely unknown to us, and therefore we cannot intuit it as an object; for such an object would have to be represented neither in

space nor in time (as mere conditions of our sensible representation), without which conditions we cannot think any intuition. Meanwhile we can call the merely intelligible cause of appearances in general the transcendental object, merely so that we may have something corresponding to sensibility as receptivity. To this transcendental object we can ascribe the whole extent and connections of our possible perceptions, and say that it is given in itself prior to all experience. But appearances are, in accordance with it, given not in themselves but only in this experience, because they are merely representations, which signify a real object only as perceptions, namely when this perception connects up with all others in accordance with the rules of the unity of experience.[60]

As we will see, Karatani is concerned with the validity of the Kantian 'thing-in-itself', much denied and misinterpreted by other philosophers, which, in Karatani's mind is responsible for Kant being taken as a philosopher of 'subjectivity'. Did Kant, Karatani asks, simply combine 'rationalism' and 'empiricism'? Before answering this question it is the real essence of the Copernican turn that must be properly understood. As Karatani points out, the idea of 'heliocentrism' had been known since ancient times, so it was not Copernicus's invention. Karatani's explanation is illuminating:

After all, the true significance of the Copernican turn lay in the hypothetical stance itself. In other words, the significance lay not in forcing any choice between geocentrism or heliocentrism, but rather in grasping the solar system as a rational structure—using the terms such as 'earth' and 'sun'—that is totally independent of empirical observed objects or event. Thus the significance of the Copernican turn was twofold.[61]

In the same manner, Karatani concludes that Kant managed to overcome the basic contradiction of the philosophy in his time, that is, between empirical senses or empiricism or rational thinking or rationalism.

> Instead, Kant introduced those structures—that is, forms of sensibility or categories of understanding—*of which one is unaware*, calling them 'transcendental' structures. Words such as 'sensibility [*Sinnlichkeit*]' and 'understanding [*Verstand*]' have long existed as conceptualizations of life experience: 'to sense' and 'to understand'. But Kant completely altered their meaning in a way similar to what Copernicus had done when he rediscovered 'sun' and 'earth' as terms within solar system qua reciprocal structure.[62]

Karatani further says that it is not necessary to repeat Kant's terminology, rather, 'What is crucial is this *architectonic* that is called "transcendental". And even if these particular words or concepts are not always used in various post-Kantian contexts, the same architectonic can be found there'.[63] Thus, for that matter, Karatani points out, the revolutionary aspects of Freudian psychoanalysis and discovery of the 'unconscious' was not 'in the idea of "unconscious controlling much of human behavior"', but rather, it was in his attempt 'to see what existed in the gap between consciousness and unconscious vis-à-vis the form of language. In the course of this attempt, he came to extract the unconscious qua transcendental structure'.[64] Along this line of argument, Karatani goes on to emphatically dispute the idea of Kant as the philosopher of subjectivity and asserts:

> What Kant really did, however, was to present the boundaries of limits of human subjective faculties, and in so doing

> criticizes metaphysics as an arrogation that oversteps those boundaries. Much like Freud's 'id, ego, and superego', Kant's 'sensibility, understanding, and reason' are not things that exist empirically. In this sense, indeed, they are *nothing*; which, however, is a 'nothing' that *exists* as a certain *function*. More precisely, transcendental apperception (or subjectivity) is the 'function as nothing' that 'bundles' the three faculties together into a single system.[65]

Kant's Copernican turn, Karatani emphasizes, is not 'toward the philosophy of subjectivity, but that toward the thing-in-itself by a detour of the scrutiny of subjectivity. It was for this objective and nothing else that Kant elaborated the transcendental structure of subjectivity'.[66] Karatani asks: 'what is the concept of *thing-in-itself*'? He argues that this concept always is related to the 'problematic of ethics [...], it is concerned, in other words, with the problematic of *the other*'.[67]

Next, Karatani moves to elucidate the Marxian *turn* along the same line of Kantian 'pronounced parallax' or *antinomy*, which will bring out the Marxian turn of *critique* while shedding a new light on the *Critique of Political Economy* not discussed anywhere before. Therefore we are left with two different readings of the critique of political economy grounded in two different philosophical argumentations that at times overlap each other: on the one hand, Žižek's reading of Marx via Hegel and Hegel via Marx, specifically where he discusses 'Beginning: The Return of the Critique of Political Economy' in *Living in the End Times*,[68] and on the other, Karatani's reading of Marx via Kant and Kant via Marx through his *transcritical* project. What both thinkers share though is the same *transcendental* approach, albeit with a different understanding or interpretation. Karatani argues that what is important is the fact that Marx's critique was 'always born from migration and the pronounced parallax that results from it'.[69] In this relation, he remarks that Hegel criticizes 'Kant's subjectivism and emphasizes objectivity', but quickly adds that in 'Hegel the pronounced parallax discovered by Kant is extinguished', in the same way that the pronounced parallax discovered by Marx was extinguished by Engels and other Marxists'.[70] As a result

> one is left with an image of Kant and Marx as thinkers who constructed solid, immovable systems. A closer reading, however, reveals that they were in fact practicing constant transposition, and that the move to different discursive systems was what brought about the pronounced parallax.[71]

Louis Althusser claimed that Marx made an 'epistemological break' with *The German Ideology*. Karatani believes that in his *transcritical* understanding, and contrary to Althusser, there were more than one break, and that this one in particular was not the most significant. If 'historical materialism' was what was established with *The German Ideology*, Karatani asserts that it was more Engels's idea, who wrote the large part of it. We must understand that, according to Karatani, capitalism is 'nothing like the economic infrastructure. It is a certain force that regulates humanity beyond its intentionality, a force that divides and recombines human beings. It is a religio-generic entity. This is what Marx sought to decode for the whole of his life'.[72] The 'Marxian turn', more significant than the previous 'breaks', Karatani contends, came with the shift from *Grundrisse* or *A Contribution to the Critique of Political Economy* to *Capital*. This was centered on the introduction of the theory of 'value form'. Marx went beyond the classical economists and the so-called 'labor theory of value' in David Ricardo directly to the mercantilist economy. Marx's radical turn came about by his 'skepticism'. It was Samuel Bailey's skepticism and his criticism of Ricardo's labor theory of value that caused Marx to move. For Ricardo, exchange-value was inherent in commodity and 'money' was just an illusion. Bailey, according to Karatani, held that the value of a commodity exists only in its relationship with other commodities and therefore 'the labor value that Ricardo insists is inherent in a commodity is an illusion'.[73] Bailey's skepticism is similar to Hume's criticism of Cartesian ego cogito that there are many egos. This claim, Karatani writes, Kant responded that

> yes, an ego is just an illusion, but functioning there is the transcendental apperception X. But what one knows as metaphysics is that which considers that the X has something essential [...] It is possible to say that an ego is not just an illusion, but a transcendental illusion.[74]

Having been stricken by Bailey's skepticism, Marx, like Kant who was similarly stricken by Hume's skepticism, took his thought to another dimension that Karatani calls a 'transcendental reflection on value'.[75] Karatani notes that Bailey did not question money which relates commodities to each other and composes the system, that is, money as 'general equivalent'. He further explains:

> Money in this sense is totally irrelevant to money as substance like gold or silver; rather, it is like a Kantian transcendental apperception of X, as it were. This position of seeing it in relation to its materiality is what Marx called fetishism. After all, money as substance is an illusion, but more correctly, it is a

transcendental illusion in the sense that it is hardly possible to discard it.[76]

Thus the Marx of *Capital*, Karatani says, stands on the side of the mercantilist (rather than Ricardo or Bailey), which means that Marx focused on what was not the objects themselves but 'the relational system in which objects are placed', in which, according to Marx, if

> gold becomes money, that is not because of its immanent material characteristics, but because it is placed in the value form. The value form—consisting of relative value form and equivalent form—makes an object that is placed in it money. Anything—*anything*—that is exclusively placed in the general equivalent form becomes money; that is, it achieves the right to attain anything in exchange.[77]

After these explorations, Karatani comes to express his thesis in an astonishing passage which goes as follows:

> One of the most crucial transposition/breaks in Marx's theory of value form lies in its attention to use value or the process of circulation. Say a certain thing becomes valuable only when it has use value to other people; a certain thing—no matter how much labor time is required to make it—has no value if not sold. Marx technically abolished the conventional division between exchange value and use value. No commodity contains exchange value as such. If it fails to relate to others, it will be a victim of 'sickness unto death' in the sense of Kierkegaard. Classical economists believe that a commodity is a synthesis between use value and exchange value. But this is only an ex post facto recognition. Lurking behind this

synthesis as event is a 'fatal leap' [*salto mortale*]. Kierkegaard saw that human being as a synthesis between finity and infinity, reminding us that what is at stake in this synthesis is inevitably 'faith'. In commodity exchange, the equivalent *religious* moment appears as 'credit'. Credit, the treaty of presuming that a commodity can be sold in advance, is an institutionalization of postponing the critical moment of selling a commodity. And the commodity economy, constructed as it is upon credit, inevitably nurtures crisis.[78]

'Crisis', Karatani further elucidates,

is the appearance of the critical moment inherent in the commodity economy, and as such it functions as the most radical critique of the political economy. In this light, it may be said that pronounced parallax brought by crisis led Marx to *Capital* [...] And all the enigmas of capital's drive are inscribed in the theory of value form. The theory of value form is not a historical reflection that follows *exchange* from barter to the formation of money. Value form is a kind of form that people are not aware of when they are placed within the monetary economy; this is the form that is discovered only *transcendentally*.[79]

At this point, I return to the beginning: A return to Marxian *critique*. We must still scrutinize the sources of 'critique' in the '*critique* of political economy' that *constitutes* the 'Marxian *turn*'. As the citation from Karatani makes clear, we *must* read Marx's corpus as *critique*. It will never ever lose its significance and relevance, no matter that the historical condition under which it appeared is rendered obsolete. We must recover the epistemological function of his critique, it will be with us for coming ages. In other words, the 'Marxian turn' in *critique* is going to be with us for a foreseeable future. As Emmanuel Wallerstein once said, it will be a hundred years from now that we will be still talking about Marxian categories. Like the critique in Kant, Marxian critique also involves incessant *transposition,* what Karatani calls *transcritique*. The Copernican turn outside the domain of science happens more than once, insofar as the *objects* in the world are composed by the *subjectivity* that the *active* subject projects into it. Before going further, I want to reiterate the standpoint of the 'transcendental': 'The transcendental position is equivalent to bracketing the imagined self-evidence of the empirical consciousness in order to reveal the (unconscious) conditions that constitute it. What is crucial here is that the transcendental standpoint inexorably accompanies a certain kind of *subjectivity*'.[80]

Capitalist society is a religious society—yet to be analyzed. It is not correct to say, as Max Weber said in his *The Protestant Ethic and the Spirit of Capitalism* that 'Protestant ethics', or Religious Reformation *qua* superstructure, gave rise to the 'spirit of capitalism' or the development of the industrial capitalist base. As Karatani points out, the Reformation could not have come into existence without a certain social transformation that accompanied the market economy in the first place.[81]

The critique of political economy first begins with the criticism of religion. In 'Toward a Contribution to the Critique of Hegel's *Philosophy of Right*: Introduction' Marx wrote:

> For Germany the *criticism of religion* has been essentially completed, and criticism of religion is the premise of all criticism [...] The basis of irreligious criticism is: *Man makes religion*, religion does not make man. And indeed religion is the self-consciousness and self-regard of man who has either not yet found or has already lost himself. But *man* is not an

> abstract being squatting outside the world. Man is *the world of men*, the state and society. The state and this society produce religion, which is an *inverted consciousness of the world* because they are an *inverted world*.[82]

Significantly, in this overturning Marx evoked the Copernican turn:

> Criticism has plucked imaginary flowers from the chain, not so that man will wear the chain that is without fantasy or consolation but so that he will throw it off and pluck the living flower. The criticism of religion disillusions man so that he thinks, acts, and shapes his reality like a disillusioned man who has come to his senses, so that he revolves around himself and thus around his true sun. Religion is only the illusory sun that revolves around man so long as he does not revolve about himself. Thus it is the *task of history*, once the *otherworldly truth* has disappeared, to establish the *truth of this world*. The immediate *task of philosophy* which is in the service of history is to unmask human self-alienation in its *unholy forms* now that it has been unmasked in its *holy form*. Thus the criticism of heaven turns into criticism of the earth, the *criticism of religion* into *criticism of law* and the criticism of theology into *criticism of politics*.[83]

Religion cannot be *rationally* abolished:

> The abolition of religion as people's *illusory* happiness is the demand for their *real* happiness. The demand to abandon illusions about their condition is a *demand to abandon a condition which requires illusions*. The criticism of religion is thus in *embryo* a *criticism of the vale of tears* whose halo is religion.[84]

Thus religion can never be abolished unless the real unhappiness of people which gives rise to religion is abolished. For Karatani, 'theoretical criticism of religion' cannot really 'affect religion; the religious problematic can only be solved *practically*'.[85] Marx saw in capitalist economy a 'secular religion', as it were. Therefore, 'Marx's critique of the political economy was an extension of his critique of religion. In this respect, there is no "epistemological break" as such'.[86]

The 'ultimate Marxian parallax' is between economy and politics, as Žižek, in confirmation of Karatani's analysis, states. It is between the critique of political economy and the 'political struggle with its logic of class antagonism [...] Both logics are "transcendental", not merely ontico-empirical; and each is irreducible to the other'.[87] Of course, Žižek points out,

> they point towards each other—class struggle is inscribed into the very heart of economy, yet it has to remain absent, non-thematized (recall how the manuscript of *Capital* iii [volume III] abruptly breaks off with classes) [...] Any direct translation of political struggle into mirroring of economic 'interest' is doomed to fail; just as is any reduction of the economic sphere into a secondary 'reified sedimentation of an underlying founding political process'.

In this respect, Žižek significantly uses the occasion of his sympathetic review of Karatani's work to say:

> In this sense, the 'pure politics' of Badiou, Rancière or Balibar, more Jacobin than Marxist, shares with its great opponent, Anglo-Saxon Cultural Studies, a degradation of the sphere of economy. That is to say, what all the new French (or French-oriented) theories of the Political, from Balibar through

> Rancière and Badiou to Laclau and Mouffe, aim at is—to put it in the traditional philosophical terms—the reduction of the sphere of economy (of material production) to an 'ontic' sphere deprived of 'ontological' dignity. Within this horizon, there is simply no place for the Marxian 'critique of political economy': the structure of the universe of commodities and capital in Marx's *Capital* is not just that of a limited empirical sphere, but a kind of socio-transcendental a priori, the matrix which generates the totality of social and political relations.[88]

I must now turn to Žižek's reading of Marx with Hegel specifically in relation to the 'critique of political economy'. In line with Karatani, we must consider this pairing to be a case of Transcritique on Marx and Hegel. Žižek tackles it in *Living in the End Times* in a chapter entitled 'Beginning: The Return of the Critique of Political Economy'. Later, Žižek expanded his reading of Marx via Hegel more extensively in his *Less than Nothing*. In his earlier reading, Žižek addresses the work of Moishe Postone who has presented a new interpretation of Marx's work by pursuing the 'critique of political economy' and 'Marx's Critical Theory'.[89] Žižek also uses this occasion to critique Alain Badiou's conception of History remarking that

> There is no place in Badiou's theoretical edifice for historical materialism, which is neither an imaginary narrative of History nor a positive science of history as a domain of being (social reality), but the science of the real of history as well as the critique of political economy as the science of the real of capitalism.[90]

Žižek empathically makes his case that: 'A resuscitation of the "critique of political economy" is the *sine qua non* of contemporary communist politics'.[91] He further says:

Marx and Critique

The 'hard real' of the 'logic of the capital' is what is missing in the historicist universe of Cultural Studies, not only at the level of content (the analysis and critique of political economy), but also at the more formal level of the difference between historicism and historicity proper.[92]

Before coming to his '*From Hegel to Marx ... and Back*' in the chapter in his *Living in the End Times* mentioned above, Žižek puts forward his defense of the revival of Marx's 'critique of political economy' in the section entitled 'The Labor Theory of Value Revisited'. Relying on Postone's argument, Žižek points out that it is only in capitalist society in which commodities are produced for the market that we can talk about the 'double character' of labor, that is, the division between concrete and abstract labor. In *Capital* Marx wrote:

> the exchange values of commodities must be capable of being expressed in terms of something common to them all, of which thing they represent a greater or less quantity. This common 'Something" cannot be a geometrical, a chemical, or any other natural property of commodities. Such properties claim our attention only in so far as they affect the utility of those commodities, make them use values. But the exchange of commodities is evidently an act characterized by a total abstraction from use value ... As use values, commodities are, above all, of different qualities, but as exchange values they are merely different quantities, and consequently do not contain an atom of use value. If then we leave out of consideration the use value of commodities, they have only one common property left, that of being the product of labor.[93]

Part II

Žižek remarks that, according to what Marx said, the 'universal intrinsic value' is totally different from the 'natural properties' of the commodity as an object, which endows it with a metaphysical or spiritual property. For looking at commodities as products of abstract labor, he cites Marx as saying

> there is nothing left of them in each case but the same phantom-like objectivity ... As crystals of this social substance, which is common to them all, they are values—commodity values ... Not an atom of matter enters into the objectivity of commodities as physical objects ... Commodities possess an objective character as values as physical only insofar as they are all expressions of an identical social substance, human labor, that their objective character has value is purely social.[94]

Commenting on this passage, Žižek writes:

> that (exchange) value is a social category, linked to the way the social character of production is inscribed in a commodity: the relationship between use-value and (exchange) value is not one between particularity and universality, but one between the different uses of the same commodity, first as an object that satisfies some need, then as a social object, as a token of relations between subjects. Value concerns products (commodities) as social entities, it is the imprint of the social character of a commodity, and *this is why labor is its only source*—once we see that value concerns 'relations between people,' the claim that its source is labor becomes almost a tautology. In other words, the only source of value is human labor because value is a social category which measures the participation of each individual laborer in the totality social labor—to claim that capital and labor are both 'factors'

which create value is the same as claiming that capital is, alongside the laborer, also a member of human society.[95]

After further elaborations following the above remarks, Žižek finally comes to his point in stating that

> Marx's so-called '"labor theory of Value"' is thus a kind of misnomer […] that it should in no way be read as claiming that one should discard exchange, or its role in the constitution of value, as a mere appearance which obscures the key fact that labor is the origin of value'.[96]

'One should rather', he adds,

> conceive the emergence of value as a process of mediation by means of which value 'casts off' its use—value *is* surplus-value over use-value. The general equivalent of use-value *had* to be deprived of use-value, it had to function as a pure potentiality of use-value.[97]

It is here that Žižek arrives at his *'From Hegel to Marx … and Back'* to say that

> Essence is appearance as appearance: value is exchange-value *as* exchange-value—or, as Marx put it in a manuscript version of the changes to the first edition of *Capital*: 'The reduction of different concrete private labours to this abstraction (*Abstraktum*) of the same human labor is accomplished only through exchange which effectively posits the product of different labors as equal to each other'. In other words, 'abstract labor' is a value-relationship which constitutes itself only in exchange, it is not the substantial property of a commodity independently of its relation with other commodities.[98]

Now it is at this point that Žižek brings up the neglected and misunderstood role of 'money' in the 'Leftist followers of Ricardo' and points out that 'The point of Marx's analysis is that this project ignores the formal determination of money which make fetishism a necessary effect'. He writes:

> In other words, when Marx defines exchange-value as the mode of appearance of value, one should mobilize here the entire Hegelian weight of the opposition between essence and appearance: essence exists only insofar as it appears, it does not pre-exist its appearance. In the same way, the value of a commodity is not its intrinsic substantial property which exists independently of its appearance in exchange.[99]

Žižek further argues that Marx's distinction between concrete and abstract labor is also a misnomer:

> in a Hegelian sense, 'concrete' labor (an individual working on a natural object, transforming it to make it satisfy some human need) is an abstraction from the network of concrete social relations within which it always takes place. This network of social relations inscribes itself into the category of labor precisely in the form of its opposite, of 'abstract' labor, and into its product, a commodity, in the form of its value (as opposed to its use-value).[100]

Žižek cites Postone as saying:

> Marx's theory of value provides the basis for an analysis of capital as a socially constituted form of mediation and wealth whose primary characteristic is a tendency towards its

limitless expansion ... In Marx's terms, out of a pre-capitalist context characterized by relations of personal dependence, a new one emerged characterized by individual personal freedom within a social framework of 'objective dependence.' Both terms of the classical modern antinomic opposition—the freely self-determining individual and society as an extrinsic sphere of objective necessity—are, according to Marx's analysis, historically constituted with the rise of and spread of the commodity-determined form of social relations.[101]

For Žižek it was Hegel who elaborated on this antinomy. Hegel, he says,

clearly perceived the link between antinomy in its social aspect (the coexistence of individual freedom and objective necessity in the guise of the rule of market mechanism) and in its religious aspect (Protestantism with its antinomic motifs of individual responsibility and Predestination).[102]

At this point Žižek makes a number of claims. First, he asserts that Althusser and Karatani, from different theoretical positions, dismissed reference to Hegel. He cites Karatani from *Transcritique: On Kant and Marx* where he said:

Notwithstanding the Hegelian descriptive style ... *Capital* distinguishes itself from Hegel's philosophy in its motivation. The end of *Capital* is never the 'absolute Spirit'. *Capital* reveals the fact that capital, though organizing the world, can never go beyond its own limit. It is a Kantian critique of the ill-contained drive of capital/reason to self-realize beyond its limit.[103]

Second, Žižek claims that Marx's critique is

> precisely *not* Kantian, since he conceived the notion of limit in the properly Hegelian sense—as a *positive* motivating force which pushes capital further and further in its ever-expanding self-reproduction, not in the Kantian sense of a negative limitation. In other words, what is not visible from a Kantian standpoint is how 'the ill-contained drive of capital/reason to self-realize beyond its limit' is totally co-substantial with this limit.[104]

Žižek further notes that the central 'antinomy' of capital is in fact its driving force. The 'movement of capital' is its drive to

> resolve its inherent antagonism [...] capital 'can never go beyond its own limit,' not because some noumenal Thing resists its grasp, rather because, in a sense, it is blinded to the fact that *there is nothing beyond this limit*, only a specter of total appropriation generated by the limit itself.[105]

There is not enough space here to go into depth on Žižek's evocation of Hegel in his reading of Marx's 'critique of political economy' and his critique of Karatani's approach. I should only mention here his invoking of Georg Lukács's position in his *History and Class Consciousness* and that of Alfred Sohn-Rethel in his *Intellectual and Manual Labour: A Critique of Epistemology* that he contrasts with Karatani's position by saying that the 'passage from bourgeois ideology with its formalism/dualism to the revolutionary-dialectical thought of totality is, philosophically, the passage from Kant to Hegel'.[106] What I nevertheless want to point out here is that Žižek's approach, by his own admission, is also 'transcendental', albeit not exactly of a 'Kantian' nature. This is why I consider Žižek's project of reading Marx with Hegel, in spite of everything else, to be also a Transcritique which is consistent with Karatani's method in principle.

Critique and the Unconscious

Critique is on the move—transversally and transcendentally. This time around, it distinctively moves toward the Unconscious. Following Karatani, I consider this latter move to be also *transcritical:* on Marx and psychoanalysis—*critique* of political economy via psychoanalytic *critique*. The significance of this pairing becomes all the more important considering the failure of the Freudo-Marxist attempt in the early twentieth century, mainly by Wilhelm Reich and Hebert Marcuse and the so-called 'liberation of desire and sexuality'. This is a *'change of terrain'* in the theoretical *problematic* of Critique.[107] In this move, Critique is directed towards the *negative*, which means: *One is separated from itself*. Capitalism rejects this negativity. The aim of this move is a radical one. Its objective, as Lacan once said, is the 'exit from the capitalist discourse ... for everyone'.[108] Freud's 'Copernican turn' effectively inaugurated this epochal move. The discovery of psychoanalysis brought an 'insult' to the human narcissism, complementing the two other 'insults', namely, Copernicus displacement of geocentrism by heliocentrism, which more accurately means decentering the harmonious cosmic order that, as we saw, put the 'earth' and the 'sun' in *relational structure*, thus changing their received notions; and the other, brought by Darwin, decentering life in biology and abolishing the hierarchy of beings by removing 'man' from his privileged metaphysical position.

Freud extracted *unconscious qua* transcendental structure. Recall that the *transcendental* is the notion that casts light on the *unconscious* structure that precedes empirical experience. In this regard, as previously mentioned, Freud's 'ego, id, and superego' are not the things that can exist empirically. We must remember that 'unconscious' is that thing which is 'produced' by the analysand's 'resistance' and 'disavowal' in the course of the psychoanalytical dialogue or 'talking cure'.[109]

Now Marx achieved his own 'Copernican turn', not once but several times, according to Karatani, the most important of which is when he radically overturned Feuerbach's 'materialism'. In the 'Thesis I' of his 'Theses on Feuerbach' Marx wrote:

> The chief defect of all previous materialism (that of Feuerbach included) is that things [*Gegenstand*] reality, sensuousness are conceived only in the form of the *object, or of contemplation*, but not as *sensuous human activity, practice*, not subjectively. Hence, in contradistinction to materialism, the *active* side was set forth abstractly by idealism—which, of course, does not know real, sensuous activity as such. Feuerbach wants sensuous objects, really distinct from conceptual objects, but he does not conceive human activity itself as *objective* activity.[110]

Lacan said that Marx invented the *symptom* before Freud. Based on this, Louis Althusser attempted a structuralist reading of Marx performed in *Reading Capital*. This is known as Althusser's Structural Marxism. In 'From *Capital* to Marx's Philosophy', Althusser wrote:

> Such is Marx's second reading: a reading which might well be called '*symptomatic*' (*symptomale*), in so far as it divulges the undivulged event in the text it reads, and in the same

movement relates it to *a different text*, present as a necessary absence in the first. Like this first reading, Marx's second reading presupposes the existence of *two texts*, and the measurement of the first against the second. But what distinguishes this new reading from the old one is the fact that in the new one the *second text* is articulated with the lapses in the first text. Here again, at least in the way peculiar to theoretical text (the only one whose analysis is at issue here), we find the necessity and possibility of a reading on two bearings simultaneously.[111]

Later, Althusser wrote extensively on psychoanalysis and the common ground of the work of Freud and Lacan with the work of Marx. For him, Marxist theory and Freudian theory both are *conflictual* theory. Being a *conflictual* theory, he said, Freudian theory is a '*scissionist* science; its history is marked by endlessly renewed scissions'.[112] But before Freud, of course, as Althusser puts it, it was 'Marxist science' that provides us with a conflictual and scissionist science, that is, the 'class struggle', which 'pits it against bourgeois ideology'. Althusser pointedly notes that it was not by chance that Marx subtitled his *Capital* by a simple formula: '*Critique of Political Economy*'. 'Nor is it by chance' he further remarks,

> that the meaning of the 'critique' has so often been misunderstood as a *judgment* by Marx on an undisputed and indisputable reality, reducing it to debate as to whether Smith and Ricardo did indeed understand this or that, did see surplus value behind income or not, and so on.[113]

Employing the Freudian term 'displacement', Althusser goes on to say that 'Things go infinitely further'. He notes:

> In the 'Displacement', that has him occupying proletarian class theoretical positions, Marx discovers that despite all the merits of its author, political economy as it exists is not fundamentally a *science* but a *theoretical foundation of bourgeoise ideology*, playing its role in the ideological class struggle.[114]

'That Marx was the first theoretician of the symptom implies' that, Samo Tomšič in his *The Capitalist Unconscious* incisively remarks, 'the proletariat *is* the subject of unconscious. This means that the proletariat designates more than an empirical social class. It expresses the universal subjective position in capitalism', and furthermore,

> as a symptom, that is, as a formation through which the repressed truth of the existing social order is inscribed in the political space, the proletariat entails a rejection of the false and abstract universalism imposed by capitalism, namely the universalism of commodity form.[115]

We must take a pause and examine, more precisely, how Marx could be the inventor of the symptom *avant la lettre*. Slavoj Žižek, years after Althusser's notion of 'symptomal reading', revisits Lacan's thesis and poses the question directly: 'How Did Marx Invent the Symptom?'.[116] One of the important outcomes of Žižek's extended analysis, while taking Althusser to task, is the implication it entails for the theory of Ideology, to which I will come later. In his attempt to answer the question, Žižek stands on the *transcendental* ground and poses the Kantian question on epistemological ground as to the 'condition of the possibility' of the encounter between Marxian and Freudian field and demonstrates that Lacan's thesis is not just a 'sally of wit' or a 'vague analogy', but rather stands on a firm theoretical foundation. He first asks: 'how was it possible for Marx, in his analysis of the world commodities, to produce a notion which applies also to the analysis of dreams, hysterical phenomena, and so on?'[117] There is a 'fundamental homology' between Marx's and Freud's interpretative procedure, Žižek remarks, between their analysis of commodity and of dreams. In the analogy between dream and commodity, it is not that we should attempt to penetrate the 'hidden kernel' of each in order to discover the so-called secret *behind* their forms. But rather, as Žižek tells us, it is *the 'secret' of this form itself*. We must explain 'why work assumed the form of the value of a commodity, why it can affirm its social character only in the commodity-form of its product'.[118] After some detailed analysis of Freud's terminologies of the 'latent dreams-thought', 'manifest dream' and 'dreamwork' in *Interpretation of Dreams*, Žižek comes to the 'paradox' of dream and offers his precise definition: the unconscious desire, that which is supposedly its most hidden kernel, articulates itself precisely through the dissimulation work of the 'kernel' of a dream, its latent thought, through the work of disguising this content-kernel by means of its translation into the dream-rebus.[119]

It is the same Unconscious which is at work in the 'Commodity-form', and it is in this form that we can find the 'transcendental subject'. Žižek writes:

> In other words, in the structure of the commodity-form it is possible to find the transcendental subject: the commodity-form articulates in advance the anatomy, the skeleton of the Kantian transcendental subject—that is, the network of transcendental categories which constitute the a priori frame of 'objective' scientific knowledge. Hereon lies the paradox of

> the commodity-form: it—this inner-worldly, 'pathological' (in the Kantian meaning of the word) phenomenon—offers us a key to solving the fundamental question of the theory of knowledge: objective knowledge with universal validity.[120]

Invoking the authority of Sohn-Rethel, frequently cited in his other works, Žižek reminds us again of the distinction between 'pure abstraction' in thought and 'real abstraction' (an abstraction at work in the actual process of commodity exchange) and elaborates more precisely on the notion of the 'transcendental subject':

> In this way, the transcendental subject, the support of the net of a priori categories, is confronted with the disquieting fact that it depends, in its very formal gesture, on some inner-worldly, 'pathological' process—a scandal, a nonsensical impossibility from the transcendental point of view, in so far as the formal-transcendental a priori is by definition independent of all positive contents: a scandal correspondingly perfectly to the 'scandalous' character of the Freudian unconscious, which is also unbearable from the transcendental-philosophical perspective [...] *the 'real abstraction' is the unconscious of the transcendental subject*, the support of objective-universal scientific knowledge.[121]

Based on this, Žižek claims that we can arrive at a possible definition of unconscious:

> *the form of thought whose ontological status is not that of thought*, that is to say, the form of thought external to the thought itself—in short, some Other Scene external to the thought whereby the form of thought is already articulated in

advance. The symbolic order is precisely such a formal order which supplement and /or disrupts the dual relationship of 'external' factual reality and 'internal' subjective experience.[122]

With this definition, Žižek comes to his critique of Althusser claiming that his epistemological distinction between the 'real object' and the 'object of thought', the 'real abstraction' is unthinkable, in so far as this latter term introduces a third element which subverts the very field of this distinction: 'the form of the thought previous and external to the thought—in short: the symbolic order'.[123]

The 'social effectivity' of exchange and its paradoxical relation with 'consciousness' of it, which is a kind of reality *'whose very ontological consistency implies a certain non-knowledge of its participants'*, is considered by Žižek to be a fundamental dimension of 'ideology':

> Ideology is not simply a 'false consciousness', an illusory representation of reality, it is rather this reality itself which is already to be conceived as 'ideology'—*'ideological' is a social reality whose very existence implies the non-knowledge of its participants as to its essence*—that is, the social effectivity, the very reproduction of which implies that the individuals 'do not know what they are doing'. *'Ideological' is not 'false consciousness' of a (social)being but this being itself in so far as it is supported by 'false consciousness'*.[124]

Thus Žižek concludes,

> we have finally reached the dimension of the symptom, because one of its possible definitions would be also 'a formation whose very consistency implies a certain non-knowledge

on the part of the subject': the subject can 'enjoy his symptom only in so far as its logic escapes him—the measure of the success of its interpretation is precisely its dissolution'.[125]

In further definition of Marxian symptom, Žižek detects a certain 'pathological imbalance' or asymmetry in the universal claims of the bourgeois notions of 'rights and duties'. This imbalance is constitutive. 'Symptom' is that particular element that subverts its universalism. In this sense,

> we can say that the elementary Marxian procedure of 'criticism of ideology' is already 'symptomatic': it consists in detecting a point of breakdown *heterogeneous* to a given ideological field and at the same time *necessary* for that field to achieve its closure, its accomplished form.[126]

The '*universality without its symptom*' also constitutes that logic of the Marxian critique of Hegel, as Žižek remarks, of the Hegelian notion of 'society as a rational totality'. He crucially notes that

> as soon as we try to conceive the existing social order as a rational totality, we must include in it a paradoxical element which, without ceasing to be its internal constituent, function as its symptom—subverts the very universal rational principle of this totality. For Marx, this 'irrational' element of the existing society was, of course, the proletariat, 'the unreason of reason itself' (Marx), the point at which the Reason embodied in the existing social order encounters its own unreason.[127]

According to Tomšič, after the 'excommunication' of Lacan from the International Psychoanalytical Association in 1963 and his subsequent creation of the 'Ecole freudienne de Paris', we can talk about the 'second return' of Lacan to Freud. In this return, 'Lacan progressively elaborated an alternative reading of the Freudian discovery that found its new privileged alliance in Marx's critique of political economy'.[128] In this second return, Lacan leaves behind structural linguistics on which the structural psychoanalysis was based with its central notion that 'The Unconscious is structured like a language'. 'The move away, from the linguistic paradigm', Tomšič notes,

> was accomplished immediately after May '68, though these political events were not only circumstances that contributed to the reorientation of the return to Freud. The move towards the critical paradigm was not unrelated to the limits of structuralism, notably in response to the theorization of unconscious production and growing weight given to the problem of jouissance in Lacan's teaching.[129]

In this return, it must be noted, Lacan is not denying altogether the structuralist emphasis on the logic of the 'Signifier'. In this respect, it is instructive to read what Jacques Lacan wrote in the *Seminars VI*:

> It seems to me [...] that it suffices to open the first volume of *Capital* to realize that the very first step of Marx's analysis of the fetishistic nature of commodities consists precisely in broaching the problem from the level of the signifier, even if the term is not used there. The relations between values are defined as signifying relations, and all subjectivity, and possibly even that of fetishization, comes to be inscribed within this signifying dialectic. This is true beyond a shadow of a doubt.[130]

Part II

The noticeable mark of the second return, Tomšič reminds us, is an enigmatic statement Lacan made to this effect: 'The unconscious is politics'.[131] This statement changes the notion of structure and its relation to politics. We must note that 'the unconscious is politics' does not entail that 'politics is unconscious', Tomšič notes. The 'is' between unconscious and politics is not reflexive: 'It rather concerns the formal inclusion of the subject of the unconscious in the field of politics, which, notably, after Marx's critique, thinks the constitution of social links through alienation and negativity'.[132]

After May '68 events the name of Marx appears frequently in Lacan's Seminars. The central trait of his references to Marx is the provocative 'homology between the object of *Capital* and the object of psychoanalysis'.[133] It is the theory of big Other to the small 'other' and the neologism '*objet pitit a*', the object of *jouissance* in conjunction with Marxian 'surplus value' that are all foregrounded. In his 1968-69 *Seminar XVI*, *D'un Autre à l'autre,* Lacan told the members of his Seminar that: 'I will proceed with a homological outlook based on Marx in order to introduce today the place where we need to situate the essential function of object *a*'.[134] A year later, in *Seminar XVII*, *The Other Side of Psychoanalysis*, Lacan told his audience:

> Something changed in the master's discourse at a certain point in history. We are not going to break our backs finding out if it was because of Luther, or Calvin, or some unknown traffic of ships around Genoa, or in the Mediterranean Sea, or anywhere else, for the important point is that on a certain day surplus *jouissance* became calculable, could be counted, totalized. This is what is called the accumulation of capital

> begins [...] Surplus value combines with capital—not a problem, they are homogeneous, we are in the field of values. Moreover, we are all up to our necks in it, in these blessed times in which we live.[135]

In an earlier session in the same Seminar Lacan said: 'We shall have the occasion to come back to what I am introducing now—there is no transgression here, but rather an irruption, a falling into the field, of something not unlike jouissance—surplus'.[136] And further:

> But perhaps even that has to be paid for. That is why I told you last year that in Marx the *a,* which is here, is recognized as functioning at the level that is articulated—on the basis of analytic discourse, not any of the others—as surplus jouissance. Here you have what Marx discovered as what actually happens at the level of surplus value. Of course, it wasn't Marx who invented surplus value. It's just that prior to him nobody knew what its place was. It has the same ambiguous place as the one I have just mentioned, that of excess work, of surplus work. 'what does it pay in?' he says. 'It pays in *jouissance,* precisely and this has to go somewhere.'

> What is disturbing is that if one pays in jouissance, then one has got it, and then, once one has got it it is very urgent that one squander it. If one does not squander it, there will be all sorts of consequences. Let's leave the thing up in the air for the moment.[137]

'Surplus-*jouissance'* is Lacan's term for the object of psychoanalysis in *homology,* and not in 'analogy', with Marxian 'surplus-value'—in German *Mehrwert*—in discursive practice.

Lacan proposes for it the German term, *Mehrlust*. In the same Seminar he said:

> Marx denounces this process as spoliation. It's just that he does it without realizing that its secret lies in knowledge itself, just as the secret of worker himself is to be reduced to being no longer anything but a value. Once a higher level has been passed, surplus *jouissance* is no longer surplus *jouissance* but it is inscribed simply as a value to be inscribed in or deducted from the totality of whatever it is that is accumulating—what is accumulating from out of an essentially transformed nature. The worker is merely a unit of value—an indication for those for whom this term produces an echo. What Marx denounced is surplus value is the spoliation of *jouissance*. And yet, this surplus value is a memorial to surplus jouissance, its equivalent of surplus *jouissance*. 'Consumer society' derives its meaning from the fact that what makes it the 'element,' in inverted commas, described as human is made homogeneous equivalent of whatever surplus jouissance is produced by our industry—an imitation surplus jouissance, in a word. Moreover, that can catch on. One can do a semblance of surplus jouissance —it draws quite a crowd.[138]

Tomšič notes that the coupling of value and *jouissance* had been present already in Freud and is not quite Lacan's invention. In his book on jokes, Tomšič reminds us, Freud centered his analysis of 'unconscious satisfaction on what he called *Lustgewinn*, pleasure gain'.[139] Lacan's intervention brought back Freud's idea of 'surplus-object' that had been relegated to oblivion. It is that 'Lacan aimed at the same status as Marx with regard to the political-economic debates regarding surplus-value'.[140] Lacan:

> The object *a,* in a certain sense I invented it, just as one can say that Marx's discourse invented something. What does this mean? Marx's discovery is surplus-value. It is not that object *a* was not approached before my discourse, of course, but it was approached in an insufficient way, as insufficient as the definition of surplus-value was before Marx's discourse made it appear in all its rigour.[141]

Žižek frequently refers to Lacan's homology between surplus-value and surplus-*jouissance*. In an early text, he notes that Marxism did not take into consideration the 'surplus-object', the leftover of the Real that eludes symbolization. It is surprising, he adds, if we recall the fact that Lacan modeled his notion of surplus-enjoyment on the Marxian Surplus-value. He further explains:

> The proof that Marxian surplus-value announces effectively the logic of the Lacanian *objet petit a* ['the object cause of desire'] as the embodiment of surplus-enjoyment is already provided by the decisive formula used by Marx, in the third volume of *Capital*, to designate the logical-historical limit of capitalism: 'the limit of capital is capital itself, i.e., the capitalist mode of production'.[142]

Žižek relates the importance of Lacanian homology to the internal conflict of capitalism itself, that is, the so-called conflict between forces of production and relation of production and its simplistic-crude 'resolution'. Žižek points out that a 'surplus' is not something that 'normally' attaches itself to enjoyment,

> because enjoyment as such emerges only in his surplus, because it is constrictively an 'excess'. If we subtract the

surplus we lose enjoyment itself, just as capitalism, which can survive only by incessantly revolutionizing its own material conditions, ceases to exists if it 'stays the same', if it achieves an internal balance. This then is the homology between surplus-value—the 'cause' which sets in motion the capitalist process of production—and surplus-enjoyment, the object-cause of desire.[143]

The whole point is that Marx failed to deal with the paradoxes of surplus-*jouissance*, Žižek remarks. In the Preface to the *Critique of Political Economy*, Žižek notes, 'he proceeds *as if he does not know it*', by presenting a simplistic or 'vulgar evolutionist dialectics' between 'material production forces' and 'already existing relations of production'.[144]

The Lacanian homology between surplus-value and surplus-*jouissance* still needs further clarifications.[145] In Marx, surplus-value originates in unpaid surplus labor the worker performs. The value of worker's labor is named 'labor power', a commodity that the worker sells to the capitalist. It is only with the advent of industrial capitalism that labor- power became a commodity. Capital transforms labor power into commodity giving it a specific exchange-value. The worker sells his 'labor power' to the capitalist, in one period, which, in its first instance, is *equal* and *free*, according to the wages the worker receives from the capitalist in the market place. Marx wrote in *Capital*:

> During one period, the worker produces a value that is only equal to the value of his labour-power, i.e., he produces its equivalent. Thus the capitalist receives, in return for advancing the price of the labour-power, a product of the same price. It is the same as if he had bought the product ready-made

in the market. During the other period, the period of surplus labour, the utilization of the labour-power creates a value for the capitalist without costing him any value in return. He is thus able to set labour-power in motion without paying for it. It is in this sense that surplus labour can be called unpaid labour.

Capital, therefore, is not only the command over labour, as Adam Smith thought. It is essentially the command over unpaid labour. All surplus-labour, whatever particular form (profit, interest or return) it may subsequently crystalize into, is in substance the materialization of unpaid labour-time. The secret of self-valorization of capital resolves itself into the fact that it has at its disposal a definite quantity of the unpaid labour of other people.[146]

Marx's surplus-value is valorization of surplus labor for which the laborer is not paid for. Marx in *Grundrisse* wrote:

Half of the working day costs capital *nothing*; it thus obtains a value for which it has given no equivalent. And the multiplication of values can take place only if a value in excess of the equivalent has been obtained, hence *created*. Surplus value in general is value in excess of the equivalent. The equivalent, by definition, is only the identity of value with itself.[147]

As Fabio Vighi remarks, 'The object of Marx's critique is the relentless extraction of surplus-value from labour-power'.[148] In *Capital* we read:

Capitalist production is not merely the production of commodities, it is, by its very essence, the production of surplus-value. The worker produces not for himself, but for the capital. It is no longer sufficient, therefore, for him simply to produce. He must produce surplus-value. The only worker who is productive is one who produces surplus-value for the capitalist, or in other words contributes towards the self-valorization of capital. If we may take an example from outside the sphere of material production, a school-master is a productive worker when, in addition to belabouring the heads of his pupils, he works himself into the ground to enrich the owner of the school. That the latter laid out his capital in a teaching factory, instead of a sausage factory, makes no difference to the relation. The concept of a productive worker therefore implies not merely a relation between the activity of work and its useful effect, between the worker and the product of his work, but also specifically social relation of production, a relation with a historical origin which stamps the worker as capital's direct means valorization. To be a productive worker is therefore not a piece of luck, but a misfortune.[149]

Therefore the goal of capital is aimed at *valorization* resulting in the appropriation of surplus-value. It is not geared to the satisfaction of human needs, and this is the point that, in Vighi's view, needs to be re-politicized in our time. Marx wrote in *Capital* that 'We mean by labour-power, or labour capacity, the aggregate of those mental and physical capabilities existing in the physical form, the living personality. Of a human being, capabilities which he sets in motion whenever he produces a use-value of any kind'.[150] Vighi explains what remains unexplored by other commentators is that Marx's surplus-value 'is already, it itself coterminous with Lacan's surplus-*jouissance*, for it not only refers to the worker's unpaid labour-time, but also to the excessive, incalculable of labour-as-such'.[151] Vighi points out that Marx did not develop this insight. Lacan's thesis, by contrast, is that the

> genesis of surplus-value—this invisible turbine at the heart of capitalist appropriation and accumulation—should be conceived less as a supplementary lapse of non-remunerable labour-time than as the entropic and non-quantifiable intrinsic to labour-as-such. If the labour-power offered by the free workers on market, as Marx put it, 'exists only as an ability, a capacity [*Vermögen*] of his bodily existence', and 'has no existence apart from that' it is precisely as an amorphous and intrinsically 'virtual' power lacking presence that we should associate it with the entropic Real of jouissance.[152]

Lacan calls his homology between surplus-value and surplus-jouissance 'our psychoanalytical belvedere', as Vighi notes, insofar as it stands for 'specious valorization of the entropic surplus of labour'.[153] Vighi cites Alenka Zupančič who has written insightfully about this homology: 'There is something in the status of work (or labour) which is identical to the status of enjoyment, namely, that it is essentially appears as entropy, as loss, or an unaccounted-for surplus (by-product) of signifying operation'.[154] Discussing the notion of 'the opacity of knowledge', Vighi perceptively reflects that 'knowledge is unconscious before being pedagogical', and further,

> This is how knowledge-at-work, *savoir fair*, is originally related to what it lacks. It is this opaque (unconscious) kernel of knowledge that is therefore intimately related to surplus-*jouissance*, and as such can be legitimately regarded as the invisible matrix of any 'performed knowledge'. This is why to know something, to have learnt our way around in a certain field

(*savoir fair*, know-how), always means that, without knowing it, we are 'within the horizon of the sexual', that is at the mercy of the unconscious from which surplus-enjoyment emerges, together with *objet a* and the articulation of desire.[155]

The result of this is that capitalism holds on to this opaque knowledge to bring it into the orbit of value in order to reproduce it as enjoyment: 'It is clear, then, that the ruse of capitalism embodied by the mythical quality of commodity that enjoins us to enjoy, originally implies the conversion of the surplus of *jouissance* into surplus-value'.[156]

It is the notion of the 'signifier' in Lacan that indicates the limitation of Marx's discovery, Vighi argues. The unpaid 'labor-power', which is the origin of the creation of surplus-value is 'ultimately nothing but the constitutive, non-symbolizable libidinal surplus that accompanies any intervention of the signifier, that is to say any knowledge'.[157] As Lacan wrote:

> What is important is that, whether natural or not, it is well and truly as bound to the very origin of the signifier's coming into play that it is possible to speak of *jouissance*. Nobody will ever know anything about what the oyster or the beaver enjoys, because, in the absence of the signifier, there is no distance between *jouissance* and the body.[158]

Vighi elaborates:

> when Lacan claims that knowledge is a means of *jouissance* he explains that when at work, knowledge produces entropy, a point of loss, which is 'the sole regular point at which we have access to the nature of *jouissance*. This is what the effect the signifier has upon the fate of speaking being translates

into, culminates in, and is motivated by'. Insofar as it overlaps with entropy, surplus-*jouissance* has not use-value: it is waste, a quantity of libido *that is both produced by and lost to any working activity*, for we cannot gain control over it—it remains other.[159]

> What Marx denounced as surplus value is the spoliation of *jouissance*. And yet, this surplus value is a memorial to surplus jouissance, its equivalent of surplus *jouissance*. 'Consumer society' derives its meaning from the fact that what makes it the 'element,' in inverted commas, described as human is made homogeneous equivalent of whatever surplus jouissance is produced by our industry—an imitation surplus jouissance, in a word. Moreover, that can catch on. One can do a semblance of surplus jouissance —it draws quite a crowd.

Apropos of this, Zupančič writes: 'The revolution related to capitalism is none other than this: it founds the means of making the waste count. Surplus value is nothing else but the waste or loss that counts, and the value of which is constantly being added to or included in the loss of capital'.[160]

I can now bring my exposition of the last case of Transcritique—the pairing of Marx and psychoanalysis, or Marx and Lacan—to an end and conclude this chapter by stating that my readings of Slavoj Žižek and Kojin Karatani lead me to conclude that, in the present conjuncture, it is the Kantian transcendental *gesture* that is worth *repeating*. But since Kant avoided the consequences of his revolutionary breakthrough, as Žižek would say, it remained to the revolutionary thinkers after him to *return* to it. Thus the validity of the claim that Marx, Hegel, Freud and Lacan must be considered to be *transcendental* thinkers. In the center, which is the *absence* of a center, lies the Unconscious in relation to the transcendental in the light of Karatani's definition that: the transcendental casts its light on the *unconscious structure* that precedes experience. For me, it is on this *transcendental ground* that the theory of Critique must be founded—the theory of *critique* is either in the *unconscious*, or it is *not* critique. Marx's '*critique* of political economy', the foundation of all other critiques, is itself the construction of the *problematic* of the Subject named the 'Subject of the Unconscious'. It is this subject that goes against the *narcissistic* subject of capitalism. Critique has to come to terms with this theory of the Subject.

Notes

1 See Kojin Karatani, *Transcritique: On Kant and Marx* (Cambridge: The MIT Press, 2005), 37. My discussion on Critique in this chapter is informed by Karatani's remarkable book, especially his novel notion of 'Transcritique'. Much of my understanding of Kant and Marx is shaped by Karatani's groundbreaking analyses.
2 See Willi Goetschel, *Constituting Critique: Kant's Writing as Critical Praxis* (Durham and London: Duke University Press, 1994). For my reflections on the notion of Critique in Kant I am basically following the argument presented in this book.
3 Willi Goetschel, *Constituting Critique*, 1.
4 Willi Goetschel, *Constituting Critique*, 2.
5 Willi Goetschel, *Constituting Critique*, 2.
6 Willi Goetschel, *Constituting Critique*, 3..
7 Willi Goetschel, *Constituting Critique*, 3.
8 Willi Goetschel, *Constituting Critique*, 4.
9 Willi Goetschel, *Constituting Critique*, 4.
10 Willi Goetschel, *Constituting Critique*, 4–5.

11 Immanuel Kant, *Critique of Pure Reason*, trans. and ed. Paul Guyer and Aalen Wood (Cambridge: Cambridge University Press, 1998), Preface <A>, 100–101.
12 In this respect see Colin McQuillan, 'Beyond the Limits of Reason: Kant, Critique and Enlightenment', in Karin de Boer and Ruth Sonderegger, eds., *Conception of Critique in Modern Contemporary Philosophy* (New York: Palgrave, 2012).
13 Willi Goetschel, *Constituting Critique*, 1–2.
14 Immanuel Kant, 'An Answer to the Question: What is Enlightenment (1784)', in *Perpetual Peace and Other Essays*, trans. Ted Humphrey (Indianapolis: Hackett, 1983), 41.
15 Immanuel Kant, 'An Answer to the Question: What is Enlightenment (1784)', 41.
16 Immanuel Kant, 'An Answer to the Question: What is Enlightenment (1784)', 44.
17 Immanuel Kant, 'An Answer to the Question: What is Enlightenment (1784)', 42.
18 Based on an admirable essay by Mladen Dolar entitled 'The Legacy of Enlightenment: Foucault and Lacan' in *New Formations* 14 (1991), I extensively discussed the 'public use of reason' in my *An Architecture Manifesto: Critical Reason and Theories of a Failed Practice* (London and New York: Routledge, 2019). Also see Onora O'Neill, *Constructions of Reason, Explorations of Kant's Practical Philosophy* (Cambridge: Cambridge University Press, 1989), chapter 2, 'The public use of reason'.
19 Immanuel Kant, 'An Answer to the Question: What is Enlightenment (1784)', 42.
20 Immanuel Kant, 'An Answer to the Question: What is Enlightenment (1784)', 42.
21 See Slavoj Žižek, *First as Tragedy, Then as Farce* (London and New York: Verso, 2009), in part 2, 'The Communist Hypothesis'. Žižek for his discussion sharply contrasts Kant with the liberal philosopher Richard Rorty.
22 Slavoj Žižek, *First as Tragedy, Then as Farce*, 104.
23 Slavoj Žižek, *First as Tragedy, Then as Farce*, 104.
24 Slavoj Žižek, *First as Tragedy, Then as Farce*, 105.
25 Kojin Karatani, *Transcritique, On Kant and Marx*, 36.
26 Kojin Karatani, *Transcritique, On Kant and Marx*, 36.
27 Kojin Karatani, *Transcritique, On Kant and Marx*, 36.

Part II

28 See Henry Home, Lord Kames, *Elements of Criticism* (London: Elibron Classics, 2005).
29 Kojin Karatani, *Transcritique, On Kant and Marx*, 37. Karatani makes reference to Hans Vaihinger's work entitled *Kommentar zu Kants Kritik der reinen Vernunft* (2 vols., 1881–1892).
30 Kojin Karatani, *Transcritique, On Kant and Marx*, 37. Karatani remarks that 'Home had sought a universality of the judgment of taste—a measure of beauty and ugliness—in principles immanent in human essence. He insisted on the a priori nature of human sensibility with respect to beauty and ugliness. At the same time, however, Home employed empirical and inductive methods of observing the general rules of taste, collecting and categorizing materials from all the domains related to art and literature from antiquity to present. Confronting the necessity of critical judgment, he refused to take any particular principle for granted and charged himself with the task of questioning the foundational principles of infallible measures of criticism', 37.
31 See Ellen Meiksins Wood, *Democracy Against Capitalism, Renewing Historical Materialism* (Cambridge: Cambridge University Press, 1995), 177.
32 Ellen Meiksins Wood, *Democracy Against Capitalism*, 177.
33 Kojin Karatani, *Transcritique, On Kant and Marx*, viii.
34 Karl Marx, 'Towards A Critique of *Hegel's Philosophy of Right*: Introduction', in *Karl Marx, Selected Writings*, ed. Lawrence H. Simon (Indianapolis: Hackett, 1994), 34; also quoted in Kojin Karatani, *Transcritique, On Kant and Marx*, xi–xii.
35 Kojin Karatani, *Nation and Aesthetics: On Kant and Freud* (New York: Oxford University Press, 2017).
36 See Slavoj Žižek, *The Parallax View* (Cambridge: MIT Press, 2006).
37 Alfred Sohn-Rethel, *Intellectual and Manual Labour: A Critique of Epistemology* (Atlantic Highland: Humanities Press, 1977). For Žižek's critique of Karatani see Slavoj Žižek, *Living in the End Times* (London and New York: Verso, 2010), chapter 3. Also see Žižek's book review of *Transcritique: On Kant and Marx* entitled 'The Parallax View', in *New Left Review* 25 (Jan.–Feb. 2004).
38 See Slavoj Žižek, *Living in the End Times*, 217.
39 See Slavoj Žižek, *Less Than Nothing: Hegel and the Shadow of Dialectical Materialism* (London and New York: Verso, 2012), and Slavoj Žižek, *Absolute Recoil: Towards A New Foundation of Dialectical Materialism* (London and New York: Verso, 2014).

40 Žižek said this in connection with his endorsement of Samo Tomšič's *The Capitalist Unconscious* (London and New York: Verso, 2015). I will discuss this important book later.
41 Among their numerous publications, see for example Mladen Dolar's *A Voice and Nothing More* (Cambridge: The MIT Press, 2006), and Alenka Zupančič's *Ethics of the Real* (London and New York: Verso, 2000). For an informative discussion of the original formation of the Slovenian intellectual circle see the useful "Preface' by Ernesto Laclau to Slavoj Žižek's *The Sublime Object of Ideology* (London and New York: Verso, 1989).
42 For the key texts and a comprehensive discussion about this Circle in Paris see Peter Hallward and Knox Peden, *Concepts and Form*, two volumes (London and New York: Verso, 2012). For a very helpful analysis and interpretation of the intellectual discourse of the Circle see Tom Eyers's *Post-Rationalism, Psychoanalysis, Epistemology, and Marxism in Post-War France* (London: Bloomsbury, 2013).
43 See Louis Althusser et al., *Reading Capital: The Complete Edition* (London and New York: Verso, 2015).
44 See Immanuel Kant, 'Dreams of a Visionary Explained by Dreams of Metaphysics' [1766], in *The Philosophy of Kant*, ed. and intro. Carl. J. Friedrich (New York: The Modern Library, 1993), 15.
45 Kojin Karatani, *Transcritique, On Kant and Marx*, 47.
46 Kojin Karatani, *Transcritique, On Kant and Marx*, 48.
47 Kojin Karatani, *Transcritique, On Kant and Marx*, 48.
48 Kojin Karatani, *Transcritique, On Kant and Marx*, 48.
49 Kojin Karatani, *Transcritique, On Kant and Marx*, 4.
50 Kojin Karatani, *Transcritique, On Kant and Marx*, 4.
51 See Slavoj Žižek, *The Parallax View*, 17.
52 Slavoj Žižek, *The Parallax View*, 17.
53 See Slavoj Žižek, *The Parallax View*, 17. Or, Žižek further puts it in Lacanian terms and says that 'the subject's gaze always-already inscribed into the perceived object itself, in the guise of its "blind spot," that which is "in the object more than the object itself," the point from which the object itself returns the gaze', quoting Lacan as having said that 'Sure, the picture is in my eye, but, I, I am also in the picture', 17.
54 See Slavoj Žižek, *The Parallax View*, 7. However, the importance of the term 'parallax gap' for Žižek, who moves from Kant to Hegel in his interpretation, is more related to his concern about rehabilitations of *dialectical materialism*

with a view of the current crisis of 'Marxism' to which *The Parallax View* is devoted.
55 Slavoj Žižek, *The Parallax View*, 7.
56 Slavoj Žižek, *The Parallax View*, 4.
57 Slavoj Žižek, *The Parallax View*, 4.
58 Kojin Karatani, *Transcritique, On Kant and Marx*, 1.
59 Kojin Karatani, *Transcritique, On Kant and Marx*, 29.
60 Immanuel Kant, *Critique of Pure Reason*, trans. and ed. Paul Guyer and Allen W. Wood (Cambridge: Cambridge University Press, 1998), 512–513, A494/B523, also in Kojin Karatani, *Transcritique, On Kant and Marx*, 29–30.
61 Kojin Karatani, *Transcritique, On Kant and Marx*, 31.
62 Kojin Karatani, *Transcritique, On Kant and Marx*, 31.
63 Kojin Karatani, *Transcritique, On Kant and Marx*, 31.
64 Kojin Karatani, *Transcritique, On Kant and Marx*, 32.
65 Kojin Karatani, *Transcritique, On Kant and Marx*, 34.
66 Kojin Karatani, *Transcritique, On Kant and Marx*, 34.,
67 Kojin Karatani, *Transcritique, On Kant and Marx*, 34–35.
68 See Chapter 3 'Beginning: The Return of the Critique of Political Economy' in Slavoj Žižek, *Living in the End Times*.
69 Kojin Karatani, *Transcritique, On Kant and Marx*, 3.
70 Kojin Karatani, *Transcritique, On Kant and Marx*, 3.
71 Kojin Karatani, *Transcritique, On Kant and Marx*, 3.
72 Kojin Karatani, *Transcritique, On Kant and Marx*, 5.
73 Kojin Karatani, *Transcritique, On Kant and Marx*, 5.
74 Kojin Karatani, *Transcritique, On Kant and Marx*, 6.
75 Kojin Karatani, *Transcritique, On Kant and Marx*, 6.
76 Kojin Karatani, *Transcritique, On Kant and Marx*, 6.
77 Kojin Karatani, *Transcritique, On Kant and Marx*, 7.
78 Kojin Karatani, *Transcritique, On Kant and Marx*, 8.
79 Kojin Karatani, *Transcritique, On Kant and Marx*, 8. Karatani notes that in the preface to the second edition of *Capital*, 'Marx "openly avowed [himself] to be the pupil of that mighty thinker" Hegel. In fact, Marx sought to describe the capitalist economy as if it were a self-realization of capital qua the Hegelian Spirit. Notwithstanding the Hegelian descriptive style, however, *Capital* distinguishes itself from Hegel's philosophy in its motivation. The end of *Capital* is never the "absolute Spirit." *Capital* reveals the fact that capital, though organizing the world, can never go beyond its own limit. It

is a Kantian critique of the ill-contained drive of capital/reason to self-realize beyond the limit', 9.

80 Kojin Karatani, *Transcritique, On Kant and Marx*, 82.

81 Kojin Karatani, *Transcritique, On Kant and Marx*, 139.

82 Karl Marx, Towards a Critique of *Hegel's Philosophy of Right*: Introduction', 28.

83 Karl Marx, 'Towards a Critique of *Hegel's Philosophy of Right*: Introduction', 28–29. About these remarks of early Marx and tracing the origin of religious criticism in the circle around Marx, Karatani reflects on the 'Marxian turn' and writes: 'The early Marx, who was one of the Young Hegelians, was faithful to Feuerbach's materialist overturning of Hegelian idealism. Feuerbach's critique of religion argued that God is a self-alienation on the generic essence (or the species-being) of humans, and that individuals as sensuous beings should recover their generic essence. The early Marx basically relied upon this critique, except that he transposed and extended the account of "self-alienation" to the domains of the monetary economy and state [...] The materialist overturn may appear to be decisive, but it is still incomplete. The true Copernican turn of Marx later expressed itself when he criticized this materialism and affirmed an active moment, conversely, in the idealism [quoting Marx from his Thesis on Feuerbach]: "The chief defect of all previous materialism—that of Feuerbach included—is that the object [*Gegenstand*], reality, and sensuousness are conceived only in the form of the *object*, or *contemplation*, but not as *human sensuous activity, practice*, and not subjectively. Hence it happened that the active side, in contradiction to materialism, was set forth by idealism—but only abstractly, since, of course, idealism does not know real, sensuous activity as such"', 137–138.

84 Karl Marx, 'Towards a Critique of *Hegel's Philosophy of Right*: Introduction', 28.

85 Kojin Karatani, *Transcritique, On Kant and Marx*, 212.

86 Kojin Karatani, *Transcritique, On Kant and Marx*, 212.

87 In Slavoj Žižek, 'The Parallax View', in *The Left Review* 25 (Jan.–Feb. 2004), 127. This is the review of Karatani's *Metacritique, On Kant and Marx* in which Žižek brings out the importance of Karatani's 'formidable' work and says it is a must reading for 'everyone who wants to break the deadlock of "cultural" resistance to capitalism, and reassert the actuality of Marx's critique of political economy', 134.

Part II

88 Slavoj Žižek, 'The Parallax View', 128.
89 See Moishe Postone, *Time, Labor, and Social Domination: A Reinterpretation of Marx's Critical Theory* (Cambridge: Cambridge University Press, 1993). Also see Moishe Postone with Viren Murthy and Yasuo Kobayashi, *History and Heteronomy: Critical Essays* (Tokyo: UTCP, 2009), also Moishe Postone, 'Rethinking Marx (in a Post-Marxist World) (I)', 90th Annual Meeting of the American Sociological Association [Washington, D.C., August 19, 1995.]
90 Slavoj Žižek, *Living in the End Times*, 185.
91 Slavoj Žižek, *Living in the End Times*, 185. Žižek further writes: 'Badiou dismisses every History that goes beyond a particular World as an ideological fiction, and one should not miss the implication of his thesis that there is no general theory of History: it amounts to no less than the full abandonment of Marxist historical materialism. The irony here is that, while "creative" Marxists of the twentieth century advocated historical materialism without dialectical materialism (dismissing the latter as the regression of Marxism to a "materialist worldview," a new general ontology), Badiou aims for a dialectical materialism (or, more precisely, materialist dialectics) without historical materialism', in Slavoj Žižek, *Living in the End Times*, 185.
92 Slavoj Žižek, *Living in the End Times*, 185. It is here that Žižek praises Moishe Postone's pursuit of the 'critique of political economy' and for his attempt 'to rethink the actuality of Marx in the conditions following the disintegration of the Communist regimes in 1990', 185.
93 Quoted in Slavoj Žižek, *Living in the End Times*, 206.
94 Quoted in Slavoj Žižek, *Living in the End Times*, 206.
95 Slavoj Žižek, *Living in the End Times*, 207.
96 Slavoj Žižek, *Living in the End Times*, 213.
97 Slavoj Žižek, *Living in the End Times*, 213.
98 Slavoj Žižek, *Living in the End Times*, 213. Žižek further remarks that 'For orthodox Marxists, such a "relational" notion of value is already a compromise with "bourgeois" political economy which they dismiss as a "monetary theory of value"—however, the paradox is that these very "orthodox Marxists" themselves effectively regress to the "bourgeois" notion of value: they conceive of value as being immanent to the commodity, as its property, and this naturalizes its "spectral objectivity" which is the fetishized appearance of its social character', 213–214.
99 Slavoj Žižek, *Living in the End Times*, 214.
100 Slavoj Žižek, *Living in the End Times*, 214.
101 Quoted in Slavoj Žižek, *Living in the End Times*, 215.

102 Slavoj Žižek, *Living in the End Times*, 215.
103 Quoted in Slavoj Žižek, *Living in the End Times*, 216.
104 Slavoj Žižek, *Living in the End Times*, 216.
105 Slavoj Žižek, *Living in the End Times*, 216–217.
106 Slavoj Žižek, *Living in the End Times*, 218–219. Žižek here adds that according to this second position, Hegel's dialectic is the mystified form of the revolutionary process of emancipatory liberation: the matrix should remain the same, one should merely, as Lukács put it explicitly, replace in the role of the subject-object of history, the absolute Spirit with the proletariat', 219.
107 Here I use the terms 'changed terrain' and 'problematic' in the Althusserian sense. See Louis Althusser, *For Marx* (London and New York: Verso, 2005). In the 'Glossary' added by the translator, the term 'problematic' is explained as 'A word or concept' that must be viewed in the 'theoretical or ideological framework in which it is used: its problematic', and further, 'It is not the essence of the thought of an individual or epoch which can be deduced from a body of texts by an empirical, generalizing reading; it is centered on the *absence* of problems and concepts within the problematic as much as their presence; it is therefore only to be reached by a symptomatic reading (*lecture symptomale* q.v.) on the model of the Freudian analyst's reading of the patient's utterance', 254–254.
108 Quoted in Samo Tomšič, *The Capitalist Unconscious* (London and New York: Verso, 2015), 233, also see Jacques Lacan, *Autres écrits* (Paris: Seuil, 2001), 520.
109 Karatani reminds us of this Freudian production of the Unconscious in the actual process of psychoanalytical dialogue between the 'analyst' and the 'analysand', see.Kojin Karatani, *Transcritique, On Kant and Marx*, 33.
110 Karl Marx, 'Theses on Feuerbach' in Karl Marx with Friedrich Engels, *The German Ideology* (Amherst: Prometheus Books, 1998), 569. Includes: Theses on Feuerbach and the introduction to the *Critique of Political Economy*.
111 Louis Althusser, 'From *Capital* to Marx's Philosophy', in Louis Althusser, Étienne Balibar, Roger Establet, Pierre Macherey and Jacques Rancière, *Reading Capital: The Complete Edition* (London and New York: Verso, 2015), 27.
112 In Louis Althusser, *Writings on Psychoanalysis: Freud and Lacan*, trans. Jeffrey Mehlman (New York: Columbia University Press, 1996), 109.
113 Louis Althusser, *Writings on Psychoanalysis*, 113.
114 Louis Althusser, *Writings on Psych*, 113.

Part II

115 Samo Tomšič, *The Capitalist Unconscious*, 6.
116 In Slavoj Žižek, *The Sublime Object of Ideology* (London and New York: 1989), see chapter 1. Also see Pierre Bruno, *Lacan, passeur de Marx, L'invention du symptôme* (Toulouse: Edition Ere, 2010).
117 Slavoj Žižek, *The Sublime Object of Ideology*, 11.
118 Slavoj Žižek, *The Sublime Object of Ideology*, 11.
119 Slavoj Žižek, *The Sublime Object of Ideology*, 13.
120 Slavoj Žižek, *The Sublime Object of Ideology*, 16. Žižek here draws again on the work of Sohn-Rethel and notes that 'After series of detailed analyses, Sohn-Rethel came to the following conclusion: the apparatus of categories presupposed, implied by the scientific procedure (that, of course of the Newtonian science of nature), the network of notions by means of which it seizes nature, is already present in the social effectivity, already at work in the act of commodity exchange. Before thought could arrive at pure *abstraction*, the abstraction was already at work in the social effectivity of the market. The exchange of commodities implies a double abstraction: the abstraction from the changeable character of commodities during the act of exchange and the abstraction from the concrete, empirical, sensual, particular character of the commodity (in the act of exchange, the distinct particular qualitative determination of a commodity is not taken into account; a commodity is reduced to an abstract entity which—irrespective of its particular nature, of its "use-value"—possesses "the same value" as another commodity for which it is being exchanged)', 16–17.
121 Slavoj Žižek, *The Sublime Object of Ideology*, 17. Žižek further adds that 'If, then, the "real abstraction" has nothing to do with the level of "reality", of the effective properties, of an object, it would be wrong for that reason to conceive of it as a "thought-abstraction", as a process taking place in the "interior" of the thinking subject: in relation to this "interior", the abstraction appertaining to the act of exchange is in an irreducible way external, decentered—or, to quote Sohn-Rethel's concise formulation: "the Exchange abstraction *is not* thought, but it has the *form* of thought', 19.
122 Slavoj Žižek, *The Sublime Object of Ideology*, 19.
123 Slavoj Žižek, *The Sublime Object of Ideology*, 19.
124 Slavoj Žižek, *The Sublime Object of Ideology*, 21.
125 Slavoj Žižek, *The Sublime Object of Ideology*, 21
126 Slavoj Žižek, *The Sublime Object of Ideology*, 21. As Žižek further adds, 'This procedure thus implies a certain logic of exception: every ideological Universal—for example freedom, equality—is "false" in so far as it

necessarily includes a specific case which breaks its unity, lays open its falsity, Freedom, for example: a universal notion comprising a number of species (freedom of speech and press, freedom of consciousness, freedom of commerce, political freedom, and so on) but also, by means of structural necessity, a specific freedom (that of the worker to sell freely his own labour on the market) which subvert this universal notion', 21–22.

127 Slavoj Žižek, *The Sublime Object of Ideology*, 23.
128 Samo Tomšič, *The Capitalist Unconscious*, 16.
129 Samo Tomšič, *The Capitalist Unconscious*, 16.
130 In Jacques Lacan, *Desire and Its Interpretation: The Seminar of Jacques Lacan, Book VI*, ed. Jacques-Alain Miller, trans. Bruce Fink (Cambridge: Polity, 2019), 313.
131 Tomšič mentions that Lacan made this statement in the introductory lecture of the unpublished *Seminar XIV*. This statement, as Tomšič notes, resonates in Fredric Jameson's important *The Political Unconscious* (London: Routledge, 1983). Jameson's title is the inspiration for Tomšič's own book as he states; for more see Samo Tomšič, *The Capitalist Unconscious*, 20.
132 Samo Tomšič, *The Capitalist Unconscious*, 22.
133 See Samo Tomšič, *The Capitalist Unconscious*, 47. Tomšič notes that 'The title of corresponding seminar resumes the underlying orientation of Lacan's second return to Freud, *D'un Autre à l'autre*: from the big Other, the field of language and absolute autonomy of the signifier, to small other, object *a*, the object of jouissance, but also the object that is logically associated with surplus-value', 47.
134 Quoted in Samo Tomšič, *The Capitalist Unconscious*, 49.
135 See Jacques Lacan, *The Other Side of Psychoanalysis: The Seminar of Jacques Lacan, Book XVI*, trans. Russell Grigg (New York and London: W.W. Norton, 2007), 177–178.
136 Jacques Lacan, *The Other Side of Psychoanalysis*, 19–20.
137 Jacques Lacan, *The Other Side of Psychoanalysis*, 20.
138 Jacques Lacan, *The Other Side of Psychoanalysis*, 81.
139 Samo Tomšič, *The Capitalist Unconscious*, 49.
140 Samo Tomšič, *The Capitalist Unconscious*, 50.
141 Quoted in Samo Tomšič, *The Capitalist Unconscious*, 50. See also Jacques Lacan, *D'un Autre à l'autre*, 45–46.
142 In Slavoj Žižek, *The Sublime Object of Ideology*, 50–51.
143 Slavoj Žižek, *The Sublime Object of Ideology*, 52–53.

Part II

144 Here is the exact passage in the Preface to the *Critique of Political Economy*: 'At a certain level of their development the material productive forces of society come into contradiction with the already existing relations of production, or in what is merely a legal expression for this, with the property relations within which they had previously functioned. From forms of development of the productive forces these relations turn into their fetters. Then an epoch of social revolution commences. With the alteration of the economic foundation the whole colossal superstructure is more or less rapidly transformed. In examining such transformations one must always distinguish between the transformation in the economic conditions of production, to be established with the accuracy of physical science, and the legal, political, religious, artistic or philosophical, in short ideological forms in which men become conscious of this conflict and fight it out', in *Marx, Later Political Writings*, ed. Terrel Carver (Cambridge: Cambridge University Press, 1996), 160.

145 In what follows I will be following Fabio Vighi's clear exposition of Lacan's homology in his *On Žižek's Dialectics: Surplus, Subtraction, Sublimation* (London: Continuum, 2010), specially chapter 3 entitled 'From Surplus-Value to Surplus-Jouissance'.

146 Karl Marx, *Capital, Volume One* (London: Penguin Books, 1990), 671–672.

147 Karl Marx, *Grundrisse* (London: Penguin Books, 1993), 324; also see Fabio Vighi, *On Žižek's Dialectics*, 40.

148 Fabio Vighi, *On Žižek's Dialectics*, 40.

149 Karl Marx, *Capital, Volume One*, 644.

150 Karl Marx, *Capital, Volume One*, 270; also see Fabio Vighi, *On Žižek's Dialectics*, 41.

151 Fabio Vighi, *On Žižek's Dialectics*, 41.

152 Fabio Vighi, *On Žižek's Dialectics*, 41–42.

153 Fabio Vighi, *On Žižek's Dialectics*, 42.

154 In Fabio Vighi, *On Žižek's Dialectics*, 42; also see Alenka Zupančič, 'When Surplus Enjoyment Meets Surplus Value', in Justin Clemens and Russell Griggs, eds. *Reflections on Seminar XVII. Jacques Lacan and the Other Side of Psychoanalysis* (Durham: and London: Duke University Press, 2006), 162.

155 Fabio Vighi, *On Žižek's Dialectics*, 43.

156 Fabio Vighi, *On Žižek's Dialectics*, 43.

157 Fabio Vighi, *On Žižek's Dialectics*, 44.

158 Jacques Lacan, *The Other Side of Psychoanalysis*, 177; also see Fabio Vighi, *On Žižek's Dialectics*, 44.
159 Fabio Vighi, *On Žižek's Dialectics*, 44–45. Vighi further explains that '*Jouissance* per se is a mythical entity, while surplus-jouissance is the libido materializing the loss that emerges from this myth—which means that whenever we speak of *jouissance* we refer to a surplus that can only be given as entropy, a plus that, as it were, coincides with minus; and that for this reason it cannot perform work', 45.
160 Alenka Zupančič, 'When Surplus Enjoyment Meets Surplus Value', 170; also quoted in Fabio Vighi, *On Žižek's Dialectics*, 48.

Chapter 4

Transcritique of architecture

The sublime object of critique

To what *domain* does a *building* belong? Is it the *aesthetic* domain or the *ethical* domain or the *economic* domain? What kind of an *object* is a building? Appositely, what is the 'object' *in the building* that is the object of *critique*? Under what 'condition of possibility' does *critique* finds its object in the building? Is this object a 'transcendental object'? The academic discourse of 'critical criticism' is too hopelessly confused, if not Romantic and reactionary, to be entrusted to provide intellectual answers to these questions. The so-called 'critical theory' in the academy is fundamentally an assault on the 'rational kernel' of architecture and, therefore, no more than *aestheticization-sensibilization* of Reason in building. Worse, aestheticization of building theory and practice in the present conjuncture, as we will see later, has verged on the border of *pure anaesthetization*.

In the framework of the conceptual-theoretical structure I present in this chapter I will contend that the three domains of *aesthetic*, *ethical* and *economic* must form a *Borromean Knot* (in Lacanian theory) that will establish an inextricable link between the three domains. In the center of this Borromean

Knot lies the Marxian 'value-form' to which we will come later. The domain of *economics* in the Borromean Knot is fundamentally a *political* one. Economics in a Marxian sense is always a *political* economy. It is this political economy that is the target of critique in bourgeois society. The underlying thesis I want to advance goes as follows: In *building* there resides an *object* henceforth named as the Sublime Object. It is this *object* which is the object of *critique*. As we have learned from Slavoj Žižek, this Sublime Object is the same as the '*sublime object of ideology*'. In the previous chapter I have already alluded to this complex theory of ideology that goes beyond all other theories of ideology and 'ideology critique', including the influential one by Louis Althusser. The distinct genealogy of the notion of the Sublime Object, I must provisionally state here, runs from Kant to Lacan, that is, from Kantian Sublime to the algebraic '*objet petit a*', the 'object cause of desire'—from Kantian ethics to Lacan's '*ethics of psychoanalysis*'. The latter is indebted to the philosophical notion of the former but goes beyond it.

But critique must ultimately confront a fundamental dialectics: between *freedom* and *necessity* (nature), or 'theoretical reason' and 'practical reason'—with the *primacy* of the latter over the former. Underlying the proposed theses above and anticipating the analysis that will follow, it is first necessary to reflect on the 'doctrine of the method' by which the three domains in the Borromean Knot enter into a relationship with each other. For this I will turn to Kojin Karatani. But first we must see how Kant lays the ground for Karatani.

In *Critique of Power of Judgment* Kant wrote: 'We can trace all faculties of the human mind without exception back to these three: 'the faculty of cognition, the feeling of pleasure and displeasure, and the faculty of desire'.[1] And further:

> Now the faculty of cognition in accordance with concepts has its *a priori* principles in the pure understanding (in its concept of nature), the faculty of desire, in pure reason (in its concepts of freedom), and there remains among properties of mind in general an intermediate faculty or receptivity, namely the feeling of pleasure and displeasure, just as there remains among the higher faculties of cognition an intermediate one, the power of judgment. What is more natural than to suspect that the latter will also contain *a priori* principles for the former?[2]

Expanding on Kant's structure of the faculty of Judgment, and within the problematic of the relation between Freedom and Nature, Karatani writes: 'When we confront the world, we have at least three kinds of judgment at the same time: cognitive judgment of true or false, ethical judgment of good or bad, and aesthetic judgement of pleasure or displeasure'.[3] In 'real life', Karatani further remarks, these three kinds of judgments are 'intermixed', thus difficult to distinguish or disentangle. He therefore offers a guiding notion to deal with these interlocking judgments: '*transcendental bracketing*'. He clarifies the term:

> Scientists make observations by bracketing ethical and aesthetic judgements: Only by this act can the objects of cognition come into existence. In aesthetic judgement, the aspects of true or false and good and bad are bracketed, only at the precise moment that artistic objects come into existence. These operations are emphatically not done naturally. Rather one is always *ordered* to bracket by the external situation, [and being accustomed to it,]'one forgets that one brackets, and thinks that the objects—scientific or artistic or moral—exist by themselves.[4]

Karatani importantly reminds us that 'bracketing' is not the same as 'negation'. Bracketing is, rather, in relation with the notion of *interest*. As to the relation of 'economics', the domain I have suggested in the Borromean Knot above, Karatani's explanation is instructive: 'the commodity economy brackets all the differences of use value and thus reduces everything to exchange value. Disinterestedness as a key function of an aesthetic context certainly signifies an act of bracketing economic as well as utilitarian interests. However, aesthetic function does not prevent aesthetic value from transferring itself to commodity value'.[5] He further notes that:

> In his critique of utilitarianism, Kant regarded happiness as a matter of affection, which was in reality a matter of interest. For instance, eudemonism (or utilitarianism) is very much that which reduces morality to interest. Henceforth, contemporary ethics, based as it is upon utilitarianism, is essentially economy centered (in the sense of neoclassical economics), because its goal is how to realize, as Jeremy Bentham said, 'the greatest happiness of the greatest number of people'. It follows that the function of Kant's critique of eudemonism lies in making us confront morality directly, once more, by bracketing interest.[6]

With specific reference to the question of 'morality', Karatani notes that for Kant, morality is a matter of *freedom* and not related to matters of goodness or badness; the latter nevertheless cannot exist without the former. Moreover, 'Freedom is synonymous to being *causa sui*, self-motivated, subjective, and autonomous'. In this respect, Karatani refers to Kant's proposed antinomy in the 'third conflict of the transcendental ideas' in *Critique of Pure Reason:*

Part II

> Thesis—the causality according to laws of nature is not the only one from which all the appearances of the world can be derived. It is also necessary to assume another causality through freedom in order to explain them.
>
> Antithesis—There is no freedom, but everything in the world happens solely in accordance with laws of nature.[7]

Noting that this antinomy has its sources in Spinozian determinism and not in modern science, Karatani remarks that everything in the world is determined by necessity, yet causality is so important that we have no choice but to assume the position of 'freedom and contingency'. Therefore, for Kant, as Karatani points out, the determination of 'free will' is *always already* by the 'complex causalities'. Kant in *Critique of Practical Reason* wrote the following:

> I am never free at the point of time in which I act. Indeed, even if I assume that my whole existence is independent from any alien cause (such as God), so that the determining grounds of my causality and even of my whole existence are not outside me, this would not in the least transform that natural necessity into freedom. For, at every point of time I still stand under the necessity of being determined to action by *that which is not within my control*, and the series of events infinite a parte priori which I can only continue in accordance with a predetermined order would never begin of itself: it would be a continuous natural chain, and therefore my causality would never be freedom.[8]

As Kant wrote in *Groundwork of the Metaphysics of Morals*, 'There is therefore only a single categorical imperative, and it is this: *act only according to that maxim through which you can at the same time will that it become a universal law*', and further, 'the universal imperative of duty could also be expressed as follows: *act as if the maxim of your action were to become by your will a* universal law of nature'.[9] Karatani contests that these maxims make Kant a 'subjectivist' as it is usually thought. 'The most crucial point here is that of responsibility, the responsibility for the result. Only when we are considered free agents, though we are not at all in reality, do we become responsible'.[10] Kant's subjectivity, Karatani concludes, is grounded in the *will* to perform 'transcendental bracketing'.

To illustrate the mechanism of 'bracketing', Karatani nicely brings up the case of Marcel Duchamp. Duchamp submitted, anonymously, his urinal signed 'R Mutt' and titled 'Fountain' to the exhibition of the Society of Independent Artists held in New York in 1917. Without getting into vast art historical analyses written on this special (in)famous 'artwork' in the early twentieth century, Karatani sees in it an 'exhibit' of the 'Kantian problematic', meaning that Duchamp contested what makes art art, by *bracketing* the daily use of a utilitarian object and putting it in an institutional setting that would endow it the *legitimacy* of being a work of 'art'. As Karatani writes: 'Duchamp is not commanding viewers to see the urinal as an artwork by bracketing daily concerns; instead, the context—being installed in an exhibition—is itself commanding viewers to see it as artwork, though most viewers are not aware of it.' Therefore this conclusion:

Likewise, the fact that the transcendental stance itself contains the imperative is forgotten, and finally the fact that the transcendental stance is spurred by an imperative is forgotten. Where does the transcendental stance spring from? It is spurred on by the existence of *others*. In this sense, it can be said that the *transcendental standpoint is ethical*.[11] [emphasis mine].

With the brief explication of the 'method of bracketing' instructive for conceptualizing the knot tying the three domains of critique proposed above, I can now come to the problematic of the *object of critique* itself, with the concept of the Sublime Object in its center. The genealogy of the concept of Sublime, as is well known, runs from Kant to Freud to Lacan. Besides Slavoj Žižek, among contemporary Marxist thinkers who have written on this notion on philosophical-political grounds, I have found Karatani's 'Transcritique on Kant and Freud' in his recent work entitled *Nation and Aesthetics: On Kant and Freud* to be insightful and relevant to my purpose at hand.[12] It is useful for the problematic of the relationship between aesthetics and ethics in the Borromean Knot I have suggested above. I will come back in the next section to the specific 'economics' domain. Here I must open a parenthesis to point out that I will not be dealing with the works of Adorno and Rancière on the question of aesthetics, especially the latter's perceptive works on the question of 'politics of aesthetics'.[13] The reason is that, in agreement with Žižek, as previously mentioned, the Marxian Critique of Political Economy is missing in their works. Moreover, Karatani at times warns us of the 'stereotypical' reading of Freud and Kant by Adorno, which is partly responsible for the failure of the attempt of Freudo-Marxian critique by the Frankfurt School. In fact, following Karatani and Žižek, I take issue with the 'Cultural Turn' in a critique of contemporary capitalism. Karatani, in the light of his reflection on the failure of Marxists to grasp the transcritical moment where workers and consumers intersect, points out that 'What Fredric Jameson calls "the cultural turn" is a form of despair inherent in Marxist practice'.[14] And, on the other hand, as Žižek has more than once pointed out, Adorno and Horkheimer in *Dialectic of Enlightenment* tried to trace the source of reification and alienation back to 'instrumental reason' and hence to

> technological/manipulation which functions as a kind of a priori of the whole of human history, but no longer rooted in any concrete historical formation. The over-arching totality is thus no longer that of capitalism, or commodity production: capitalism itself becomes one of the manifestations of instrumental reason.[15]

Here I close the parenthesis.

In *Critique of Pure Reason* Kant said that 'I call a science of all principles of *a priori* sensibility the transcendental aesthetics' and then added:

> The Germans are the only ones who now employ the word 'aesthetics' to designate that which others call the critique of taste. The ground for this is a failed hope, held by the excellent analysis of Baumgarten, of building the critical estimation of the beautiful under the principles of reason, and elevating its rules to a science. But this effort is futile. For the putative rules or criteria are merely empirical as far as their sources are concerned, and can therefore never serve as *a priori* rules according to which our judgment of taste must be directed, rather the latter constitutes the genuine touchstone of the correctness of the former. For this reason it is advisable again to desist from the use of this term and save it for that doctrine which is true science.[16]

Karatani points out that with the advance of modern science, sensibility became an important factor related only to 'sense-data, or perception', while 'sentiment' was viewed as 'nothing but a passion that the human being must overcome through understanding'.[17] He remarks that in the eighteenth century an argument emerged concerning 'sentiment' that viewed it not only as capable of 'intellectual cognition and moral judgment, but, in a sense, a faculty that exceeds understanding and reason'.[18] This was called 'aesthetics', which is not a study of the 'beautiful' that Kant opposed. Baumgarten whom Kant mentioned in the passage above wrote *Aesthetica* (1750–1758) as a 'science of sensual cognition', in which a theory of art is only a part of it. Karatani points out that Kant took issue with Baumgarten 'not because the latter used aesthetics to signify a science of the beautiful, but because Baumgarten tried to see something rational in sensibility or sentiments'.[19] In *Critique of Pure Reason*, as Karatani reminds us, Kant uses

> aesthetics only as in the sense of a science of sensibility. Here Kant is consistent in his distinction between sensibility and understanding, or between the sensible and intelligible, because thought without this distinction is metaphysics, which claims that a certain thing (God, for example) exists only because it is intelligible.[20]

For Kant the moral law is *rational*, and therefore, there is no 'morality in sentiment or sensibility'. The crux of the matter not to be missed, as Karatani stresses, is that 'the idea that some sentiments are rational a priori is to sensibilize or aestheticize morality (or reason). Kant criticizes the idea of the direct link between sensibility and understanding (or reason)'.[21] We should therefore call a thought 'aesthetic', when it is not limited to the science of beauty. For Kant,

> the problem of morality is directly linked to that of economy. For him, the core of morality is not situated in good or evil but in freedom. In that case, the moral law, which commands us to use humanity in the person of every other 'always at the same time as end [as a free being] and never merely as a means,' must not be understood without referring to actual problem of economy. The laws include the 'categorical imperative' for abolishing those politico-economic situations in which others are used exclusively as means.[22]

In his *transcritical* project of 'Kant and Freud', which is in continuation of his *transcritique* of 'Kant and Marx', given the fact that Marx and Freud were both 'ungenerous' with Kant, Karatani analyzes the 'pronounced parallax' between Kant's notion of Sublime (in its distinction with the 'Beautiful') and Freud's notions of Superego or the 'death drive'—repetition compulsion—which goes *beyond* 'the pleasure principle'.[23] For Kant, the sublime is possible only through *unpleasure*. There is a parallel, therefore, between Kant and Freud. According to Kant,

> judgment of the beautiful is caused by finding the form of 'purposiveness without purpose' in a natural object. In this case, the beautiful has its ground in the external object and imagination works together with understanding. On the other hand, the sublime emerges when we cannot find such purposiveness but still try to find another kind of purposiveness: judgment of the sublime is caused by the imagination working together with *reason*.[24]

In *Critique of the Power of Judgment* Kant wrote:

> The quality of the feeling of the sublime is that it is a feeling of displeasure concerning the aesthetic faculty of judging an object that is yet at the same time represented a purposive, which is possible because the subject's own incapacity reveals the consciousness of an unlimited capacity of the very same subject, and the mind can aesthetically judge the latter only through the former.[25]

Karatani writes that

> Without reason, which overcomes the powerlessness, no doubt there would be no sublime; otherwise it would be a religious fear and far from yielding pleasure. The sublime, however, is not a mere subjective feeling. The sublime is impossible without the existence of the overwhelming external object.[26]

Kant had already in his *Observations on the Feeling of the Beautiful and Sublime* written that:

> The sight of a mountain whose snow-covered peak rises above the clouds, the description of a raging storm, or Milton's portrayal of the infernal kingdom, arouse enjoyment but with horror; on the other hand, the sight of flower-strewn meadows, valleys with winding brooks and covered with gazing flocks, the description of Elysium, of Homer's portrayal of the girdle of Venus, also occasion a pleasant sensation but one that is joyous and smiling. In order that the former impression could occur to us in due strength, we must have a feeling of the sublime, and, in order to enjoy

the latter well, a feeling of the beautiful. Tall oaks and lonely shadows in a scared grove are sublime; flower beds, low hedges and trees trimmed in figures are beautiful. Night is sublime, day is beautiful.[27]

The extraordinary discussion that Karatani advances in drawing the parallel between Kant and Freud should not further detain us. My main purpose here is to get straight to the crux of the 'sublime object' in Lacanian theory which, as I claimed above, must *par excellence* be taken to be the *object of ideology critique*. In this respect, we can talk of another *transcritical* endeavor, that is, the 'pronounced parallax' between Kant and Lacan, which for Žižek is also a parallax between Lacan and Hegel concerning the same problematic of the Sublime.

Lacan in Seminar VII, *The Ethic of Psychoanalysis*—the only 'ethics' acceptable, according to him—tackles the notion of 'Sublimation'—unsatisfactorily treated in Freud's work—in relation to the Freudian Thing, or *Das Ding*, and in the process we get the radicalization of the Kantian ethics.[28] Lacan wrote: 'It is after all as a function of ethics that we have to judge sublimation; it creates socially recognizable values'.[29] Prior to this, he made these interesting remarks:

> Note that no correct evaluation of sublimation in art is possible if we overlook the fact that all artistic production, including especially that of the fine arts, is historically situated. You do not paint in Picasso's time as you painted in Velazquez's time; you don't write a novel in 1930 as you did in Stendhal's time. This is an absolutely essential fact that does not for the time being need to be located under the rubric of the collectivity— let's place it under the rubric of culture.[30]

As Marc de Kesel in his excellent reading of the Seminar VII points out, 'According to psychoanalysis, with the arrival of modernity, the distance or gap that separates man from the real has become unbridgeable: this gap has become constitutive of the modern subject'.[31]

Finally, in a later session of his Seminar (20 January 1960), Lacan offered his audience the famous definition of Sublimation: 'Thus, the most general formula that I can give you of sublimation is the following: it raises an object—and I don't mind the suggestion of a play on words in the term I use—to the dignity of the Thing'.[32] By 'raising the object to the dignity of the Thing', we arrive at the exact definition of the *sublime object*. Based on this definition, Žižek offers his remarks on the notion of the Sublime in Kant:

> with Kant the Sublime designates the relation of an innerworldly, empirical sensuous object to *Das an sich*, to the transcendence, trans-phenomenal, unattainable Thing-in-itself. The paradox of the Sublime is as follows: in principle, the gap separating phenomenal, empirical objects of experience from the Thing-in-itself is insurmountable—that is, no empirical object, no representation [*Vorstellung*] of it can adequately present [*darstellen*] the Thing (the supersensible Idea); but the Sublime is an object in which we can experience this very impossibility, this permenant failure of the representation to reach after the Thing. Thus, by means of the very failure of representation, we can have a presentiment of the true dimension of the Thing. This is also why an object evoking in us the feeling of Sublimity gives us simultaneous pleasure and displeasure: it gives us displeasure because of its inadequacy to the Thing-Idea, but precisely through this inadequacy it gives us pleasure by indicating the true, incomparable greatness of

the Thing, surpassing every possible phenomenal, empirical experience.[33]

In affirmation, Žižek cites a relevant passage from *Critique of Power of Judgment*:

> The feeling of the sublime is thus feeling of displeasure from the inadequacy of the imagination in the aesthetic estimation of magnitude for the estimation by means of reason, and a pleasure that is thereby aroused at the same time from correspondence of this very judgment of the inadequacy of the greatest sensible faculty in comparison with the ideas of reason, insofar as striving for them is nevertheless a law for us.[34]

To bring this section to a close: In liberal capitalist modernity, *architecture*, strictly speaking, is the product of the bourgeois society and the commodity economy. In this society, architecture assumes the task, more than any other material ideological support, of providing the necessary 'ideological consistency' for its proper functioning. The dominant *ethics* in this bourgeois society is grounded in the ideology of eudemonism or utilitarianism. Kant went against it. In his *Groundwork of the Metaphysics of Morals* he wrote: 'The practical imperative will thus be the following: *So act that you use humanity, in your own person as well as in the person of any other, always at the same time as an end, never merely as a means*'.[35] Karatani notes that it is significant that Kant stressed 'never merely as'. By inserting this phrase, Kant had already taken as a premise the 'production and the relation of production'—the domain that Marx scrutinized in *Capital*. To Kant, Karatani notes,

213

> the use of others' humanity *as a means* was already an inevitability in the 'production and the relation of production' in the commodity economy. Any account of human relations that overlooks this concern is merely a 'monastery' or 'dormitory' daydream, from the hotbeds of those who use the humanity of the 'faithful' and 'parents' merely as a means.[36]

Karatani remarks that Kantian ethics tended to be dismissed or degraded only because it is read

> as if speaking to 'an end but not means' in the place of 'an end, never merely as a means.' The kingdom of the end exists upon a material and economic basis, and the 'personalism', when the base matters are not taken into consideration, cannot help but becoming a priestly sermon.[37]

Noting that Neo-Kantian Herman Cohen once said that Kant is the 'true originator of German socialism', Karatani importantly asserts that:

> Communist society, for that matter, must be a society where others are treated as an end at the same time as a means; and communism is possible only by reorganizing the social system where people are treated merely as a means. In other words, here apodictically arrives the regulative idea of superseding capitalism.[38]

Capitalism with the dominant trend of utilitarianism considers *good* as calculable, that Jacques Lacan once named as 'servicing the goods'. It takes *good* to be synonymous with *interest*. Thus, 'ethics is reduced to economics, not to mention that it was coined from the standpoint of capitalist development'.[39]

Communism, therefore, from its conception in the nineteenth century on was always 'an ethico-economic problematic', Karatani claims. Thus Marx's communism conceived within this problematic is an 'ethical intervention'. Recall, as I previously cited in the 'Apologue' to this work, young Marx in effect wrote about the 'Categorical Imperative' of communism when in his 'A Contribution to the Critique of Hegel's *Philosophy of Right*' he wrote, 'The criticism of religion ends with the teaching that *man is the highest being for man*, hence with the *categorical imperative to overthrow all relations* in which man is a debased, enslaved, forsaken, despicable being'.[40] Stressing that this 'categorical imperative' is a thread lingering in Kant's thinking, Karatani concludes that 'Communism as practice is neither merely economic nor merely moral. To adapt Kant's rhetoric, communism without economic basis is *empty*, while communism without moral basis is *blind*'.[41]

I have begun this chapter by setting the stage for an exposition of *critique* in architecture that I have called, after Karatani, a 'transcritique of architecture'. Underlying its premise is that the theory of critique must contest the *ethical* criteria of architecture dictated by the eudemonism of the bourgeois society. I confront this ethical stance, *uncompromisingly*, by another ethical criterion, as will become clearer in this chapter.

At the end, but for a beginning, I want to invoke the alteration of a motto—used by both Hegel and Marx—*Hic Rhodus, hic saltus*—that Žižek has put in the distinct ethical dictum of psychoanalysis as: *Ibi Rhodus, ibi saltus*. With this motto, I want to enjoin the 'architect-critic' with Žižek's command which emulates Kant's 'categorical imperative': 'Act in such a way that your activity does not rely on any figure of the big Other as its ontological guarantee'.[42] Translation: Do not act in accordance with the eudemonism of the bourgeois society.

Part II

Phantasmagoria of architecture

Two names must be conjoined: Marx and Benjamin. Under one critical concept: Phantasmagoria. This concept allows us to open a space of *transcodings* between two *critiques*: the Benjaminian critique and the Marxian critique. The former critiqued architecture by invoking the critical conceptual tool the latter had provided. After Karatani, I will name the space of this transcoding as 'Transcritique on Marx and Benjamin'. Between them intervenes the psychoanalytical theory whose terms underlie the interpretation of Phantasmagoria. We can tell of Marx, bringing out this concept, that he had *already* anticipated Freud and Lacan, or he was a good reader of them *avant la lettre*.

From the terms of this Transcritique I infer a thesis for architecture valid for the entire era of liberal capitalist modernity. It goes as follows: *Architecture is structured like a phantasmagoria*.[43] It must not be missed that I fashion this thesis in analogy to Lacan's famous phrase, 'the unconscious is structured like a language', a definition that came out of the *first* return of Lacan to Freud. In the next section I will construct yet another Transcritique based on the results of the *second* return of Lacan to Freud as has perceptively been analyzed by Samo Tomšič. Here I must point out that both critiques above are grounded in the Unconscious, in particular the 'Unconscious of Commodity-Form'. It in turn underlines a theory of *ideology-critique* which stands in contradistinction with all other theories.

The most *enigmatic* critical construction of *capital*, the high point of Marx's philosophy, seemingly simple but notoriously difficult to decipher, what Marx called 'the mystical character of the commodity', as is well known, is written in Chapter 1 of *Capital, Volume One*, entitled 'The Commodity'. In Section

4: 'The Fetishism of the Commodity and its Secret', Marx begins to say:

> *A commodity appears at first sight an extremely obvious, trivial thing. But its analysis brings out that it is a very strange thing, abounding in metaphysical subtleties and theological niceties.* So far as it is a use-value, there is nothing mysterious about it, whether we consider it from the point of view that by its properties it satisfies human needs, or that it first takes on these properties as the product of human labour. It is absolutely clear that, by this activity, man changes the forms of the materials of nature in such a way as to make them useful to him. The form of wood, for instance, is altered if a table is made out of it. Nevertheless the table continues to be wood, an ordinary, sensuous thing. But as soon as it emerges as a commodity, it changes into a thing which transcends sensuousness. It not only stands with its feet on the ground, but, in relation to all other commodities, it stands on its head, and evolves out of its wooden brain grotesque ideas, far more wonderful that if it were begin dancing of its own free will.[44] [emphasis mine].

We will come back to this 'dancing table', this 'sensuous nonsensuous' Thing, to whose analysis Jacques Derrida devoted a number of pages in his *Specters of Marx*.[45] Let us continue with our reading:

> Whence, then, arises the enigmatic character of the product of labour, as soon as it assumes the form of commodity? Clearly, it arises from this form itself. The equality of the kinds of human labour takes on a physical form in the equal objectivity of the products of labour as values; the measure of

> the expenditure of human labour-power by its duration takes on the form of the magnitude of the value of the products of labour; and finally the relationships between the producers, within which the social characteristic of their labours are manifested, take on the form of a social relation between the product of labour.[46]

And further:

> The mysterious character of the commodity-form consists therefore simply in the fact that the commodity reflects the social characteristics of men's own labour as objective characteristics of the product of labour, as the socio-natural properties of these things. Hence it also reflects the social relation of the producers to the sum total of labour as a social relation between objects. Through this substitution, the products of labour become commodities, sensuous things which are at the same time suprasensible or social. In the same way, the impression made by a thing on the optic nerve is perceived not as a subjective excitation of that nerve but as the objective form of a thing outside the eye. In the act of seeing, of course, light is really transmitted from one thing, the external object, to another thing, the eye. It is a physical relation between physical things. As against this, the commodity-form, and the value-relation of the products of labour within which it appears, have absolutely no connection with the physical nature of commodity and the material [*dinglich*] relations arising out of this. *It is nothing but the definite social relation between men themselves which assumes here, for them, the fantastic form of a relation between things.* In order, therefore, to find an analogy we must take a flight into the misty realm of religion. There the products of the human brain

appear as autonomous figures endowed with a life of their own, which enter into relations both with each other and with the human race. So it is in the world of commodities with the products of men's hands. I call this the fetishism which attaches itself to the product of labour as soon as they are produced as commodities, and is therefore inseparable from the production of commodities.[47] [emphasis mine]

Before going further, we must make a note of the term rendered as 'fantastic form' in the passage above, an inadequate and unfortunate translation of the German term Marx used which is '*dies phantasmagorische Form*'. If properly rendered in English, it should have been 'Phantasmagoria'. Before I examine this term I cite one more passage for the purpose at hand. Marx goes on to say:

Value, therefore, does not have its description branded on its forehead; *it rather transforms every product of labour into a social hieroglyphic.* Later on, men try to decipher the hieroglyphic, to get behind the secret of their own social product: for the characteristic which objects of utility have of being values is as much men's social product as is their language. The belated scientific discovery that the products of labour, in so far as they are values, are merely the material expressions of the human labour expended to produce them, marks an epoch in the history of mankind's development, but by no means banishes the semblance of objectivity possessed by the social characteristics of labour.[48] [emphasis mine].

At this point some brief remarks on the words 'value', 'use-value' and 'exchange-value' are in order. Marx in *A Contribution to the Critique of Political Economy* points out that:

Part II

> The commodity is a use-value for its owner only so far as it is an exchange-value. The commodity therefore *has* still *to become* a use-value, in the first place a use-value for others. Since it is not a use-value to its owner, it must be a use-value to owners of other commodities [...] Commodities do not acquire a new economic form *in the course* of their mutual relations as use-values. On the contrary, the specific form which distinguished them as commodities disappears [...] To become use-values commodities *mis nust* be altogether alienated; they must enter into an exchange process; exchange however is concerned merely with their aspects as exchange-values. Hence, only by being realized as exchange-values can they be realized as use-values.[49]

Elucidating 'The Form of Value' in Marx, Karatani suggests that there is a distinction between *Capital* and the previous works such as *A Contribution to the Critique of Political Economy* or *Grundrisse*. He points out that there was a more 'radical epistemological break', not only as Althusser had claimed between *The German Ideology* and *Capital*, but between *Grundrisse* and *Capital*, 'which was rendered by the theory of value form'.[50] According to Karatani,

> securitizing commodity form thus necessitates a transcendental elucidation of the form that makes objects commodity and/or money. In the 'simple form of value,' the value of commodity A is expressed by the use-value commodity B. Therein commodity A is in the relative form of value, while commodity B is in the equivalent form.[51]

Karatani then takes Marx's example that The simple form of value is expressed in the following equation:

20 yards of linen = I coat

(relative form of value) (equivalent form)

What this equation indicates is that twenty yard of linen cannot express its value by itself; its value can be presented in its natural form only after being posited in the equivalency with one coat. On the other hand, one coat is in the position that it can always be exchanged with the former. It is the equivalent form that makes the coat seem as if it had exchange-value (direct exchangeability) in itself. 'The equivalent form of commodity, accordingly, is the form in which it is directly exchangeable with other commodities.' The enigma of money is lurking behind the equivalent form. Marx called it 'fetishism of the commodity'.[52] That enigma is inscribed in the 'theory of value form'. The 'value form', Karatani writes: 'is a kind of form that people are not aware of when they are placed within the monetary economy; this is the form that is discovered only *transcendentally*'.[53]

At this point, returning to the example of the 'table' evoked by Marx, I want to make an analogical comparison between the *table* and *building* by drawing a precise *equivalence* between the two, as the two 'sensuous, non-sensuous' Things. As Derrida, reflecting on the 'dancing table' and making his well known case on the distinction between 'specter' and 'spirit(s)', ghost and apparition, between '*hauntology* and ontology', remarks:

> Marx does not say sensuous *and* non-sensuous, sensuously supersensible. Transcendence, the movement of *super-*, the step beyond (*über, epekeina*), is made sensuous in that very excess. It renders the non-sensuous sensuous [...] The

commodity thus haunts the thing, its specter is at work in use-value.[54]

I take a step further and conceive *building* like the *table*, moving from 'a séance of the table' to 'a séance of the building' in the *theatrical* sense of which Derrida speaks, as 'Commodity-Form' with an Unconscious—as 'sensuous non-sensuous', at the same time. Thus, consider this equation: Table-commodity=Building-commodity. The *building* must be staged if it is to become a building, exactly like a table with four legs. Grounding this equivalence in 'The Unconscious of the Commodity-Form' (Žižek's term) it has then to be delineated in the concept of Phantasmagoria, which contains a theory of Ideology that, as we saw before, Žižek extracts from Marx while at the same time distancing himself from Derrida's version of 'spectrology'.[55]

Now to the notion of Phantasmagoria itself. The word *phantasmagoria* derives from the Greek *phantasma* literally an 'assembly of phantasms'.[56] Etymologically it is composed of *phantasma* (phantom, ghost) and *agoreuein* (to speak in public). However, according to *Le Robert* French dictionary, phantasmagoria is composed of *phantasma* and *gourere* (to deceive, to fool). The latter meaning is probably closer to Etienne-Gaspard Robertson who invented the term in the late eighteenth century. Robertson in the 1970s ran 'magic lantern' shows in Paris. By the late eighteenth century and early nineteenth century, magic lantern shows had become a popular form of entertainment in Paris and London. Dispensing with the conventional theatrical stage, Robertson used a projector, or Fantascope. His technological device used 'lighting sources and effects in the projector itself by placing it behind a large flat screen like a theatrical scrim'.[57] The projector derived from the *camera obscura* and is the forerunner of the devices which came later in the form of the slide projector and the cinema. In their original sense, Phantasmagorias were machines to produce illusions, fantasies, ghosts, and hallucinations in horror shows.[58]

In the passage I cited above from *Capital*, Marx used a visual metaphor to drive home his point about the 'fantastic form' [phantasmagoria] in commodity fetishism. To remind ourselves I repeat the passage:

> In the same way, the impression made by a thing on the optic nerve is perceived not as a subjective excitation of that nerve but as the objective form of thing outside the eye. In the act of seeing, of course, light is really transmitted from one thing, the external object, to another thing, the eye. It is a physical relation between physical things. As against this, the commodity-form, and the value-relation of the products of labour within which it appears, have absolutely no connection with the physical nature of commodity and the material [*dinglich*] relations arising out of this. It is nothing but the definite social relation between men themselves which assumes here, for them, the fantastic form of a relation between things. In order, therefore, to find an analogy we must take a flight into the misty realm of religion.

Marx (with Engels) in *The German Ideology* used the *camera obscura*—invented before the magic lantern—as a metaphor for his theory of ideology as *inversion*. It is in the section on Feuerbach and the 'Opposition between Materialist and Idealist Outlooks', where Marx states that ideas, conceptions, and consciousness are 'directly interwoven' with the material conditions of men and their actual life-process. The same applies to mental productions expressed variously in legal, political, religious, and metaphysical forms. According to Marx, 'If in all ideology men and their relations appear upside-down as in *camera obscura*, this phenomenon arises just as much from their historical-life process as the inversion of objects on the retina does from their physical life-process'.[59]

In her excellent *Camera Obscura of Ideology*, Sarah Kofman argues convincingly that the *camera obscura* analogy is used here to stress the two components of this device. 'In ideology', she remarks,

> ideas are put under lock and key room, cut off from the real material base which alone can confer upon them light and truth. The dark chamber 'is a place where light can only enter through a hole an inch in diameter to which one applies a glass which, letting the rays from external object pass onto the opposite wall, or onto a curtain held there, allows what is outside to be seen inside'.[60]

Moreover, for Kofman, the *camera obscura* presents a model of vision that does away with the Euclidean conception 'according to which it is from the eye that emanates the luminous ray, and that the model of camera obscura implies the existence of a "given" which would offer itself as already inverted'.[61] According to Kofman,

> Marx draws attention to the privileged status of religious ideology as exemplary, even, constitutive, of ideology as such. He notes, as well, that the ideological inversion is a hierarchical inversion which substitutes, for a real foundation, an imaginary one. The inversion of the inversion involves departing from 'real premises,' founded on real bases, the empirically

observable 'material bases,' and deriving, from these, those phantasmagorias which are ideological formations.[62]

Significantly, Marx never used the word 'ideology' in *Capital*. Walter Benjamin in *The Arcades Project* and the two Exposés of 1935 and 1939 subsumed the word 'ideology' and 'false consciousness' under the term Phantasmagoria as a critical category he adopted from Marx. Benjamin in affirmation of Marx's theory of Commodity Fetishism coined the phrase 'phantasmagoria of civilization' to critique the Second Empire architecture and culture, economy and technology under Napoleon III. In 'Introduction' to the 1939 Exposé he wrote:

> Our investigation proposes to show how, as a consequence of reifying representation of civilization, the new form of behavior and new economically and technologically based creations that we owe to the nineteenth century enter the universe of a phantasmagoria. Thus appear the arcades—first entry in the field of iron construction; thus appear the world of exhibitions whose link to the entertainment industry is significant. Also included in this order of phenomena is the experience of flâneur, who abandons himself to phantasmagoria of the marketplace.[63]

He further wrote, 'As for the phantasmagoria of civilization itself, it found its champion in Haussmann and its manifest expression in his transformation of Paris', and pointedly noted that 'Nevertheless, the pomp and splendor with which commodity-producing society surrounds itself, as well as its illusory sense of security, are not immune to dangers; the collapse of the Second Empire and Commune of Paris remind it of that'.[64]

Part II

Some conclusions can be drawn: From the time of Bonapartism in the Second Empire under Napoleon III to our own time that I call Neo-Bonapartism, we have been in the 'civilization of phantasmagoria'. Certain obvious differences between the two periods notwithstanding, together they constitute the 'civilization' of liberal capitalist modernity. Inheriting the term from Marx and Benjamin, the notion of Phantasmagoria remains the key critical category for the critique of architecture and culture for our time. The analysis of the *building* must first begin by conceiving it as a 'commodity-form' in analogy with Marx's 'dancing table' while keeping in mind that 'A commodity appears at first sight an extremely obvious, trivial thing. But its analysis brings out that it is a very strange thing, abounding in metaphysical subtleties and theological niceties'. Building as Value must be looked at as a 'social hieroglyphic': 'Value therefore', to repeat again what Marx said, 'does not have its description branded on its forehead; it rather transforms every product of labour into a social hieroglyphic'—inclusive of *building*. After the conceptualization of the building as *value*, it is appropriate here to remember Paul Valéry, who after his reading of *Capital* arrived at the conclusion that 'art' is a *value* caught in the process of production and consumption, as I brought it up in 'Exordium' at the beginning of this book. Ultimately, the *value* of 'building-commodity' arises from the separation of production and consumption and the 'impenetrability of the gap' between them. We must then perform a '*transcendental bracketing*' to determine the pedagogical categories in the domains of *ethics*, *economics*, and *aesthetics* that, within the structure of the Borromean Knot suggested before, will constitute the critique of architecture. At the most general level, architecture in the Second Empire underwent *sensibilization-aestheticization*. In our time of Neo-Bonapartism, under the 'monarchy of capital', architecture, determinately and irreversibly, has undergone a process of *anaesthetization*, thus *numbing* the human sensorium and *emptying* the Subject of its political-ethical content.[65] The combined effects of both, to put it in Hegelian terms, constitute nothing but a frontal assault on the 'Rational Kernel' of architecture. Both are the forms that help architecture remain as an instrument in reproduction of the capitalist forms of domination, and an *imaginary* resolution of its fundamental social antagonism.

Architecture and the capitalist Unconscious

A link between psychoanalytical critique and Marx's Critique of Political Economy as two discursive practices is brought about by a movement of 'transposition' or 'pronounced parallax'. Samo Tomšič in his *The Capitalist Unconscious* establishes the epistemological and political aspects of this parallax. He outlines his argument as follows:

> Marx thus continuously moves on two different but intimately related levels, that of the *logic of production*, which explains how the abstract and seemingly neutral relations between values support and reproduce concrete social antagonisms, and that of the *logic of fantasy*, which examines the reproduction of objective appearances, whose function is to repress, distort and mystify the existing structural contradictions. The logic of production and the logic of fantasy are the two basic components of Marx's notion of critique.[66]

As we will see, it is the specific theory of the Subject which will establish the link between Marx and Lacan. Tomšič links the critique of political economy and psychoanalysis through

Structural Linguistics. We should recall that it was through this link that Althusser's so-called Structuralist reading of Marx and Lacan's 'structural psychoanalysis' was achieved. We must also remember that what punctuates the Freudian break from the Jungian 'Romantic' brand of psychoanalysis is fundamentally the presence of 'linguistics' in Freud's work—and its lack in Jung—well before the appearance of Saussure's Structural Linguistics. According to Tomšič, putting the main accent on the role of 'labour' in the discovery of the unconscious, Freud outlined a '*labour theory of the unconscious*'. But, importantly, as Tomšič points out, in this discovery, a theory of 'production' was needed that Saussurean Structural Linguistics could not provide. It was left to Marx to offer it. It is therefore useful to briefly examine here the relation between political economy and linguistics.

In capitalism no product is produced without *labor*. Labor is of course the substance of *value*. But as Karatani points out, what makes a product a value is rather the 'form of value'. This value-form means that the commodity must be analyzed within the 'relational system' or the system of *difference*. The link between political economy and linguistics, through 'exchange', is ultimately grounded on the system of difference in language as social product. This is why Marx wrote that 'every product of labour' that is transformed by *value* 'into social hieroglyphic' is a social product in analogy with *language*. Both are 'men's social product'. Recall the passage from *Capital* cited above:

> Value, therefore, does not have its description branded on its forehead; it rather transforms every product of labour into a social hieroglyphic. Later on, men try to decipher the

hieroglyphic, to get behind the secret of their own social product: for the characteristic which objects of utility have of being values is as much men's social product as is their language.

Karatani astutely compares Marx's notion of commodity as 'social hieroglyphic' with Derrida's '*archi-écriture*' in his *Of Grammatology*.[67] He writes:

philosophy since Plato has entailed a hostility to letters, while admiring the direct and transparent exchange-communication. And the same has been going on in the political economy as hostility towards money [...] the hatred of money of Ricardo and Prouhdon corresponds to the hatred of writing. Both are hatreds of mediated communication, going hand in hand with the fantasy of direct and transparent exchange.[68]

Emphasizing that it was linguistics that was in the first place shaped by political economy—hence the primacy of Marx over de Saussure—Karatani invokes the prominent twentieth-century Prague linguist Roman Jakobson (much admired and cited by Lacan) and writes:

In the century-old history of economics and linguistics, questions of uniting both disciplines have arisen repeatedly. One may recall that economics of the Enlightenment period used to attack linguistic problems [...] as, for example, Anne-Robert-Jacques Turgot, who compiled a study on etymology for the *Encyclopédie* (1756), or Adam Smith, who wrote on the origin of language (1770). G. Tarde's influence on Saussure's doctrine in such matters as circuit, exchange, value, output-input, and producer-consumer is well known. Many common topics, as, for instance, 'dynamic synchrony,' contradictions within the system, and its continual economic concepts are repeatedly subjected to tentative semiotic interpretation.[69]

The *first* return of Lacan to Freud is marked by reading Freud with structural linguistics resulting in the claim that Freud's theories anticipated Saussure and Jakobson's theories of language. In this reading 'metonymy and metaphor, the two central operations in language, are discovered in the way the unconscious processes manipulate the conscious and preconscious material. The two linguistic operations translate into condensation and displacement, the main achievements of unconscious labour'.[70] Therefore, as Tomšič reminds us, this linguistic return to Freud marking Lacan's 'structural psychoanalysis', yielded the famous formula, 'The unconscious is structured as a language', as was mentioned before, and therefore the 'theory of signifier', that led to the notion of the 'barred subject, $', the subject of signifier. As Lacan said:

> With Saussure and the Prague linguistic circle linguistics is constituted on a cut, which is the bar placed between the signifier and signified in order to expose the difference, on which the signifier is constituted in an absolute way, and through which it effectively obtains its autonomy.[71]

Ferdinand de Saussure in his *Course in General Linguistics* exposed the *arbitrary* relation between two component parts of the linguistic sign, signifier and signified, and the bar separating them from each other. He discovered language as a 'system of difference'.[72] Structural linguistics recognizes the autonomy of the signifier. The bar in question does not aim at the external relation between words and things but at the internal consistency of linguistic signs. It thus designates the absence of any substantial, essential or immanent link between the two components, which implies that the relation between the signifier (the series of sounds) and the signified (the associated mental representation) is actually a non-relation: an instable, shifting and groundless link.[73]

By exposing the 'structural functioning of the bar' and the autonomy of the signifier, the underlying structure can be then formulated as this: '*the structure is a cut*',[74] thus confirming what Lacan said above. Tomšič writes:

> By failing to envisage the difference between labour-process and labour-power, as well as between labour-power and other commodities, Saussure situates production outside the science of language. For him, language knows no surplus and the use of language remains throughout communicative and meaningful. This will eventually become the central point of Lacan's critique of Saussure.[75]

In *Encore* Lacan said:

> Communication implies reference. But one thing is clear—language is merely what scientific discourse elaborates to account for what I call *lalangue*. Language serves purposes that are altogether different from that of communication … If communication approaches what is effectively at work in the *jouissance* of lalanguage, it is because communication implies a reply, in other words, dialogue. But does lalanguage serve, first and foremost, to dialogue? As I said before, nothing is less certain.[76]

Tomšič writes:

> The bar between the signifier and the signified initiated an epistemological revolution in human science, because the structuralist paradigm disrupted the historical predominance of 'Aristotelianism' in linguistics and in philosophy of language. Before the emergence of structuralism, language was almost exclusively conceived in reference to Aristotle's notion of *organon*, which enabled the definition of language as a tool and an organ of communication and of social relation, an abstract convention between autonomous, rational and conscious subjects. Through the lenses of structural linguistics, language turns out to be a far more paradoxical and complex subject, a system of differences that resists totalization, and because it is untotalisable, it is both autonomous and inexistent—hence the Lacanian use of the very same bar that in Saussure separates the signifier from the signified, in order to designate the inexistence of the Other and the split of the Subject.[77]

What is at the crux in all of these with which we are concerned—as related to the notion of language as the *system of difference*—is the notion of 'Surplus' and its corollary in Marx, that is, the 'Surplus-Value'. In her *$urplus: Spinoza, Lacan*, A. Kiarina Kordela, who puts a strong emphasis on the close proximity between Spinoza and Lacan, brings up precisely this notion of Surplus while arguing that 'Spinoza is the first philosopher to grasp the structure of secular causality, as immanent or differential causality', when it was popularized by linguistics. What enabled Spinoza to see this structure, she argues, is the fact that he conceived nature, 'insofar as it is inhabited by human beings, as a system of signifier'.[78] She explains that 'Far from being autonomous physical things, with inherent qualities, signifiers are differential values. *And differential values, by structural necessities, constitute a system of disequilibrium, that is a system that always produces a surplus*'[79] [emphasis mine]. She then argues that Marx's 'one major innovation' is the realization that the

> structure of capital, too, is a manifestation of the structure of secular causality on the level of economy. What enabled Marx to see this was the fact that he conceived of nature as a system of commodities, that is, again, differential values.[80]

Underlying her argument is the same negation of Aristotelian notion of 'causality' that we saw above. Recall that for Aristotle, knowledge is basically the knowledge of causes, which he identified as four cardinal causes. Kordela explains them in this way:

> (1) the material cause, the substrate or substance of which an object is made, such as stones that make up a house; (2) the formal cause, the shape or form of the substance, such as the specific design of the stone house; (3) the final cause, the use, purpose, or end for the sake of which something is made, such as habitation in the case of a house; and (4) the efficient cause, the primary instigator of the process of change, such as the agent who commissioned the construction of the house.[81]

What is important to notice is the passage from Aristotle to medieval scholasticism and finally to secularized thought in the attempt 'to ground truth on human reason itself' that, as Kordela points out, came about with the Cartesian *cogito* with its own Theory of God.[82] Kordela goes into length to elaborate the aspects of the 'secular causality' in modern secular capitalism and the notion of *causa sui* in Spinoza that should not detain us here. What concerns us here is the linguistic passage from *surplus* caused by 'differential systems of value' to the Marxian notion of 'surplus-value' in economy, and how finally this will lead us to the notion of the Uncurious in capitalism. Let us examine how Marx initially put the whole matter in *Capital*.

At the end of Chapter 1 in *Capital* Marx writes:

> If commodities could speak, they would say this: our use-value may interest men, but does not belong to us as objects. What does belong to us as objects, however, is our value. Our own intercourse as commodity proves it. We relate to each other merely as exchange-values.[83]

Then, at the end of Chapter 5, Marx wrote:

> The sphere of circulation or commodity exchange, within whose boundaries the sale and purchase of labour-power goes on, is in fact a very Eden of the innate rights of man. It is the exclusive realm of Freedom, Equality, Property and Bentham. Freedom, because both buyer and seller of a commodity, let us say of labour-power, are determined only by their free will. They contract as free persons, who are equal before the law. Their contract is the final result in which their joint will finds a common legal expression. Equality, because each enters into relation with the other, as with a simple owner of commodities, and they exchange equivalent for equivalent. Property, because each disposes only of what is his own. And Bentham, because each looks only to his own advantage. The

only force bringing them together, and putting them into relation with each other, is selfishness, the gain and the private interest of each. Each pays heed to himself only, and no one worries about the others. And precisely for that reason, either in accordance with the pre-established harmony of things, or under the auspices of an omniscient providence, they all work together to their mutual advantage, for the common weal and the common interest.[84]

In the above passage we must pay attention to the four fundamental principal elements of liberal capitalism that Marx succinctly articulates, that is, Freedom, Equality, Property, and Bentham (or private interest). Marx explains the *forms* of 'value' and 'surplus value' in the following manner:

One sum of money is distinguishable from another only by its amount. The process M-C-M does not therefore owe its content to any qualitative difference between its extremes, for they are both money, but solely to quantitative changes. More money is finally withdrawn from circulation than was thrown into it at the beginning. The cotton originally bought for £100 is for example re-sold at £100+£10, i.e. £110. The complete form of this process is therefore M-C-M', where M' = M+ Δ M, i.e. the original sum advanced plus an increment. This increment or excess over the original value I call 'surplus value' [*Mehrwert*].[85]

And further:

The simple circulation, the value of commodities attained at the most a form independent of their use-values, i.e. the form of money. But now, in the circulation M-C-M, value suddenly presents itself as a self-moving substance which passes through a process of its own, and for which commodities and money are both forms. But there is more to come: instead of simply representing the relations of commodities, it now enters into a private relationship with itself, as it were. It differentiates itself as original value from itself as surplus-value, just as God the Father, differentiates himself from himself as God the Son, although both are of the same age and form, in fact one single person; for only by the surplus-value of £10 does the £100 originally advanced become capital, and as soon as this has happened, as soon as the son has been created and, through the son, the father, their differences vanishes again, both become one, £110.[86]

Karatani asks how does industrial capitalism earn surplus value? He explains to us that, first of all, Marx's unique contribution is the way in which he sought to understand industrial capitalism within the same general formula M-C-M'. To Marx,

what distinguishes industrial capitalism from merchant capitalism was, first and foremost, that the former discovered a 'special commodity' that the latter had not known—the commodity of labor power. Industrial capitalism purchases this most special commodity in human history—labor power—in order to produce products, and then sells those products to the commodity itself—laborers—in order to earn surplus value.[87]

This means that surplus value must be considered, as Karatani notes, as *total social product*, and not at the level of individual capital. In this respect, Karatani brings out the moment of crisis in the twentieth century when in the 1930s with the Great

Depression capital changed course and so-called Fordism and with it the 'consumer society', as we know it, came into existence. Karatani writes that,

> These incidents were however not beyond Marx's theoretical reach. Fordism and Keynesianism signify the intervention of the total social capital to restrain the egoism of individual capitals in order to avoid total collapse, and in turn, secure profit for the individual capitals. It appears to be contrary to the conviction of Adam Smith that everyone's egoistic strive for profit is in the end beneficial to everyone. Also it appears to be a denial of the Weberian spirit of capitalism—Protestantism that encourages 'diligence' and 'saving'. But they are nothing unimaginable within Marxian theory. It was shocking only for the view that detects the realization of surplus value in individual capitals alone or in the process of production alone. [88]

As is known, Marx made a distinction between *absolute surplus value* and *relative surplus value*. The industrial capitalism

> earns surplus value by producing new value systems *temporally* and *continually*. The surplus value proper to industrial capital is thus *relative surplus value*. This is attained by the following procedure: Technological innovation shortens labor time; this lowers the values of commodities that are necessary for the production of labor power; then the value of labor-power is lowered as a practical effect. Relative surplus value is an exploitation in the double sense—*development* to *take advantage of*'.[89]

Going back to the notion of *difference*, and based on the fact that Marx employed the term *industrial* in a much broader sense, Karatani perceptively observes that,

Part II

> In this sense, capital does not care whether it gets surplus value from solid object or fluid information. So it is that the nature of capital is consistent even before and after its dominant production shifted from heavy industry to the information industry. It lives on by the difference. And as the father of cybernetics, Norbert Wiener, suggested, information is originally nothing but *difference*.[90]

The most crucial 'point of distinction for Marx', Karatani further remarks, 'is the one between production in general and value production; value productivity is not determined by what it produces, but by whether or not it produces *difference*'.[91]

With this brief discussion of the economic notion of 'surplus-value' we can now return to its function in the Unconscious and its relationb to capitalism. Kordela in her *Being, Time, Bios: Capitalism and Ontology*, attempts to establish a relation between Spinoza and Marx in relation to 'pantheism' and the new configuration between thing and word after the collapse of the *organic* bond between them.[92] She cites Lacan who said that Spinoza's 'pantheism' means nothing other than 'the reduction of the field of God to the universality of the signifier'.[93] Kordela explains that

> For, to conceive of God as the immanent cause of the World amounts to conceiving of the world as a system of deferential relations, in which there is no cause transitively preceding and determining them. This is exactly what the signifier is: a system of differential relations. To say that God is Nature entails nature *is* a system of signifiers. This is the sole possible meaning of 'pantheism' once God is the immanent cause of the world.[94]

Based on this, she claims that although Freud is known to be the one who introduced the 'unconscious thought', it is Marx who, besides being the first inventor of 'symptom' as Lacan said, is also the inventor of unconscious. He did so in a way that 'makes amply clear that no reduction of the world to ideas is involved in the concept of pantheism'.[95] Kordela further points out that once 'objects' are transformed into commodities they are no longer material things but also signifiers, 'by the dint of the fact that they are now become abstract exchange-values'. Hence Marx's drawing on the ontological difference between the realm of exchange-value and that of use-value. As Marx said in *Capital*:

> Not an atom of matter enters into the objectivity of commodities as values; in this it is the direct opposite of the coarsely sensuous objectivity of commodities as physical objects. We may twist and turn a single commodity as we wish; it remains impossible to grasp it as a thing possessing value. However, let us remember that commodities possess an objective character as values only in so far as they are all expressions of an identical social substance, human labour, that their objective character as values is therefore purely social.[96]

'Commodities *qua* exchange-value' become 'suprasensible', or the 'language' of human, as Kordela reflects,

> since both exchange-values and signifiers are determined purely differentially within their synchronic systems, in which there is not 'an atom of matter.' By being economic values, commodities become also signs, linguistic or semantic values, since both obey the same law.[97]

Money as exchange-value and commodity as use-value are 'different modes of existence of value itself', as Marx writes. Objects of utility and exchange-values as signs are *empirically* given. But, and this is crucial not to miss, 'surplus-value' nowhere is given to be seen, it cannot be given in reality. It is therefore, a *transcendental* category, which Kordela calls 'purely *metaphysical*'. In her reasoning, employing the familiar Hegelian categories of 'in-itself' and 'for-itself', she goes on to argue that,

> Through Marx we understand that, while use-value and exchange-value are the phenomenological in-itself and for-itself, respectively, value-in-itself (surplus) is the *meta-phenomenological or metaphysical* being-in-itself-for-itself, the substance whose attributes are expressed empirically in the phenomenological being-in-itself and being-for-itself.[98]

Linking the 'unconscious' to 'surplus value' Kordela continues her line of reasoning, which in a way is close to Tomšič's argument in his *The Capitalist Unconscious*, as we have seen before. Kordela forcefully contends that, 'In the specific capitalist modulation of surplus and surplus-value, the unconscious of capital become surplus-value'. One might object here, isn't capital's most conscious intention the accumulation of surplus-value? No: capitalism's conscious intention is the increase of exchange-value. The two statements may be taken as saying the same thing *practically*, but as we saw emphatically insist, they do not *ontologically*, since surplus-value is not something I can ever have in my hand, unlike exchange-value (money) which I can. The 'Cunning' of capital, in precisely Hegelian sense, is that while it sees its essence and sole purpose of existence in the perpetual accrual of exchange-value, in truth and generally without knowing it, it serves the perpetual accumulation of something transcendent to its empirical reality, surplus-value'.[99] According to this argument, the *surplus* in capitalism remains unconscious, that is, it is not given to experience, or is the thing that is supported transcendentally. Finally, drawing on the close homology between economics and linguistic sign or 'semantic field', Kordela remarks that 'The economic modulation of ontological surplus as surplus-value within capitalism entails that a similar distortion must occur also in the semantic field and, by extension in human subjectivity', insofar as Lacan said, 'subject is the subject of signifier'.[100]

In conclusion: Architecture enters the logic of capitalism at two interrelated levels—the *logic of production* and the *logic of fantasy*. As we have seen, these two levels set the standard of the Marxian-psychoanalytical critique. Building as *signifier*, is simultaneously an *economic* sign and a *linguistic* sign. By definition, it is a *surplus-building*, as a differential structure or system of difference, which will signify 'what is in building more than building itself', on the analogy of 'what is in body more than the body itself', bearing in mind that, according to Lacan, there is only one *substance* known in the body: *jouissance*. This *jouissance*, or the 'surplus-enjoyment' is *valorized* by capitalism for its own profit. Building has a use-value not in itself but for other people. It attains *value*, when it is the object of exchange, that is, when it is *sold*, thus becoming a *commodity-building*. The *surplus* it generates undergoes *valorization* in the capitalist exchange. Since, as Karatani informed us, Marx 'technically abolished the conventional division between exchange-value and use-value',[101] building, by inference contains no exchange value as such. Building, therefore, becomes a use-value when it undergoes an exchange value, *ex post facto*. It becomes a commodity-building, which is its *salto-mortale* ('fatal leap'), when it is *sold* in the market, after the fact. This is the moment when building begins to speak. Building is prosopopoeia: *Ça parle*—It speaks. The commodity-building speaks, in the *social link*, when it becomes an exchange-value. It is only then that it becomes a use-value. Thus, building, as *value*, is the embodiment of 'labor' in the process of production and consumption, exactly in the same way Paul Valéry said that art is *value* (in his reading of *Capital*) when it enters into the circle of production and circulation thus becoming an exchange-value. Buildings as signifiers do not have *meaning*, they are linguistic *values*, they are the objects of *exchange* in the social network. Moreover, building, by appearing in the *capitalist unconscious*, enters the discourse of the *political*. If we follow Lacan's saying that 'the unconscious is political',[102] and follow Fredric Jameson's notion of the 'Political Unconscious', the moment that architecture, as the symbolic discourse functioning as a factor in *social antagonism*, enters in the 'capitalist discourse'—identified as the *fifth* discourse in the classification of Lacan's Four Discourses—it attains an Unconscious—a *political unconscious*.[103] As an element in the political unconscious in the symbolic discourse of society, architecture, as I have said elsewhere, is a fundamental *structure of fantasy*, at the level of ideology, functioning as an *imaginary* resolution of the Real social antagonism. [104]

Notes

1 Immanuel Kant, *Critique of the Power of Judgment*, ed. Paul Guyer, trans. Paul Guyer and Eric Mathews (Cambridge: Cambridge University Press, 2000), in 'First Introduction', 11, 20:206. Kant further remarks: 'To be sure, philosophers who otherwise deserve nothing but praise for the

thoroughness of their way of thinking have sought to explain this distinction as merely illusory and to reduce all faculties to the mere faculty of cognition. But it can be easily be demonstrated, and has already been understood for some time, that this attempt to bring unity into multiplicity of faculties, although undertaken in a genuinely philosophical spirit, is futile. For there is always a great difference between representation belonging to cognition, insofar as they are related merely to the object and the unity of the consciousness of it, and their objective relation where, considered as at the same time the cause of the reality of this object, they are assigned to the faculty of desire, and finally, their relation merely to the subject, where they are considered merely as grounds for preserving their own existence in it and to this extent in relation to the feeling of pleasure; and the latter is absolutely not a cognition, nor does it provide one, although to be sure it may presuppose such a cognition as a determining ground', 11.

2 Immanuel Kant, *Critique of the Power of Judgment*, 12, 20:208.
3 Kojin Karatani, *Transcritique: On Kant and Marx* (Cambridge: The MIT Press, 2005), 114.
4 Kojin Karatani, *Transcritique: On Kant and Marx*, 114.
5 Kojin Karatani, *Transcritique: On Kant and Marx*, 318, n. 47.
6 Kojin Karatani, *Transcritique: On Kant and Marx*, 318, n. 47.
7 Kojin Karatani, *Transcritique: On Kant and Marx* (Cambridge: The MIT Press, 2005), 115. Also see Immanuel Kant, *Critique of Pure Reason*, trans. and ed. Paul Guyer and Allen W. Wood (Cambridge: Cambridge University Press, 1998), 484–485, A444/B472–A445/B473.
8 Cited in Kojin Karatani, *Transcritique: On Kant and Marx*, 115–116. Also see Immanuel Kant, *Critique of Practical Reason*, trans. and ed. Mary Gregor, intro. Allen W. Wood (Cambridge: Cambridge University Press, 1997), 80, 5:94.
9 Kant, *Groundwork of the Metaphysics of Morals*, Revised Edition, ed. Mary Gregor and Jens Timmermann, intro. Christian M. Korsgaard (Cambridge: Cambridge University Press), 34, 4:421.
10 Kojin Karatani, *Transcritique: On Kant and Marx*, 117.
11 Kojin Karatani, *Transcritique: On Kant and Marx*, 119.
12 See Kōjin Karatani, *Nation and Aesthetics: On Kant and Freud* (New York: Oxford University Press, 2017).
13 Among the relevant works of Jacques Rancière in this area see the early, *The Politics of Aesthetics*, trans. and intro. Gabriel Rockhill, with afterword by Slavoj Žižek (London: Continuum, 2004), and *Aesthetics and Its Discontents*

(Cambridge: Polity, 2009), and the more recent, Jacques Rancière and Peter Engelmann, *Politics and Aesthetics* (Cambridge: Polity, 2019).

14 Kojin Karatani, *Transcritique: On Kant and Marx*, 21. In a different context Karatani returns to the same term 'cultural turn' saying: 'After the failure of the struggle centered on workers' occupation of factories, Gramsci, in his prison cell, came to realize that it was due to the state's and capital's control of the reproduction process of the labor power, and he found it imperative to render the struggle in institutions—such as in the family, school, and church—over cultural hegemony. This might be deemed the very initiation of the "cultural turn" (Fredric Jameson) of Marxism', 291.

15 See Slavoj Žižek, *Living in the End Times* (London and New York: 2010), 204.

16 Immanuel Kant, *Critique of Pure Reason*, trans. and ed. Paul Guyer and Allen W. Wood (Cambridge: Cambridge University Press, 1998), 156. In the translation that Karatani uses, the quoted paragraph continues as follows: '(In doing so we would also come closer to the language of the ancients and its meaning: among the ancients the division of cognition into *aiotheta kai noeta* [the sensible and the intelligible] was quite famous). The other alternative would be for the new *aesthetic[s]* to share the name with speculative philosophy; we would then take the name partly in its transcendental sense, and partly in the psychological meaning', in Kōjin Karatani, *Nation and Aesthetics: On Kant and Freud*, 16.

17 Kōjin Karatani, *Nation and Aesthetics: On Kant and Freud*, 16.

18 Kōjin Karatani, *Nation and Aesthetics: On Kant and Freud*, 16.

19 Kōjin Karatani, *Nation and Aesthetics: On Kant and Freud*, 17.

20 Kōjin Karatani, *Nation and Aesthetics: On Kant and Freud*, 17.

21 Kōjin Karatani, *Nation and Aesthetics: On Kant and Freud*, 18.

22 Kōjin Karatani, *Nation and Aesthetics: On Kant and Freud*, 19.

23 See Sigmund Freud, *Beyond the Pleasure Principle*, The Standard Edition, intro. Peter Gay (New York and London: W.W. Norton, 1961).

24 Kōjin Karatani, *Nation and Aesthetics: On Kant and Freud*, 49–50.

25 Immanuel Kant, *Critique of the Power of Judgment*, 142; also cited in Kōjin Karatani, *Nation and Aesthetics: On Kant and Freud*, 50.

26 Kōjin Karatani, *Nation and Aesthetics: On Kant and Freud*, 50.

27 As quoted in Kōjin Karatani, *Nation and Aesthetics: On Kant and Freud*, 49.

28 Jacques Lacan, *The Seminar of Jacques Lacan, Book VII: The Ethics of Psychoanalysis, 1959–1960*, ed. Jacques-Alain Miller, trans. Denis Porter (New York and London: W.W. Norton, 1992).

29 Jacques Lacan, *The Seminar of Jacques Lacan, Book VII: The Ethics of Psychoanalysis, 1959–1960*, 107.
30 Jacques Lacan, *The Seminar of Jacques Lacan, Book VII: The Ethics of Psychoanalysis, 1959–1960*, 107.
31 See Marc de Kesel, *Eros and Ethics: Reading Jacques Lacan's Seminar VII*, trans. Sigi Jöttkandt (Albany: State University of New York, 2009), 103–104.
32 Jacques Lacan, *The Seminar of Jacques Lacan, Book VII: The Ethics of Psychoanalysis, 1959–1960*, 112.
33 In Slavoj Žižek, *The Sublime Object of Ideology* (London and New York: Verso, 1989), 202–203.
34 Cited in Slavoj Žižek, *The Sublime Object of Ideology*, 203. I have used the new translation in previously cited Immanuel Kant, *Critique of the Power of Judgment*, 141. On this notion of the Sublime, Žižek bring his familiar Hegelian stance by noting that 'Hegel, of course, retains the basic dialectical moment of the Sublime, the notion that the Idea is reached through purely negative presentation—that the very inadequacy of the phenomenality to the Thing is the only appropriate way to present it. The real problem lies elsewhere: Kant still presupposes that the Thing-in-itself exists as something positively given beyond the field of representation, of phenomenality; the breakdown of phenomenality, the experience of phenomena, is for him only an "external reflection", only a way of indicating, within the domain of phenomenality, this transcendent dimension of the Thing which persists in itself beyond phenomenality'. Hegel's position is, in contrast, that 'there is *nothing* beyond phenomenality, beyond the field of representation. The experience of radical negativity. Of the radical inadequacy of all phenomena to the Idea, the experience of the radical fissure between the two—this experience is already *Idea itself as "pure", rational negativity.* Where Kant thinks that he is still dealing only with a negative presentation of the Thing, we are already in the midst of Thing-in-itself—*for this Thing-in-itself is nothing but this radical negativity*', 205–206.
35 See Kant, *Groundwork of the Metaphysics of Morals*, 41.
36 Kojin Karatani, *Transcritique: On Kant and Marx*, 128–129.
37 Kojin Karatani, *Transcritique: On Kant and Marx*, 129.
38 Kojin Karatani, *Transcritique: On Kant and Marx*, 129.
39 Kojin Karatani, *Transcritique: On Kant and Marx*, 129.
40 Karatani cites this same paragraph remarking that 'This drew from Ernst Bloch who had criticized the Marburg School as a Kantian revisionism of

tive" is by no means, as alleged by the bisectors of Marx, confined to the unyoung Marx. No Part of it was suppressed when Marx transferred what he had formerly termed "real Humanism" into the materialist philosophy of history', Kojin Karatani, *Transcritique: On Kant and Marx*, 130.
41 Kojin Karatani, *Transcritique: On Kant and Marx*, 130.
42 See Slavoj Žižek, *Sex and the Failed Absolute* (London: Bloomsbury, 2020), 11.
43 This definition was initially put forward in my co-authored book (with Libero Andreotti) entitled, *The Architecture of Phantasmagoria, Specters of the City* (Abingdon: Routledge, 2017), here I am expanding on it within the framework of the suggested Transcritique.
44 Karl Marx, *Capital, Volume One* (London: Penguin Books, 1990 [1976]), 163–164.
45 See Jacques Derrida, *Specters of Marx, The State of the Debt, the Work of Mourning and the New International*, trans. Peggy Kamuf, intro. Bernard Magnus and Stephen Cullenberg (London and New York: Routledge, 1994), especially chapter 5, 'The apparition of Inapparent'.
46 Karl Marx, *Capital, Volume One*, 164.
47 Karl Marx, *Capital, Volume One*, 164–165.
48 Karl Marx, *Capital, Volume One*, 167.
49 Karl Marx, *A Contribution to the Critique of Political Economy*, ed. and intro. Maurice Dobb (New York: International Publisher, 1970), 42–43.
50 Kojin Karatani, *Transcritique: On Kant and Marx*, 193.
51 Kojin Karatani, *Transcritique: On Kant and Marx*, 198.
52 Kojin Karatani, *Transcritique: On Kant and Marx*, 198–199.
53 Kojin Karatani, *Transcritique: On Kant and Marx*, 9.
54 Jacques Derrida, *Specters of Marx*, 151.
55 See Slavoj Žižek, 'Introduction: The Specter of Ideology' in Slavoj Žižek, ed. *Mapping Ideology* (London and New York: Verso, 1994). Žižek writes: 'Such a reading of spectrality as that which fills out the unrepresentable abyss of antagonism, of non-symbolized real, also enables us to assume a precise distance from Derrida, for whom spectrality, the apparition of the Other, provides the ultimate horizon of ethics', 26–27.
56 See Martin Warner, *Phantasmagoria: Spirit Visions, Metaphor, and Media into the Twentieth-First Century* (Oxford and New York: Oxford University Press, 2006), 147. Also see Libero Andreotti and Nadir Lahiji, *The Architecture of Phantasmagoria: Specters of the City* (New York: Routledge, 2017).

57 Martin Warner, *Phantasmagoria: Spirit Visions, Metaphor, and Media into the Twentieth-First Century*, 147.
58 In our time, Phantasmagorias are exclusively a means to produce what is technically called *simulacra* by means of high-tech digital media. For more see Libero Andreotti and Nadir Lahiji, *The Architecture of Phantasmagoria: Specters of the City*.
59 See Karl Marx with Friedrich Engels, *The German Ideology* (Amherst: Prometheus Books, 1998), 42.
60 See Sarah Kofman, *Camera Obscura of Ideology*, trans. Will Straw (Ithaca and New York: Cornell University Press, 1998), 13. Also see Libero Andreotti and Nadir Lahiji, *The Architecture of Phantasmagoria: Specters of the City*, 28.
61 Sarah Kofman, *Camera Obscura of Ideology*, 3.
62 Sarah Kofman, *Camera Obscura of Ideology*, 2.
63 See Walter Benjamin, 'Paris, Capital of the Nineteenth century', Exposé of 1939, in *The Arcades Project* (Cambridge: The Belknap Press of Harvard University Press, 1999), 14.
64 Walter Benjamin, 'Paris, Capital of the Nineteenth century', Exposé of 1939, 14–15.
65 For an extended analysis of 'anaesthetization' based on Susan Buck-Morss's reading of Walter Benjamin's 'The Work of Art in the Age of Technical Reproductivity' see Libero Andreotti and Nadir Lahiji, *The Architecture of Phantasmagoria: Specters of the City*.
66 Samo Tomšič, *The Capitalist Unconscious: Marx and Lacan* (London and New York: Verso, 2015), 5.
67 See Jacques Derrida, *Of Grammatology*, trans. Gayatri Chakravorty Spivak (Baltimore: Johns Hopkins University Press, 1976).
68 Kojin Karatani, *Transcritique: On Kant and Marx*, 232.
69 Quoted in Kojin Karatani, *Transcritique: On Kant and Marx*, 229.
70 Samo Tomšič, *The Capitalist Unconscious: Marx and Lacan*, 16.
71 Quoted in Samo Tomšič, *The Capitalist Unconscious: Marx and Lacan*, 17.
72 See Ferdinand de Saussure, *Course in General Linguistics* (New York: Philosophical Library, 1959).
73 Samo Tomšič, *The Capitalist Unconscious: Marx and Lacan*, 17.
74 Samo Tomšič, *The Capitalist Unconscious: Marx and Lacan*, 17.
75 Samo Tomšič, *The Capitalist Unconscious: Marx and Lacan*, 37.
76 Quoted in Samo Tomšič, *The Capitalist Unconscious: Marx and Lacan*, with a modified translation, 37; see Jacques Lacan, *Encore: The Seminar of*

Part II

> *Jacques Lacan, Book XX, On Feminine Sexuality, the Limits of Love and Knowledge 1972–1973*, ed. Jacques-Alain Miller, trans. Bruce Fink (New York and London: W.W. Norton, 1998), 138.

77 Samo Tomšič, *The Capitalist Unconscious: Marx and Lacan*, 18.
78 See A. Kiarina Kordela, *$urplus: Spinoza and Lacan* (Albany: State University of New York Press, 2007), 1.
79 A. Kiarina Kordela, *$urplus: Spinoza and Lacan*, 1.
80 A. Kiarina Kordela, *$urplus: Spinoza and Lacan*, 2.
81 A. Kiarina Kordela, *$urplus: Spinoza and Lacan*, 27–28. Kordela points out that 'Scholasticism adopted this Aristotelian model to its own purpose, namely to prove that the cause for the existence of all things lies in the creating will of God. God is both the first or efficient cause and the final cause, because of, and for the sake of which, all materials and formal causes exist. Scholasticism did not challenge the number of causes. In his *Summa Theologiae*, Thomas Aquinas, one of the major revisionists of Aristotle, maintained that all physical beings are subject to four kinds of change or motion (*motus*), fashioned after the model of the Aristotelian four cardinal causes. But, going beyond Aristotle, he also argued that the process in which A moves B, B moves C, and so on, cannot go on to infinity, for such an infinity would not explain anything. There must, therefore, be a different kind of "mover," a first mover not moved by another, and hence not a matter of the chain of movers and not of the same nature as all movable, bodily things. This mover is what Christianity calls God', 28.
82 A. Kiarina Kordela, *$urplus: Spinoza and Lacan*, 28.
83 Karl Marx, *Capital, Volume One*, 176–177.
84 Karl Marx, *Capital, Volume One*, 280.
85 Karl Marx, *Capital, Volume One*, 251.
86 Karl Marx, *Capital, Volume One*, 256.
87 Kojin Karatani, *Transcritique: On Kant and Marx*, 235. Karatani further explains that 'Meanwhile, the surplus value of industrial capitalism is attained *in a sort of* circulation process: capital purchases labor power from living laborers, who in consequence, buy back what they produce from capital (and at this very moment, *laborers are totally equal to consumers*). It is not that the individual workers buy the very same things they produce, but that in *totality*—and herein the concept of *totality* intervenes as a sine qua non—laborers qua consumers buy what they produce', 235.
88 Kojin Karatani, *Transcritique: On Kant and Marx*, 236.
89 Kojin Karatani, *Transcritique: On Kant and Marx*, 237.

90 Kojin Karatani, *Transcritique: On Kant and Marx*, 267. See also, Norbert Wiener, *Cybernetics: or Control and Communication in the Animal and the Machine* (Cambridge: The MIT Press, 1984).
91 Kojin Karatani, *Transcritique: On Kant and Marx*, 267.
92 See A. Kiarina Kordela, *Being, Time, Bios: Capitalism and Ontology* (Albany: State University of New York Press, 2013).
93 Quoted in A. Kiarina Kordela, *Being, Time, Bios*, 15.
94 A. Kiarina Kordela, *Being, Time, Bios*, 15.
95 A. Kiarina Kordela, *Being, Time, Bios*, 15. Kordela further argues that 'If Marx, unlike his contemporary economists, grasped the mechanism of capital, it is because he replicated the Spinozian reduction of the world to the universality of the signifier on the level of economy: He subjected all (commodified) nature to (exchange-)value, whereby nature—including humans and their labor as "objectified," "congealed," or "abstract human labor"—is not only the vast flock of "objects of utility" (use-value, i.e., no abstract value but a concrete physical, material thing) but also the aggregation of "sensuous things which are at the same time suprasensible or social," that is, "values ... as their [men's] language"', 15–16.
96 Karl Marx, *Capital, Volume One*, 138–139.
97 A. Kiarina Kordela, *Being, Time, Bios*, 16.
98 A. Kiarina Kordela, *Being, Time, Bios*, 18–19.
99 A. Kiarina Kordela, *Being, Time, Bios*, 20; also see A. Kiarina Kordela, *Epistemology in Spinoza-Marx-Freud-Lacan: The (Bio)Power of Structure* (New York and London: Routledge, 2018).
100 A. Kiarina Kordela, *Being, Time, Bios*, 21.
101 Kojin Karatani, *Transcritique: On Kant and Marx*, 8.
102 See Samo Tomšič, *The Capitalist Unconscious: Marx and Lacan*, 20.
103 For the notion of the 'capitalist discourse' in Lacan see Samo Tomšič, *The Capitalist Unconscious: Marx and Lacan*, Chapter 4: 'What is the Capitalist Discourse?' See Fredric Jameson, *The Political Unconscious: Narrative as a Socially Symbolic Act* (Ithaca: Cornell University Press, 1981); also see Nadir Lahiji, ed., *The Political Unconscious of Architecture: Re-Opening Jameson's Narrative* (Surrey: Ashgate, 2011).
104 See Nadir Lahiji, *An Architecture Manifesto: Critical Reason and Theories of a Failed Practice* (London and New York: Routledge, 2019).

Part III

Chapter 5

Toward a philosophy of shelter

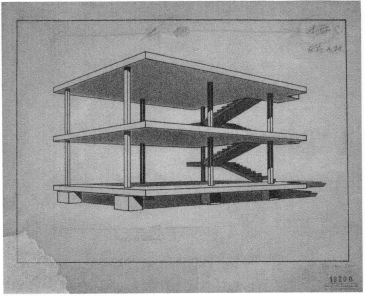

Figure 5.1 Le Corbusier, *Maison Dom-Ino* (Dom-Ino House), 1914. Credit: © F.L.C. / ADAGP, Paris / Artists Rights Society (ARS), New York 2019

Shelter, not a lofty tower

'Even if we do not need a lofty tower, we need shelter', writes Onora O'Neill in her exploration of Kant's Practical Philosophy. The key term in her commentary is 'Constructions of Reason'. Kant knew that we cannot 'turn our backs on the task of construction' when he said 'we cannot refrain from building a secure home'.[1] Alluding to the biblical story of Babel in Genesis in 'The Transcendental Doctrine of Method' of his *Critique of Pure Reason* Kant employed the metaphor of *building* in analogy to completion of his formidable philosophical task. He wrote:

> If I regard the sum total of all cognition of pure and speculative reason as an edifice for which we have ourselves at least the idea, then I can say that in the Transcendental Doctrine of Elements we have made an estimate of the building materials and determined for what sort of edifice, with what height and strength, they would suffice. It turned out, of course, that although we had in mind a tower that would reach the heavens, the supply of materials sufficed only a dwelling that was just roomy enough for our business on the plain of experience and high enough to survey it; however, that bold undertaking had to fail from lack of material, not to mention the confusion of languages that unavoidably divided the workers over the plan and dispersed them throughout the world, leaving each to build on his own according to his own design. Now we are concerned not so much with materials as with the plan, and, having been warned not to venture some arbitrary and blind project that might entirely exceed our entire capacity, yet not being able to abstain from erection of a sturdy dwelling, we have to aim at an edifice in relation to the supplies given to us that is at the same time suited to our needs.[2]

The first act in meeting the need for shelter, if we are not to be condemned to a 'nomadic' existence, consists of the '*plan*' to meet the deepest human needs including the 'needs of *reason*', O'Neill notes. At this point, an equation can be obtained: the needs of shelter = the needs of reason. Kant in the First Preface to *Critique of Pure Reason* tells us of the 'insatiable needs of human reason' which is at the 'heart of our very predicament':

> Human reason has the peculiar fate in one species of its recognition that it is burdened with questions which it cannot dismiss, since they are given to its problems by the nature of reason itself, but which it also cannot answer, since they transcend every capacity of human reason.[3]

When it is said that 'We may not need a lofty tower that reaches the heavens, but we do need at least a modest cottage [home]',[4] this must be strictly understood within the Kantian *ethics* of the Categorical Imperative. To recall, Kant in *Groundwork of the Metaphysics of Moral* wrote: 'There is therefore only a single categorical imperative, and it is this: *act only according to that maxim through which you can at the same time will that it becomes a universal law*'.[5] The Categorical Imperative, as O'Neill notes, is the 'supreme principle not just of practical but of all reasoning'.[6] Recall that Marx invoked the same Categorical Imperative:

> The criticism of religion ends with the doctrine that *man is the highest being for man*, hence with the *categorical imperative to overthrow all conditions* in which man is a degraded, enslaved, neglected, contemptible being—conditions that cannot better be described than by the exclamation of a

Frenchman on the occasion of a proposed dog tax: Poor dogs! They want to treat you like human beings![7]

In her reading of *Groundwork of the Metaphysics of Moral*, O'Neill notes that in Kantian moral law 'Instinct provides an inadequate basis for human life'.[8] This remark has a relevance for my purpose. Recall, again, Le Corbusier's dictum in the last chapter of *Toward an Architecture* I have cited repeatedly before: '*It is a primal instinct of every living being to ensure a shelter*'. The question is: Was the 'architect of the century' aware of this *inadequacy of instinct* when he used the term 'primal instinct' in this statement? Here I need to go back to the points I raised in 'Pedagogy' at the beginning of this book. There I claimed that Le Corbusier's statement, in essence, is an *egalitarian* maxim, in spite of the architect himself. I also raised a question about the term 'living being' in his statement. I suggested that this term must be associated with the Marxian notion of 'species being' or 'species life'. These are the points to which I can now come back. Le Corbusier was not of course a reader of Marx—far from it. He was rather afraid that by not paying attention to the problem of the 'housing shortage' we might get 'revolution'. To recall, this is what he said: '*la crise des logements aménera à la révolution, Préoccupez-vous de l'habitation*' ('the housing shortage will bring about revolution. Be alert to housing').[9]

After Le Corbusier issued his warning almost a hundred years ago—naïve as it may sound—we must reopen it for a critical examination in conjunction with what he said about shelter. I want to submit it to philosophical categories of *ethics* and *universality* and put it under the jurisdiction of the Idea of *equality*. More specifically, I want to put the Idea of *shelter* in an association with the Marxian term *proletariat*, hence identifying it with the *principle of universality*. I hasten to say that the thesis which I will derive from this association would be utterly unrecognizable to Le Corbusier, if not politically offensive to his *bourgeois* sensibility.

Anticipating what will come later, I first make a transition from Kant to Hegel to discuss the Right to shelter linked to the terms 'ethical life' and 'civil society' grounded in Hegel's *Philosophy of Right*. In a second move, I make a transition from Hegel to Marx and his scathing critique of the Philosophy of Right. The premise of my argument is that, in modern capitalist society, if we must discuss 'shelter' we must *also* discuss 'poverty'. In establishing a homology between *shelter* and *proletariat* and by grounding both in a discourse of *equality*, I follow Frank Ruda's remarkable reading of *The Philosophy of Right* in his *Hegel's Rabble*. I rely on the persuasive move which Ruda makes at the end of his inquiry in transiting from Hegel to Marx pointing out Hegel's failure in his political philosophy when he confronted poverty in bourgeois civil society.[10]

Marx brought up the notion of 'proletariat' for the first time in his 'Toward A Contribution to the Critique of Hegel's *Philosophy of Right*: Introduction':

> Where then is the *positive* possibility of German emancipation? *Answer*: in the formation of a class with *radical chains*, a class in civil society that is not of civil society, a class that is the dissolution of all classes, a sphere of society having a universal character because of its universal suffering and claiming no *particular* right because no *particular wrong* but *unqualified wrong* is perpetrated on it; a sphere that can invoke no *traditional* title but only a *human* title, which does not partially oppose the consequences but totally opposes

257

> the premises of the German political system; a sphere, finally, that cannot emancipate itself without emancipating itself from all the other spheres of society, thereby emancipating them; a sphere, in short, that is the *complete loss* of humanity and can only redeem itself through the *total redemption of humanity*. This dissolution of society existing as a particular class is the *proletariat*. [...] Heralding the *dissolution of the existing order of things*, the proletariat merely announces the *secret of its own existence* because it *is* the *real* dissolution of this order.[11]

The 'proletariat' is the non-part which is at the same time the Whole, 'a class in civil society that is not of civil society, a class that is the dissolution of all classes'. Strictly speaking, there is only one class, the *bourgeoisie*, and then a 'class' which is a non-class, the *proletariat*, a universal 'class' with no properly defined place within society. In other words, the proletariat is the *symptom*! Recall that, as we said, Marx was the inventor of the 'symptom', before Freud. The *wrong* that is done to the proletariat is the test of its *universality*. It is the *subjectivization* of this same universality. A point of dissolution of the same society that excluded it, or what Jacques Rancière has named 'the part-of-no-part'. As Slavoj Žižek has said, a 'proletarian subject' is in fact 'the evanescent point of the Cartesian *cogito*, deprived of its substantial content'.[12] What I want to say here is that, *shelter is a symptom*, a subject emptied of its 'substantial content', a point of the universality of building that has gone through a process of so-called 'proletarianization'. In this respect, we should not confuse the *empirical* building with the transcendental notion of 'shelter', exactly in the same way that we must distinguish the empirical 'working class' from the 'preliterate'. In this sense, the notion of shelter must not be confused with the scandalous *shacks* of the 'Planet of Slums' (to use the title of Mike Davis's book).

The *idea* of shelter, I claim, inherently entails *equality*. It is reported that Anatole France once sarcastically said that 'both the rich and the poor had an equal right to sleep under the bridges of Paris'.[13] Marx was not sarcastic though when he condemned—emphatically—the society in which people are accorded only 'formal' rights where there remain social and material inequalities. In his *Critique of the Gotha Programme* he wrote:

> This *equal right* is still— at least in principle—a *bourgeois right*, although principle and practice are no longer at loggerheads, [...] This equal right is an unequal right for an unequal labour. It acknowledges no distinctions of class, because everyone is a worker just like everyone else, but it tacitly recognizes unequal individual talent and hence productivity in labour as natural privilege. *Therefore in content this is a right to inequality, like all rights.* By its nature a right can only consist in the application of a common standard; but unequal individuals (and they would not be different individuals if they were not unequal) are only commensurable in terms of common standard, if they are brought within a common purview, grasped only in terms of *specific* aspects, e.g. considered in a given case *only as workers*, and nothing else about them is taken into account, all else being disregarded.[14]

This notion of *bourgeois right* will be 'transcended' in a communist society, as Marx told us:

> In a higher phase of communist society, after the subjection of the individual to the division of labour, and thereby the

antithesis between mental and physical labour, has disappeared; after labour has become not merely a means to live but the foremost need in life; after the multifarious development of individuals has grown along with their productive power, and all the springs of cooperative wealth flow more abundantly—only then can the limited horizon of Bourgeois right be wholly transcended, and society can inscribe on its banner: from each according to his abilities, to each according to his needs![15]

Earlier, in his *Economic and Philosophic Manuscript of 1844*, Marx wrote:

Equality is nothing but a translation of the German "Ich=Ich" into the French, i.e., political form. Equality as the *groundwork* of communism is its *political* justification, and it is the same as when the German justifies it by conceiving man as *universal self-consciousness*. Naturally, the transcendence of the estrangement always proceeds from that form of the estrangement which is the *dominant* power: in Germany, *self-consciousness*; in France, *equality*, because politics; in England, real, material, practical need taking only itself as its standard. It is from this standpoint that Proudhon is to be criticized and appreciated.

If we characterize *communism* itself because of its character as negation of the negation, as the appropriation of the human essence which mediates itself with itself through the negation of private property—as being not yet the *true*, self-originating position but rather a position originating from private property, [...]

Since in that case the real estrangement of the life of man remains, and remains all the more, the more one is conscious of it as such. It may accomplish solely by putting communism into operation.

In order to abolish the *idea* of private property, the *idea* of communism is completely sufficient. It takes *actual* communist action to abolish actual private property. History will come to it; and this movement, which in *theory* we already know to be a self-transcending movement, will constitute in *actual fact* a very severe and protracted process.[16]

Now I return to the term 'living being', the term Le Corbusier used in his dictum above, a term that needs to be taken apart from 'instinct' and instead be returned to the *object* of *labor* and the universality of *freedom*. Marx in the same *Economic and Philosophic Manuscript* wrote:

Man is a species being, not only because in practice and in theory he adopts the species as his object (his own as well as those of other things), but—and this is only another way of expressing it—but also because he treats himself as the actual, living species; because he treats himself as a *universal* and therefore a free being.

The life of the species, both in man and in animals, consists physically in the fact that man (like the animal) lives on inorganic nature; and the more universal man is compared with an animal, the more universal is the sphere of inorganic nature on which he lives. Just as plants, animals, stones, the air, light, etc., constitute a part of human consciousness in the realm of theory, partly as objects of natural science, partly as objects of art—his spiritual inorganic nature, spiritual nourishment which he must first prepare to make it palatable and digestible—so too in the realm of practice they constitute a part of human life and human activity. Physically man lives

> only on these products of nature, whether they appear in the form of food, heating, clothes, a dwelling, or whatever it may be. The universality of man is in practice manifested precisely in the universality of which makes all nature his *inorganic* body—both inasmuch as nature is (1) his direct means of life, and (2) the material, the object and the instrument of his life-activity. Nature is man's *inorganic* body—nature, that is, insofar as it is not itself the human body. […] For in the first place, labor, *life-activity, productive life* itself, appears to man merely as a *means* of satisfying a need—the need to maintain the physical existence. Yet the productive life is the life of the species. It is life-engendering life. The whole character of a species—its species character—is contained in the character of its life-activity; and free, conscious activity is man's species character. Life itself appears only as a *means to life*. […] Man makes his life-activity the object of his will and of his consciousness.[17]

Further Marx writes that

> Man therefore also forms things in accordance with the laws of beauty, it is just in the working-up of the object world, therefore, that man first really proves himself to be a *species being*. This production is his active species life. Through and because of this production, nature appears as *his* work and his reality. The object of labor is, therefore, the *objectification of man's species life*.[18]

Later in *Grundrisse* Marx will take up the same notion of 'species being' and equates it with '*human being*' when discussing how the product of one satisfies the need of the other, and vice versa, that one is capable of producing the object of the need of the other, and that each confronts the other as owner of the object of the other's need, this proves that each of them reaches beyond his own particular need, etc., as *human being*, and that they relate to one another as human beings; that their common species-being [*Gattungswesen*] is acknowledged by all.[19]

Alain Badiou in a conversation with Jean-Luc Nancy brings up the importance of the Manuscript of 1844 for his philosophy by renaming Marx's 'species-being' as 'generic humanity'. He says:

But I'd just like to add that there is something in the manuscript of 1844 that is decisive for me, namely the idea that the aspect of humanity that comes to the fore in Marx's historical era (which to a certain extent is also our era) is what he calls *generic humanity*. And generic humanity is very much a philosophical category. The whole problem is to identify, in existing societies, the trace, the recognizable figure, of this generic humanity. This is linked to the idea that human activity itself ought to be generic rather than specialized—to the critique of the division of labour […], on the basis of the idea that every individual should become a polymorphous worker— and to the very important notion of the end of the opposition between intellectual and manual workers. There is a whole Marxist anthropology on the future of the value of humanity as such, a value conditioned on what we might define as the generic dimension of humanity.[20]

In spite of the fault I find in Le Corbusier's way of putting his dictum, '*It is a primal instinct of every living being to ensure a shelter*', it must nevertheless be acknowledged that, once translated into his Maison Dom-Iino project of 1914, his dictum potentially contains all the germs of an emancipatory project for achieving *equality in shelter* for the *'generic humanity'*—then and now. I therefore hazard this equation: Maison Dom-Ino = Shelter + Generic Humanity. It is the fault of Le Corbusier's critics and admirers who attempt to *sensibilize-aestheticize* the Maison Dom-Ino project through excessive formalistic analysis, not to mention Le Corbusier's own fault to *sensibilize* the industrial products of his time that he would then rhetorically put it in the service of *aestheticization* of architecture, in order to provide a secure ground for the direction he took toward 'An Architecture'.

Universality of shelter and the philosophy of right

Shelter is a necessity, *Ius necessitatis*. The 'right to shelter' is embedded in '*The Right of Necessity*' that defines the limits of law. Kant in *The Metaphysics of Morals* wrote that 'the right of necessity says: "Necessity has no law (*necessitas non habet legem*)"'.[21] Geoff Mann reminds us that Kant, who was called the 'philosopher of the French Revolution', wrote these words three years after Robespierre's arrest and his execution on 27July 1794—9 Thermidor, Year II in the Revolutionary calendar. 'In truth, he only came to grips with *necessitas* through Robespierre and the Revolution. History realized what Kant then tried to rationalize, but ultimately failed to grasp'.[22] Yet, we must be mindful of what was envisioned by Kant on the ground of the *practical reason*, the moral law leading to the long-run of the 'kingdom of ends': from *necessity* to *freedom*. Here, coming back to the main concern I expressed in the beginning of this work, I must point out that the passage from necessity to freedom, and

Toward a philosophy of shelter

for that matter, the necessity of shelter, and ultimately the freedom from it, is not possible in a liberal bourgeois order, not without revolution, *pace* Le Corbusier—not after finishing the *unfinished* work of the French Revolution. In this regard, it is proper to note what Robespierre once said concerning 'honorable poverty':

> I envy not at all the advantageous share you have received, since this inequality is a necessary or incurable evil: but at least do not take from me the imprescriptible property of which no human law can strip me. Let me even be proud sometimes of an honorable poverty.[23]

As Mann comments,

> If a social order could exist in which material inequality has no moral or political relevance, in which one's wealth and income had no impact on one's participation as *citoyen*, then bourgeois liberalism might well be commensurable with the new world inaugurated by the Revolution. Only when he no longer believed the bourgeois order capable of accommodating an honorable poverty did Robespierre abandon this position and commit himself to the necessarily violent construction of a new society founded on a more radical equality, one in which poverty would not exist and hence would have no meaning.[24]

I will add that the *idea* of shelter and its necessity would have no meaning and will disappear once a new society is constructed on the foundation of this *radical equality*. We must keep in mind that liberal bourgeoisie is established on 'formal' equality, positing a clean division between abstract equal legal-political 'rights' and 'freedom' and concrete economic inequality of labor. Mann mentions the ideological differences, often stated, between the Girondins and the Jacobins concerning the difference between 'liberty' and 'equality'. But, he says, for either one, liberty and equality were both essential. For Robespierre, the link between them is necessity, the unrelenting constraint on the material and moral structure of all organized forms of social life. [...] Recognizing and accepting this constraint is not an unfortunate amendment to our common liberty, but essential to it: "freedom consists in obeying the laws we make for ourselves" [Robespierre]. If necessity imposes itself upon us, freedom consists in its embrace, in recognizing it as our own principle. Indeed, Robespierre turns this necessity into virtue. Acknowledging our irreducible equality before the law of necessity is an eminently *practical* morality. It establishes the one obligation that always holds, precisely because it is obliged to respect no other—*necessitas non hebet legem*.[25] When Robespierre asked the Convention: 'Citizens, would you want a revolution without revolution?', it was *equality*, Mann points out, 'that determined the distinction between an event and true transformation'.[26] I have already surmised how Le Corbusier would have responded to this famous rhetorical question.

Hegel in his political philosophy would follow Robespierre on the relation between freedom and necessity—the fact that the former cannot be abstracted from the latter. In his *Philosophy of Right* Hegel names the problem of necessity *Notrecht*, 'the right of law [*recht*] of necessity [*Not*]'.[27] He wrote:

In extreme danger and in collision with the rightful property of someone else, this life may claim (not in equity, but as a right) a *right of necessity* [*Notrecht*]; for the alternatives are

Toward a philosophy of shelter

an infinite injury [*Verletzung*] to existence with total loss of rights, and an injury only to an individual and limited existence of freedom, whereby right as such and the capacity for rights of the injured party, who has been injured only in *this* specific property, continue to be recognized.[28]

And further in *Addition*:

Life, as the totality of ends, has a right in opposition to abstract right. If, for example, it can be preserved by stealing a loaf, this certainly constitutes an infringement of someone's property, but it would be wrong to regard such an action as common theft. If someone whose life is in danger were not allowed to take measures to save himself, he would be destined to forfeit all his rights; and since he would be deprived of life, his entire freedom would be negated. [...] But the only thing that is necessary is to live *now*; the future is not absolute, and it remains exposed to contingency. Consequently, only the necessity [*Not*] of the immediate present can justify a wrong action, because its omission would in turn involve committing a wrong—indeed the ultimate wrong, namely the total negation of the existence of freedom.[29]

The problem of necessity addressed by the notion of *Notrecht* is always bound up with the problem of freedom. 'The recognition of immediate necessity is prerequisite to concrete freedom'.[30] In all of these Hegel is concerned with the plight of the poor. He tackles the problem in two key sections of *Philosophy of Right* on 'Civil Society' and 'The State'. Hegel's conception of 'civil society' goes beyond Kant's '*bürgerliche Gesellschaft*'. More accurately called 'bourgeois civil society', arising from the Industrial Revolution, is the society in which the distinction is made between bourgeois and *citoyen*, between political and civil condition, between 'private citizen and the state, standing side by side'.[31] As David Smith in his *Hegel's Philosophy of Right* explains, 'Hegel associates the citizen (Bürger) as bourgeois specifically with civil society [...] and he describes the bourgeois as private, that is to say, someone who is concerned with the satisfaction of his needs and lacks any political relation, unlike the *citoyen*'.[32] Hegel's theory of modern ethical life—*Sittlichkeit*—allows us to 'think of the contented *bourgeois* as being someone who identifies himself with the laws and institutions of modern ethical life for purely prudential reason, and thus remains a bourgeois rather than also becoming a *citoyen*'.[33] In Hegel, the idea of *Sittlichkeit*, the 'ethical life', unfolds in three moments of the family, civil society, and the state. In Hegel's view 'formalistic freedom', associated with liberalism, 'sanctions massive material inequalities between subjects through juridical equality in "the right of property" and leads civil society to develop an "external order" to ensure property rights [...] the "external state"'.[34]

Now it is from the very bosom of civil society with its liberal 'formal equality', and 'formal freedom' that what Hegel calls 'rabble' emerges. He crucially wrote that: 'This shows that, despite an *excess of wealth*, civil society is *not wealthy enough*—i.e. its own distinct resources are not sufficient—to prevent an excess of poverty and the formation of rabble'.[35] Hegel gives the example of England:

> The example of *England* permits us to study these phenomena [*Erscheinungen*] on a large scale, especially the result achieved by poor-rates, boundless donations, and equally limitless private charity, and above all by the abolition [*Aufheben*]

of the corporations. There (especially in Scotland), it has emerged that the most direct means of dealing with poverty, and particularly with the renunciation of shame and honor as the subjective bases of society and with the laziness and extravagance which gives rise to a rabble, is to leave the poor to their fate and direct them to beg from the public.[36]

In Mann's view, rabble 'conjures up both the sans-culottes of Paris 1793 and the mincing "people" Robespierre habitually recalled to chasten the Convention; it is both the revolutionary force and looming threat of revolution'.[37] Haunting *The Philosophy of Right*, and as a key figure in Hegel's political philosophy, the rabble, as Mann points out, is a product of civil society itself and, as such, is a modern phenomenon. 'And, since the rabble is the inevitable precipitate of an unregulated bourgeois civil society enjoying its "freedom"—which generates as much "deprivation and want" as it does riches—it is the inevitable outcome of the neglect of necessity'.[38] As Hegel wrote:

> When a large mass of people sinks below the level of a certain standard of living—which automatically regulates itself at the level necessary for a member of the society in question—that feeling of right, integrity [*Rechtlichkeit*], and honor which comes from supporting oneself by one's own activity and work is lost. This leads to the creation of a *rabble*, which in turn makes it much easier for disproportionate wealth to be concentrated in a few hands.[39]

And further in *Addition*:

> The lowest level of subsistence [*Subsistenz*], that of the rabble, defines itself automatically, but this minimum varies

greatly between different peoples. In England, even the poorest man believes he has his rights; this differs from what the poor are content with in other countries. Poverty in itself does not reduce people to a rabble; a rabble is created only by the disposition associated with poverty, by inward rebellion against the rich, against society, the government, etc. It also follows that those who are dependent on contingency become frivolous and lazy, like the *lazzaroni* of Naples, for example. This in turn gives rise to the evil that rabble do not have sufficient honour to gain their livelihood through their own work, yet claim that they have a right to receive their livelihood. No one can assert a right against nature, but within the conditions of society hardship at once assumes the form of a wrong inflicted on this or that class. The important question of how poverty can be remedied is one which agitates and torments modern societies especially.[40]

Disturbed by the problem of poverty in modern civil society, Hegel further said that

The emergence of poverty is in general a consequence of civil society, and on the whole it arises necessarily out of it … Poverty is a condition in civil society which is unhappy and forsaken on all sides. […] Because the individual's freedom has no existence, the recognition of universal freedom disappears. From this condition arises that shamelessness that we find in the rabble. A rabble arises chiefly in a developed civil society.[41]

This remark prompts Mann to say that we are back to Robespierre: '*Bourgeois civil society—liberalism—renders honorable poverty categorically impossible.* In "*this specific *society*," there is no honor in poverty, and the poor are, by definition, without honor'.[42]

In *Hegel's Theory of the Modern State*, Shlomo Avineri is among the earliest authors who brought up the notion of poverty in civil society as discussed in Hegel's *Philosophy of Right*. He significantly points to one area where Hegel was utterly unable to propose a solution for a problem that he rightly detected in modern industrial society. Avineri writes: 'After thus discarding the various possible alternative for the elimination of poverty, Hegel gloomily remarks that it remains inherent and endemic to modern society'.[43] This is the 'only time', according to Avineri, that Hegel 'raises a problem—and leaves it open'. Avineri further explains:

> Though his theory of the state is aimed at integrating the contending interests of civil society under a common bond, on the problem of poverty he ultimately has nothing more to say than that it is one of 'the most disturbing problems which agitate modern society'. On no other occasion does Hegel leave a problem at that.[44]

This last statement serves as point of departure for Ruda in his discussion of poverty and the problem of rabble in Hegel's *Philosophy of Right*, making a novel attempt at the old 'transition from Hegel to Marx'. The result of this attempt articulated in his *Hegel's Rabble* is extraordinary. Like Avineri, Ruda also starts with the notion that Hegel in his *Philosophy of Right* was confronted with a problem of poverty he could not resolve but goes a step beyond Avineri to show 'how poverty is only a necessary condition of a more fundamental problem that Hegel addresses under the name, "rabble"'.[45] But more importantly, Ruda begins with the idea that the 'appearance' of the rabble in Hegel's philosophy is a 'problem *of* philosophy and *within* philosophy but a problem with something other than philosophy: a problem with politics'.[46] The name of this problem, Ruda says, is 'rabble'. Hegel's failure on the problem of rabble, therefore, prompts us to conceive yet a different transition from Hegel to Marx: It is the transition from rabble to the proletariat. Ruda writes:

> If Hegel's theory is, as Marx had it, a theory of the *modern* state, it is because within it Hegel attempts to link two things: 1. The free self-realization of rational subjects whose historical advent he relates to the Reformation and 2. The condition of a legally regulated equality and justice that emerges with the French Revolution. If Hegel fails because of the rabble, this failure takes place under specifically modern conditions. The Marxian transformation of philosophy therefore has to be grasped as transformation that attempts to be appropriate to the historical conditions of modernity. If Hegel's *Philosophy of Right* is marked by its claim to think a relation between a conception of subjectivity in which the active realization of freedom is inscribed and a notion of justice—under the condition of state-secured systems of rights—one already attains the essential coordinates according to which the Marxian transformation of philosophy orients itself: subject, justice, equality.[47]

Marx, in contrast to Hegel, is not a thinker of the rabble but that of the proletariat, Ruda reminds us. This is the difference between the two; which must mark the new thinking of the old idea of the 'transition' from Hegel to Marx. From the moment that the word 'proletariat' appeared in the early Marx, precisely in 1844, in 'A Contribution to Critique of

Hegel's *Philosophy of Right*—Introduction', we must understand the word, as Stathis Kouvelakis points out, as the 'negative result of—or antagonistic force immanent in—bourgeois society' that reveal the 'void' constitutive of this bourgeois order, which would signify that 'Proletarian rule is not an ideal state to be realized in the future, not a negative version of bourgeois monarchy; it is that which, in bourgeois society [...] confronts that society with its own impossibility, its pure difference'.[48] Marx diagnosed that, as Ruda notes, 'civil society from a certain historical point of its development constantly produces the conditions which makes the emergence of the proletariat thinkable. Therein the proletariat, as the Hegelian rabble, is determined by a complete "improvement"'.[49] Its particularity, hence, is its universality. Anyone—*anyone*—in bourgeois civil society is latently proletarian. This is why the 'proletariat is a class which is no class and therefore constitutively distinguished from the working class'.[50]

The early Marx, the Marx of 'humanism', according to Ruda, is a thinker of proletariat as a 'subject of process of universal production in which the universality of human species-being is understood starting from non-being as equality of anyone in the form of unfolding eternal truths' that will prompt us to say that the humanism of early Marx is an '*angelo-humanism*, a humanism of impossibility. Its principle is: Man only truly lives when man is an angel to man'.[51] Ruda then asserts that this Marx of angelo-humanism turns politics which appears in Hegel's philosophy in the 'rabble' against him, that is, 'he puts the logic of politics through the name "proletariat" forth against the logic of philosophy and (re)introduces the condition of politics into philosophy. Philosophy is, at least, *after* Marx conditioned by the singularity of politics'.[52] From this Ruda concludes that 'There is no political philosophy which could escape the Marxian rupture without again returning, in one way or another, to the Hegelian problem of rabble. Marx introduced the true primacy of practice into philosophy, the primacy of the autonomy of political practice'.[53]

Based on the above argument, I come back to qualify the title 'philosophy of shelter' I have proposed. This philosophy must be ruptured, interrupted, interrogated, and disrupted by the *logic* of *politics*. It is the politics of Poverty and its political economy that must be problematized. The *idea* of shelter as *universality*, and as universality of production, which is production of universality, insofar as the Marxian 'species-being' is concerned, must go beyond the aegis of civil society and the state. We can say that the 'political philosophy' of shelter, at the same time, is a philosophy of shelter that has been interrupted by politics. When Le Corbusier said that '*It is a primal instinct of every living being to ensure a shelter*', he forgot to say that this 'primal instinct' is repressed and the need of shelter is denied, because he could not know that *the society which produces wealth is the same society which produces poverty*, and therefore it *cannot*, by definition, satisfy these needs. Le Corbusier did not have a political theory for what he advocated. He was *optimistically* naïve. He was not alone. The architect, in modernity, with very few exceptions, is incapable of political thinking. Moreover, Le Corbusier was incapable of putting the problem of shelter within the ethical imperatives of the civil society and the state, relegating its responsibility to the authority of a *state-secured system of rights*. Le Corbusier did not take to task the same industrial capitalism in which he uncritically put his full trust. He never understood that this system, this society, is inherently an *unjust* society. Le Corbusier confronted a problem that he could not solve: the 'housing problem'. 'Ensuring a shelter' is ironically a name for Le Corbusier's *failure*. It remained just an *idea*. While we must praise him for his *egalitarian* intention, we must not be shy in reminding him of his failure! At the same time, we must not be shy in defending him against *all* other architects who never walked same path as his, a risky and a frustrating path. The problem of shelter, as the problem of poverty, will continue to agitate modern liberal capitalist society. Architecture or revolution—No, revolution!

Notes

1 See Onora O'Neill, *Constructions of Reason: Explorations of Kant's Practical Philosophy* (Cambridge: Cambridge University Press, 1989), 12.
2 Emmanuel Kant, *Critique of Pure Reason*, trans. and ed. Paul Guyer and Allen W. Wood (Cambridge: Cambridge University Press, 1998), 627. As the editors note, Kant specifically is alluding to the 'biblical story of Babel (Genesis 11. 1–9)', 750.
3 Emmanuel Kant, *Critique of Pure Reason*, 99. The same passage is rendered in slightly different translation in O'Neill's citation: 'Human reason has this peculiar fate that in one species of its knowledge it is burdened by questions which, as prescribed by the very nature of reason itself, it is not able to ignore, but which, as transcending all its powers, it is also not able to answer', in Onora O'Neill, *Constructions of Reason: Explorations of Kant's Practical Philosophy*, 12.
4 Onora O'Neill, *Constructions of Reason: Explorations of Kant's Practical Philosophy*, 12.
5 Kant, *Groundwork of the Metaphysics of Morals*, revised edition, ed. Mary Gregor and Jens Timmermann, intro. Christine M. Korsgaard (Cambridge: Cambridge University Press, 2012), 34. Prior to this passage Kant explains that, 'When I think of a *hypothetical* imperative as such I do not know in advance what it will contain, until I am given the condition. But when I think of a *categorical* imperative I know at once what it contains. For since besides the law the imperative contains only the necessity of the maxim to conform with this law, whereas the law contains no condition to which it was limited, nothing is left but the universality of a law as such, with which the maxim of the action ought to conform, and it is this conformity alone that the

imperative actually represents as necessary', 33–34. The notion of 'maxim' is explained as follows: 'A *maxim* is the subjective principle for acting, and must be distinguished from the *objective principle*, namely the practical law. The former contains the practical rule that reason determines in conformity with the conditions of the subject (quite often his ignorance, or his inclinations), and is thus the principle according to which the subject *acts*; but the law is the objective principle, valid for every rational being, and the principle according to which it *ought to act*, i.e., an imperative', 33–34.

6 Onora O'Neill, *Constructions of Reason: Explorations of Kant's Practical Philosophy*, 20.

7 Karl Marx, 'Toward A Critique of Hegel's *Philosophy of Right*: Introduction' in *Karl Marx, Selected Writings*, ed. Lawrence H. Simon (Indianapolis and Cambridge: Hackett, 1994), 34.

8 Onora O'Neill, *Constructions of Reason: Explorations of Kant's Practical Philosophy*, 12. The relevant sections in O'Neill reading Kant's *Groundwork of the Metaphysics of Moral* are 4: 395–397.

9 See Jean-Louis Cohen's 'Introduction' in Le Corbusier, *Toward an Architecture* (Los Angeles: The Getty Research Institute, 2007), 67, n. 102. Translation was slightly modified.

10 See Frank Ruda, *Hegel's Rabble: An Investigation into Hegel's Philosophy of Right* (London: Continuum, 2011).

11 Karl Marx, 'Toward a Contribution to the Critique of Hegel's *Philosophy of Right*: Introduction', 38; for a slightly different translation see 'A Contribution to the Critique of Hegel's "Philosophy of Right". Introduction', in *Critique of Hegel's 'Philosophy of Right'*, ed., Joseph O'Malley (Cambridge: Cambridge University Press, 1970), 141–142.

12 See Slavoj Žižek , *Living in the End Times* (London and New York: Verso, 2010), 241.

13 See Steven B. Smith, *Hegel's Critique of Liberalism: Rights in Context* (Chicago and London: The University of Chicago Press, 1989), 101.

14 Karl Marx, 'Critique of the Gotha Programme', in *Marx: Later Political Writings*, ed. Terrel Carver (Cambridge: Cambridge University Press, 1996), 214.

15 Karl Marx, 'Critique of the Gotha Programme', 214–215.

16 Karl Marx, *Economic and Philosophic Manuscripts of 1844*, trans. Martin Milligan (Amherst: Prometheus Books, 1988), 123.

17 See Karl Marx, *Economic and Philosophical Manuscript of 1844*, 75–76.

18 Karl Marx, *Economic and Philosophical Manuscript of 1844*, 77.
19 See Karl Marx, *Grundrisse*, trans. and Foreword by Martin Nicolaus (London: Penguin Books, 1973), 243.
20 See Alain Badiou and Jean-Luc Nancy, *German Philosophy, A Dialogue*, ed. with Afterword by Jan Volker, trans. Richard Lambert (Cambridge: The MIT Press, 2018), 39–40.
21 See Kant, *The Metaphysics of Morals*, ed. Mary Gregor (Cambridge: Cambridge University Press, 1996), 28. Also cited in Geoff Mann, *In the Long Run We Are All Dead: Keynesianism, Political Economy and Revolution* (London and New York: Verso, 2017), 88.
22 Geoff Mann, *In the Long Run We Are All Dead*, 88.
23 Quoted in Geoff Mann, *In the Long Run We Are All Dead*, 90.
24 Geoff Mann, *In the Long Run We Are All Dead*, 90.
25 Geoff Mann, *In the Long Run We Are All Dead*, 99–100. Mann further remarks that 'To take from those who put their property rights or freedom of commerce before their neighbor's hunger is no crime against justice or peace, and to the extent that the poor must assert the right of necessity to the detriment of social order, that social order is exposed as neither just nor peaceful. For Robespierre, therefore, it is true that the principle of equality in this fuller sense became the foundation of revolution—as, some say, it must always be', 100.
26 Geoff Mann, *In the Long Run We Are All Dead*, 101.
27 See Geoff Mann, *In the Long Run We Are All Dead*, 148. In what follows I draw extensively on Chapter 6 of Mann's book entitled 'Necessity and Rabble'. I will also follow the analysis by David James in his *Hegel's Philosophy of Right: Subjectivity and Ethical Life* (London: Continuum, 2007).
28 Hegel, *Elements of the Philosophy of Right*, ed. Allen W. Wood, trans. H. B. Nisbet (Cambridge: Cambridge University Press, 1991), 154, §127, 154.
29 Hegel, *Elements of the Philosophy of Right*, §127, 155.
30 Geoff Mann, *In the Long Run We Are All Dead*, 150.
31 Geoff Mann, *In the Long Run We Are All Dead*, 151.
32 David James in his *Hegel's Philosophy of Right*, 70–71.
33 David James in his *Hegel's Philosophy of Right*, 110. Smith adds that 'This problem can be further illustrated with reference to the institution of modern ethical life which for Hegel provides the *bourgeois* with his main source of universal activity: the corporation', 110.

Part III

34 Geoff Mann, *In the Long Run We Are All Dead*, 152. Mann explains that 'the external state is not yet the "actuality of ethical life." It is rather the closer thing in Hegel to what we usually mean by "the state" today, that is, the Weberian state, and Hegel is in no way its champion', 152.
35 Hegel, *Elements of the Philosophy of Right*, §245, 267.
36 Hegel, *Elements of the Philosophy of Right*, §245, 267.
37 Geoff Mann, *In the Long Run We Are All Dead*, 157.
38 Geoff Mann, *In the Long Run We Are All Dead*, 157–158.
39 Hegel, *Elements of the Philosophy of Right*, §244, 266.
40 Hegel, *Elements of the Philosophy of Right*, §244, 266–267.
41 Hegel, *Elements of the Philosophy of Right*, 453n.
42 Geoff Mann, *In the Long Run We Are All Dead*, 160. Further Mann says that 'The "rabble-mentality," the product of poverty combined with a collective feeling of exclusion and dishonor, cannot be dependably neutralized by the exercise or acknowledgment of *Notrecht* alone. The necessity determining *Notrecht* is transformed in the rabble from a moment of desperate need to a structural condition', 162.
43 See Shlomo Avineri, *Hegel's Theory of the Modern State* (London: Cambridge University Press, 1972), 153.
44 Shlomo Avineri, *Hegel's Theory of the Modern State*, 154.
45 Frank Ruda, *Hegel's Rabble*, 4.
46 Frank Ruda, *Hegel's Rabble*, 4.
47 Frank Ruda, *Hegel's Rabble*, 5.
48 See Stathis Kouvelakis, *Philosophy and Revolution, from Kant to Marx*, preface by Fredric Jameson, trans. G. M. Goshgarian (London and New York: Verso, 2003), 331.
49 Frank Ruda, *Hegel's Rabble*, 170.
50 Frank Ruda, *Hegel's Rabble*, 171. Ruda points out that one must remember the Hegelian distinction between luxury and poverty rabble. If Marx in his conception of the proletariat takes up the determination of the rabble, it is obvious that he refers to the poor rabble. But what does then happen to the luxury-rabble? As soon as the 'proletariat' appears in the place of Hegelian rabble it becomes apparent that the luxury-rabble is the only true rabble. One can again see here that only poor rabble and not the rich rabble poses a problem of categorization. The poor rabble becoming-proletariat in Marx produces the insight that in civil society and the state there will always have

been one true rabble: the rich one, the luxury-rabble, the capitalist. For it the Hegelian judgments prove to be absolutely accurate: it is morally evil, i.e. corrupt, a mere negative understanding, which considers the ethical community only from the perspective of private interest', 171.
51 Frank Ruda, *Hegel's Rabble*, 179.
52 Frank Ruda, *Hegel's Rabble*, 179.
53 Frank Ruda, *Hegel's Rabble*, 179.

Coda: In defence of Marx

In his *Specters of Marx*, Jacques Derrida wrote: 'The responsibility, once again, would here be that of an heir. Whether they wish it or know it or not, all men and women, all over the earth, are today to a certain extent the heirs of Marx and Marxism'.[1] We might disagree with some of the things Derrida wrote in *Specters of Marx*, but we must at least agree with him when he says: 'one *must assume the inheritance* of Marxism'. Importantly he reminded us that 'Inheritance is never a *given*, it is always a task'.[2] Derrida put it bluntly when he asserted 'It will be always a fault not to read and reread and discuss Marx [...] Not without Marx, no future without Marx, without the memory and the inheritance of Marx'.[3] There will be no philosophical answer without Marx residing in its center. The pedagogical apparatus in the academy in general, and the architecture academy in particular, has repressed this inheritance of Marx. It conjures away 'what we will still dare to call the *spirit of Marx*'.[4]

Invoking the Freudian notion of *Unheimlichkeit* Derrida speaks of 'Marx spectrology' and asks: 'is this not our own great problematic constellation of haunting?' His own response is equally haunting:

> It has no certain border, but it blinks and sparkles behind the proper names of Marx, Freud and Heidegger: Heidegger who misjudged Freud who misjudged Marx. This is no doubt not aleatory. Marx has not been received. [...] Marx remains an immigrant *chez nous*, a glorious, scared, accursed but still a clandestine immigrant as he was all his life [rather an *exile*]. He belongs to a time of disjunction, to that 'time out of joint' in which is inaugurated, laboriously, painfully, tragically, a new thinking of borders, a new experience of the house, the home, and the economy. Between Earth and sky. One should not rush to make of the clandestine immigrant an illegal alien or, what always risks coming down to the same thing, to domesticate him. To neutralize him through naturalization. To assimilate so as to stop frightening oneself (making oneself fear) with him. He is not part of the family, but one should not send him back, once again, him too, to the border.[5]

The architecture academy has engaged in a shameless act of holding the immigrant Marx on the border behind the fence. It is afraid of him. It neither shelters him nor recognizes his right, granting him the right, as an Internationalist and an *exile*. His specter poses a threat to it and therefore must be conjured away. The academy has abdicated its *responsibility* to be an *heir*, to claim an *inheritance*—the inheritance of Marx.

Alain Badiou in *The End: A Conversation*, in a dialogue with Giovanbattista Tusa, reminds his interlocuter that when he said that Marxism is in a 'moral crisis' he was basically talking about a 'certain brand of Marxism', 'Marxism as a cultural phenomenon, shared by everyone, with its own system of historical references'.[6] He makes it clear that he was essentially talking about Marxism in a similar way to Jean-Paul Sartre, that 'Marxism is the unsurpassable horizon of our culture'.[7]

Coda: In defence of Marx

Badiou explains that Sartre was talking about Marxism insofar as 'Marxism was omni-present—whether one was for or against it, it was there'.[8] By saying there was a 'moral crisis', Badiou means that

> there is a good chance that, at some point, it will no longer exist, and indeed, I think that today it no longer exists. In this form, Marxism no longer exists. The socialist states are gone, along with any evidence of a Marxist culture, in differing states of health but present everywhere. So there was indeed a moral crisis of this particular Marxism, Marxism as an unsurpassable cultural horizon.[9]

From this he draws the conclusion that: 'we must resuscitate Marxism, but not that Marxism: as always, the resurrection is never in fact a resurrection of exactly the same thing. We must resuscitate the Marxism that we need today. And this Marxism will inevitably be resurrected'.[10] Why? Because:

> the hegemonic ideology today is liberalism. Which means that we have gone back to something like the years 1830–1840, that is to say we are in a moment when capitalism is conscious of its victory. In 1840, it was consciousness of its birth, of the enormous space that had opened up for it. Today it is consciousness of its victory. Which is not the same thing, but it has finally overcome the test, the test of the former Marxist hegemony, and has become established. And in the end we will rediscover, in a strange kind of way, at a very general level, the contradiction between liberalism and communism, the contradiction that structured the revolutionary and workers' movements throughout the whole of the nineteenth century.[11]

Coda: In defence of Marx

It is obvious, Badiou further says, that it is a 'matter of a new Marxism. The name "Marxism" itself will reappear. A communism will reappear along with it. And this is an inevitable confrontation with liberalism. [...] All of the great laws of elementary Marxism are especially visible and active today'.[12]

His interlocutor, Tusa, then poses this question to Badiou: 'What of revolutions today, then?' Badiou response is unambiguous:

> I would say that we are in an uncertain period but, in my view, a period that even so, in its own way, can be assured of resurrection of Marxism—this is the first point. In a struggle against a reconstituted liberalism, it is certain that the category of revolution must be re-examined, and will be re-examined, as a part of resurrection of Marxism, probably with an entirely new extension and signification.[13]

And further:

> As we can see, what we are looking for is a reactivation of the word 'revolution', in conditions which are no longer simply those of the violent overthrow of a hostile power, but which go in the direction of the effective construction of a society that will move beyond socialism towards communism, or will orient itself towards the sovereignty of the *common good*, as in the original definition of communism.[14] [emphasis mine]

In his impressive *The Structure of World History*, Kojin Karatani writes that

> in a sense, 1968 was a simultaneous world revolution. It arose unexpectedly and, seen from the perspective of political

power, ended in failure, yet seen from the perspective of what Immanuel Wallerstein calls 'antisystemic movements,' 1968 had a tremendous impact.[15]

Importantly, Karatani notes that 'On this point, it resembles the revolution of 1848'.[16] He further remarks that:

> In fact, 1968 was in many ways a reawakening of the outcome of the early Marx, Proudhon, Max Stirner, and Charles Fourier. What was the fate of the vision of simultaneous world revolution after this? Since 1990 it has served as a summons to reawakening the world revolution of 1968—really, of 1848.[17]

What is at stake in this determination is the notion of State. Karatani explains:

> In that sense, the notion of a simultaneous world revolution still persists today. But it is never clearly analyzed, which is precisely why it functions as a myth. If we want to avoid repeating the failures of the past, we need to subject the notion to a detailed analysis. To reiterate, simultaneous world revolution is sought by movements that seek to abolish the state from within. But the movements in different countries are characterized by large disparities in terms of their interests and goals. In particular, the deep fissure between Global North and South lingers—now taking on the rise of a religious conflict. A transnational movement will always fall prey to internal splits arising due to conflicts between states, no matter how closely its members band together. The emergence of a socialist government in one or more countries may make it possible to avoid this kind of schism, but would only lead

to a different kind of schism—that between movements that hold state power and those that do not. For this reason, any attempt to build a global union of countermovements that arise within separate countries is destined to end in failure.[18]

I insert a parenthesis here to note that if the Revolution of 1848 did not specifically contribute anything to architectural thinking, the period around the revolution of 1968 did, notwithstanding its shortcomings. The liberal-conservative academy arrogantly abandoned the pedagogical lessons of the latter revolution. What came after it is the reactionary Restoration, to evoke Badiou's designation characterizing our time since 1980.

A better understanding of industrial capitalism should lead us, Karatani says, to 'think countermovements against capitalism'.[19] For example, many people say that the core of social movements has passed from workers to consumers and citizens. Yet with the exception of those few people who make their living from unearned income (rentiers), every consumer and citizen is also a wage laborer in some form or another'. Karatani continues:

> Consumers are simply members of the prolertrait who have stepped into the site of circulation. This means that consumer movements are also proletariat movements and should be conducted as such. We should not regard citizen movements or those involving gender or minority issues as being separate from working-class movements.[20]

To wit: *We are all proletarians. We lay our claim on universality.*
Throughout this book, following our radical thinkers, I argued that Marx, and 'Marxism', for that matter, must in

Coda: In defence of Marx

our time be thought with Kant and Hegel—with a transition that moves from Kant to Hegel to Marx. Karatani, and Žižek who took the novel notion of *parallax* from Karatani's unprecedented reading of Kant, are two exemplary revolutionary thinkers in this enterprise—the former with his stimulating reading of Kant and the latter with his formidable reading of Hegel and dialectical materialism. In both, a *certain* 'spirit of Marx' is *present*, as Derrida would say. In different ways, they would concur with Badiou and the *Idea* of communism.

To conclude: to repeat with Derrida, there is *no future without Marx*. I make a leap of faith here and say: there is *also* no future for the *theory of critique* in architecture without Marx. The architecture academy must stop conjuring away the *specter* of Marx. I end with what I started: In upholding the 'Proletarian Enlightenment', recalling Fredric Jameson's phrase, I invoke French Revolution's 'Liberty, Equality, Fraternity', while at the same time making a note of Marx's insight in *Capital* that in the capitalist system, in the sphere of buying and selling labor power, the moment that a 'free' contract between a capitalist and a worker is concluded, 'is in fact a very Eden of the innate rights of man. It is the exclusive realm of Freedom, Equality, Property and Bentham'. The category 'Bentham' enters to spoil freedom/equality designated by the preceding categories, because, as Marx noted, and this is the last word,

> each looks only to his own advantage. The only force bringing them together, and putting them into relation with each other, is selfishness, the gain and the private interest of each. Each pays heed to himself only, and no one worries about the others.[21]

Coda: In defence of Marx

Notes

1 Jacques Derrida, *Specters of Marx: The State of the Debt, the Work of Mourning, and the New International*, trans. Peggy Kamuth, intro. Bernd Magnus and Stephen Cullenberg (New York and London: Routledge, 1994), 91.
2 Jacques Derrida, *Specters of Marx*, 54.
3 Jacques Derrida, *Specters of Marx*, 13.
4 Jacques Derrida, *Specters of Marx*, 53.
5 Jacques Derrida, *Specters of Marx*, 174.
6 See Alain Badiou and Giovanbattista Tusa, *The End: A Conversation* (Cambridge: Polity, 2019), 65–66.
7 Alain Badiou and Giovanbattista Tusa, *The End: A Conversation*, 66.
8 Alain Badiou and Giovanbattista Tusa, *The End: A Conversation*, 66.
9 Alain Badiou and Giovanbattista Tusa, *The End: A Conversation*, 66–67.
10 Alain Badiou and Giovanbattista Tusa, *The End: A Conversation*, 67.
11 Alain Badiou and Giovanbattista Tusa, *The End: A Conversation*, 67.
12 Alain Badiou and Giovanbattista Tusa, *The End: A Conversation*, 68.
13 Alain Badiou and Giovanbattista Tusa, *The End: A Conversation*, 70.
14 Alain Badiou and Giovanbattista Tusa, *The End: A Conversation*, 73.
15 See Kojin Karatani, *The Structure of World History: From Modes of Production to Modes of Exchange*, trans. Michael K. Bourdaghs (Durham and London: Duke University Press, 2014), 294.
16 Kojin Karatani, *The Structure of World History*, 294.
17 Kojin Karatani, *The Structure of World History*, 294. Here Karatani adds that 'as seen, for example, Antonio Negri and Michael Hardt's notion of a simultaneous worldwide revolt by the "multitude"—a multitude that is equivalent to the proletariat of 1848. To wit, the people who were called the proletariat in the 1848 uprising shouldn't be thought of as industrial workers: they were in fact the multitude', 294–295.
18 Kojin Karatani, *The Structure of World History*, 295.
19 Kojin Karatani, *The Structure of World History*, 290.
20 Kojin Karatani, *The Structure of World History*, 290.
21 Karl Marx, *Capital, Volume One* (London: Penguin, 1990), 280.

Bibliography

Afray, Janet, and Kevin B. Anderson. *Foucault and the Iranian Revolution: Gender and the Seductions of Islamism*. Chicago: The University of Chicago Press, 2005.

Althusser, Louis. *For Marx*. Translated by Ben Brewster London and New York: Verso, 2005 [1969].

Althusser, Louis, "From *Capital* to Marx's Philosophy." In *Reading Capital: The Complete Edition*, edited by Louis Althusser, Étienne Balibar, Roger Establet, Pierre Macherey and Jacques Rancière. London and New York: Verso, 2015.

Althusser, Louis. *Writings on Psychoanalysis: Freud and Lacan*. Translated by Jeffrey Mehlman. New York: Columbia University Press, 1996.

Althusser, Louis, Etienne Balibar, Roger Establet, Pierre Macherey, and Jacques Rancière. *Reading Capital, Complete Edition*. London and New York: Verso, 2015.

Andress, David. *The Terror: Civil War in the French Revolution*. London: Abacus, 2005.

Andreotti, Libero, and Nadir Lahiji. *The Architecture of Phantasmagoria, Specters of the City*. London and New York: Routledge, 2017.

Badiou, Alain. *The Century*. Cambridge: Polity, 2007.

Badiou, Alain. *Metapolitics*. London and New York: Verso, 2005.

Badiou, Alain. *The Rebirth of History: Times of Riots and Uprisings*. London and New York: Verso, 2012.

Badiou, Alain, *Trump*. Cambridge: Polity, 2019.

Badiou, Alain, and Jean-Luc Nancy. *German Philosophy: A Dialogue*, edited and afterword by Jan Völker. Cambridge: The MIT Press, 2018.

Badiou, Alain, and Giovanbattista Tusa. *The End: A Conversation*. Cambridge: Polity, 2019.

Baehr, Peter, and Melvin Richter, eds. *Dictatorship in History and Theory, Bonapartism, Caesarism, and totalitarianism*. Cambridge: Cambridge University Press, 2004.

Bensaïd, Daniel. *Marx for Our Time: Adventures and Misadventures of a Critique*. Translated by Gregory Eliott. London and New York, 2009.

Benjamin, Walter. *The Arcades Project*. Cambridge: The Belknap Press of Harvard University Press, 1999.

Benjamin, Walter. "Capitalism as Religion." In *Walter Benjamin, Selected Writings, Volume 1, 1913–1926*. Cambridge: The Belknap Press of Harvard University Press, 2004.

Benjamin, Walter, "Critique of Violence." In *Walter Benjamin, Selected Writings, Volume 1*, 1913–1926. Cambridge: The Belknap Press of Harvard University Press, 1996.

Benjamin, Walter. "Experience and Poverty." In *Walter Benjamin: Selected Writings, Volume 2, 1927–1934*. Cambridge: The Belknap Press of Harvard University Press, 1999.

Benjamin, Walter, "Paris, the Capital of the Nineteenth Century, Exposé of 1935." In The Arcades Project. Cambridge: The Belknap Press of Harvard University Press, 1999.

Benjamin, Walter. In "The Work of Art in the Age of Its Technological Reproducibility, Second Version." *Walter Benjamin: Selected Writings, vol. 3, 1935–1938*, edited by Michael W. Jennings. Cambridge: The Belknap Press of the Harvard University Press, 2002.

Bosteels, Bruno, "The Fate of Generic: Marx and Badiou." In *(Mis) Reading of Marx in Continental Philosophy*, edited by J. Habjan and J. Whyte. Palgrave: New York, 2014.

Bruno, Pierre, *Lacan, passeur de Marx, L'invention du symptôme.* Toulouse: Edition Ere, 2010.

Buck-Morss, Susan. *The Dialectics of Seeing, Walter Benjamin and the Arcades Project.* Cambridge: The MIT Press, 1989.

Carver, Terrell, ed. *Marx, Later Political Writings.* Cambridge: Cambridge University Press, 1996.

Clark, T.J. "Painting in the Year Two." *Representations* 47 (Summer 1994).

Clemens, Justin, and Russell Griggs, eds. *Reflections on Seminar XVII. Jacques Lacan and the Other Side of Psychoanalysis.* Durham and London: Duke University Press, 2006.

Cohen, Jean-Louis. *Le Corbusier and the Mystique of the Russia, Theories and Projects for Moscow, 1923–1936.* Princeton: Princeton University Press, 1992.

Comninel, Georg C. *Rethinking French Revolution, Marxism and the Revisionist Challenge*, forward, Georg Rude. London and New York: Verso, 1987.

Davidson, Neil. *How Revolutionary Were the Bourgeois Revolutions?* Chicago: Haymarket Books, 2012.

De Boer, Karin, and Ruth Sonderegger, eds. *Conception of Critique in Modern Contemporary Philosophy.* New York: Palgrave, 2012.

De Kesel, Marc. *Eros and Ethics, Reading Jacques Lacan's Seminar VII.* Translated by Sigi Jöttkandt. Albany: State University of New York, 2009.

De Saussure, Ferdinand. *Course in General Linguistics.* New York: Philosophical Library, 1959.

Derrida, Jacques, *Of Grammatology.* Translated by Gayatri Chakravorty Spivak. Baltimore: Johns Hopkins University Press, 1976.

Derrida, Jacques. *Specters of Marx, The State of the Debt, the Work of Mourning, and the New International.* Translated by Peggy Kamuf, intro. Bernd Magnus and Stephen Cullenberg. New York and London: Derrida Routledge, 1994.

Dolar, Mladen, *A Voice and Nothing More.* Cambridge: The MIT Press, 2006.

Dolar, Mladen. "The Legacy of Enlightenment: Foucault and Lacan." *New Formations* 14 (1991).

Doyle, William. *The French Revolution: A Very Short Introduction*. Oxford: Oxford University Press, 2001.

Draper, Hal. *Karl Marx's Theory of Revolution, The "Dictatorship of Proletariat"*, volume III. New York: Monthly Review Press, 1986.

Eyers, Tom, *Post-Rationalism, Psychoanalysis, Epistemology, and Marxism in Post-War France*. London: Bloomsbury, 2013.

Fehér, Ference, ed. *The French Revolution and The Birth of Modernity*. Berkeley: The University of California Press, 1990.

Fontana, Benedetto, "The Concept of Caesarism in Gramsci." In *Dictatorship in History and Theory, Bonapartism, Caesarism, and Totalitarianism*, edited by Peter Baehr and Melvin Richter. Cambridge: Cambridge University Press, 2004.

Furet, François. *Interpreting the French Revolution*. Cambridge: Cambridge University Press, and Paris: Editions de la Maison des Sciences de l'Homme, 1981.

Freud, Sigmund. *Beyond the Pleasure Principle*, The Standard Edition, intro. Peter Gay. New York and London: W.W. Norton, 1961.

Giedion, Sigfried. *Building in France, Building in Iron, Building in Ferro-Concrete*, intro. Sokratis Georgiadis, Translated by J. Duncan Berry. Santa Monica: The Getty Center for the History of art and Humanities, 1995.

Goetschel, Willi. *Construction Critique, Kant's Writing as Critical Praxis*. Durham and London: Duke University Press, 1994.

Habjan, Jernej, and Jessica Whyte. *(Mis)Readings of Marx in Continental Philosophy*. New York: Palgrave, 2014.

Hallward, Peter and Knox Peden, *Concepts and Form*, two volumes. London and New York: Verso, 2012.

Hazan, Eric, *A People's History of the French Revolution*. London and New York, 2017.

Hegel, G.W.F. *Elements of the Philosophy of Right*. Edited by Allen W. Wood. Cambridge: Cambridge University Press, 1991.

Hegel, G.W.F. *The Philosophy of History*, intro. C.J. Friedrich. New York: Dover, 1956.

Heine, Heinrich, "Religion and Philosophy in Germany." In *The Prose Writings of Heinrich Heine*. Newton Stewart: Anodos Books, 2019.

Heine, Heinrich. *The Prose Writings of Heinrich Heine*. Newton Stewart: Anodos Books, 2019.

Heinrich, Heine. *On the History of Religion and Philosophy in Germany and Other Writings*. Edited by Terry Pinkard, Translated by Howard Pollack-Milgate. Cambridge: Cambridge University press, 2007.

Home, Henry, Lord Kames. *Elements of Criticism*. London: Elibron Classics, 2005.

Hobsbawm, E.J. *Echoes of the Marseillaise, Two Centuries Look Back on the French Revolution*. London and New York: Verso, 1990.

Hobsbawm, Eric. "Goodbye To All That." *Marxism Today*, October 1999.

Hobsbawm, Eric. *How to Change the World, Reflections on Marx and Marxism*. New Haven and London, Yale University Press, 2011.

Israel, Jonathan. *Revolutionary Ideas, An Intellectual History of the French Revolution from The Right of Man to Robespierre*. Oxford and Princeton: Princeton University Press, 2014.

James, David. *Hegel's Philosophy of Right, Subjectivity and Ethical Life*. London: Continuum, 2007.

Jameson, Fredric. *An American Utopia: Dual Power and the Universal Army*. Edited by Slavoj Žižek. London and New York: Verso, 2016.

Jameson, Fredric. *The Political Unconscious, Narrative as a Socially Symbolic Act*. Ithaca: Cornell University Press, 1981.

Jameson, Fredric. *Representing Capital, A Reading of Volume One*. London and New York: Verso, 2011.

Kant, Immanuel. "An Answer to the Question: What is Enlightenment (1784)." In *Perpetual Peace and Other Essays*, translated by Ted Humphrey. Indianapolis: Hackett, 1983.

Kant, Immanuel. *Critique of the Power of Judgment*. Edited by Paul Guyer, Translated by Paul Guyer and Eric Mathews. Cambridge: Cambridge University Press, 2000.

Kant, Immanuel. *Critique of Pure Reason*. Translated and edited by Paul Guyer and Allen W. Woods. Cambridge: Cambridge University Press,1998.

Kant, Immanuel, *Critique of Practical Reason*. Translated and edited by Mary Gregor, intro. Allen W. Wood. Cambridge: Cambridge University Press, 1997.

Kant, Immanuel, "Dreams of a Visionary Explained by Dreams of Metaphysics" [1766]. In *The Philosophy of Kant*, edited by and intro. Carl. J. Friedrich. New York: The Modern Library, 1993.

Kant, Immanuel. *Groundwork of the Metaphysics of Morals*, revised edition, edited by Mary Gregor and Jens Timmerman, intro. Christian M. Korsgaard. Cambridge: Cambridge University Press, 2012.

Karatani, Kojin. *Architecture as Metaphor: Language, Number, Money*. Cambridge: MIT Press, 1995.

Karatani, Kojin. "Critique is Impossible Without Moves', An Interview with Kojin Karatani by Joel Wainwright." *Human Geography* 2, no. 1 (2012): 30–52.

Karatani, Kojin. *Nation and Aesthetics: On Kant and Freud*. New York: Oxford University Press, 2017.

Karatani, Kojin. *The Structure of World History: From Modes of Production to Modes of Exchange*. Translated by Michael K. Bourdaghs. Durham and London: Duke University Press, 2014.

Karatani, Kojin. *Transcritique: On Kant and Marx*. Cambridge: MIT Press, 2005.

Keynes, John Maynard. *The General Theory of Employment, Interest, and Money*. San Diego: Harvest/Harcourt, 1964.

Kofman, Sarah. *Camera Obscura of Ideology*. Translated by Will Straw. Ithaca and New York: Cornell University Press, 1998.

Kordela, A. Kiarina. *Being, Time, Bios: Capitalism and Ontology*. Albany: Suny Press, 2013.

Kordela, A. Kiarina, *Epistemology in Spinoza-Marx-Freud-Lacan: The (Bio)Power of Structure*. New York and London: Routledge, 2018.

Kordela, A. Kiarina. *$urplus: Spinoza, Lacan*. Albany: Suny Press, 2007.

Kouvelakis, Stathis. *Philosophy and Revolution from Kant to Marx*, preface. Fredric Jameson. London and New York: Verso, 2003.

Lacan, Jacques, *Autres écrits*. Paris: Seuil, 2001.

Lacan, Jacques. *Desire and Its Interpretation, The Seminar of Jacques Lacan, Book VI*. Edited by Jacques-Alain Miller, Translated by Bruce Fink. Cambridge: Polity, 2019.

Lacan, Jacques. *Encore: The Seminar of Jacques Lacan, Book XX, On Feminine Sexuality, the Limits of Love and Knowledge 1972–1973*. Edited by Jacques-Alain Miller, Translated by Bruce Fink. New York and London: W.W. Norton, 1998.

Lacan, Jacques. *The Ethics of Psychoanalysis, The Seminar of Jacques Lacan, Book VII, 1959–1960*. Edited by Jacques-Alain Miller. Translated Denis Porter. New York and London: W. W. Norton, 1992.

Lacan, Jacques. *The Other Side of Psychoanalysis, The Seminar of Jacques Lacan, Book XVII*. Translated by Russell Grigg. New York and London: W.W. Norton, 2007.

Lahiji, Nadir, ed. *The Political Unconscious of Architecture , Re-Opening Jameson's Narrative*. Sorrey: Ashgate, 2011.

Lahiji, Nadir. *An Architecture Manifesto: Critical Reason and Theories of a Failed Practice*. London and New York: Routledge, 2019.

Lahiji, Nadir. "The Gift of the Open Hand: Le Corbusier Reading Georges Bataille's *La Part Maudite*." *Journal of Architectural Education*, September 1996.

Le Corbusier. *The City of To-Morrow and its Planning*. New York: Dover, 1987.

Le Corbusier. *Toward An Architecture*. Translated by John Goodman, intro. Jean-Louis Cohen. Los Angeles: Getty Research Institute, 2007.

Le Corbusier. *Vers une architecture*. Paris: Flammarion, 1995.

Liedman, Sven-Eric. *A World to Win, the Life and Works of Karl Marx*. London and New York: Verso, 2018.

Löwy, Michael. *The Theory of Revolution in the Young Marx*. Chicago: Haymarket Books, 2003.

Losurdo, Dominico. *Hegel and the Freedom of Moderns*. Durham and London: Duke University, 2004.

Magee, Glenn Alexandre. *The Hegel Dictionary*. London: Continuum, 2010.

Mallet, Robert, ed. *Self-Portrait: The Gide/Valéry Letters 1890–1942*. Abridged and Translated by June Guicharnaud. Chicago and London: The University of Chicago Press, 1966.

Mann, Geoff. *In the Long Run We Are All Dead, Keynesianism, Political Economy and Revolution*. London and New York: Verso, 2017.

Marx, Karl, "A Contribution to the Critique of Hegel's 'Philosophy of Right': Introduction." In *Karl Marx: Selected Writings*, edited by Lawrence H. Simon. Indianapolis: Hackett, 1994.

Marx, Karl, *A Contribution to the Critique of Political Economy*, edited by and intro. Maurice Dobb. New York: International Publisher, 1970.

Marx, Karl, "A Contribution to the Critique of Political Economy—Preface." In *Marx, Later Political Writings*, edited by Terrell Carver. Cambridge: Cambridge University Press, 1996.

Marx, Karl. *Capital, Volume 1*. New York: Penguin Books, 1990.

Marx, Karl. *Critique of Hegel's 'Philosophy of Right'*. Translated by Annette Jolin and Joseph O'Malley, Edited by and translated by Joseph O'Malley. Cambridge: Cambridge University Press, 1970.

Marx, Karl, "Critique of the Gotha Programme." In *Marx: Later Political Writings*, edited by Terrel Carver. Cambridge: Cambridge University Press, 1996.

Marx, Karl. *Economic and Philosophical Manuscripts of 1844*. Translated by Martin Milligan. New York: Promethean Books, 1988.

Marx, Karl. *Grundrisse*. London: Penguin, 1973.

Marx, Karl. *Later Political Writings*. Edited by Terrell Carver. Cambridge: Cambridge University Press, 1996.

Marx, Karl, *The Metaphysics of Morals*, edited by Mary Gregor. Cambridge: Cambridge University Press, 1996.

Marx, Karl, "Towards A Critique of *Hegel's Philosophy of Right*: Introduction." In *Karl Marx, Selected Writings*, edited by Lawrence H. Simon. Indianapolis: Hackett, 1994.

Marx, Karl with Friedrich Engels. *The German Ideology: Includes Theses on Feuerbach and Introduction to the Critique of Political Economy*. New York: Prometheus Books, 1998.

Marx, Karl and V.I. Lenin, *Civil War in France: The Paris Commune*, with essay by Nikita Fedorovsky. New York: International Publishers, 1940.

McCole, John. *Walter Benjamin and the Antinomies of Tradition*. Ithaca and London: Cornell University Press, 1993.

McGowan, Todd. *Emancipation After Hegel, Achieving a Contradictory Revolution*. New York: Columbia University Press, 2019.

McLoad, Mary. "'Architecture or Revolution": Taylorism, Technocracy, and Social Change." *Art Journal* 43, no. 2 (Summer 1983).

McQuillan, Colin, "Beyond the Limits of Reason: Kant, Critique and Enlightenment." In *Conception of Critique in Modern Contemporary Philosophy*, edited by Karin de Boer and Ruth Sonderegger. New York: Palgrave, 2012.

Murthy, Viren and Yasuo Kobayashi, *History and Heteronomy: Critical Essays*. Tokyo: UTCP, 2009.

Negri, Antonio. "Keynes and the Capitalist Theory of the State post-1929" [1968]. In Antonio Negri, *Revolution Retrieved: Writing on Marx, Keynes, Capitalist Crisis and New Social Subjects*. London: Red Notes, 1988.

O'Neill, Onora. *Constructions of Reason, Explorations of Kant's Practical Philosophy*. Cambridge: Cambridge University Press, 1989.

Plessis, Alain. *The Rise and Fall of the Second Empire, 1852–1871*. Cambridge: Cambridge University Press and Paris: Editions de la Maison des Sciences de l'Homme, 1985.

Plessis, Alain. *The Rise and Fall of the Second Empire, 1852–1871*. Cambridge: Cambridge University Press, 1987.

Postone, Moish. *Time, Labor, and Social Domination, A Reinterpretation of Marx's Critical Theory*. Cambridge: Cambridge University Press, 1993.

Rancière, Jacques. *Aesthetics and Its Discontents*. Cambridge: Polity, 2009.

Rancière, Jacques. *The Politics of Aesthetics*. Translated and intro. Gabriel Rockhill, with afterword by Slavoj Žižek. London: Continuum, 2004.

Rancière, Jacques, and Peter Engelmann. *Politics and Aesthetics*. Cambridge: Polity, 2019.

Ritter, Joachim. *Hegel and the French Revolution, Essays on The Philosophy of Right*. Translated by Ricard Dien Winfield. Cambridge: The MIT Press, 1984.

Bibliography

Robespierre, Maximilien. *Virtue and Terror*, Intro. Slavoj Žižek. London and New York: Verso, 2007.

Robinson, Joan. "Latter Day Capitalism." *New Left Review* 1 (1962): 16.

Ruda, Frank. *Hegel's Rabble, An investigation into Hegel's Philosophy of Right*, preface by Slavoj Žižek. London: Continuum, 2011.

Scurr, Ruth. *Fatal Purity, Robespierre and the French Revolution*. New York: Holt, 2006.

Shlomo, Avinerim, *Hegel's Theory of the Modern State*. London: Cambridge University Press, 1972.

Skidelsky, Robert. *Keynes, A Very Short Introduction*. Oxford: Oxford University, 2010.

Smith, Steven B. *Hegel's Critique of Liberalism: Rights in Context*. Chicago and London: University of Chicago Press, 1989.

Smith, Steven B., "Hegel and the French Revolution: An Epitaph for Republicanism." In *The French Revolution and the Birth of Modernity*, edited by Ference Fehér. Berkeley: University of California Press, 1990.

Sohn-Rethel, Alfred, *Intellectual and Manual Labour: A Critique of Epistemology*. Atlantic Highland: Humanities Press, 1977.

Tafuri, Manfredo. *Architecture and Utopia, Design and Capitalist Development*. Cambridge: The MIT Press, 1979.

Tomšič, Samo. *The Capitalist Unconscious*. London, New York: Verso, 2015.

Vaughan, William, and Helen Weston, eds. *David's The Death of Marat*. Cambridge: Cambridge University Press, 2000.

Vighi, Fabio. *On Žižek's Dialectics, Surplus, Subtraction,, Sublimation*. London: Continuum, 2010.

Villari, Sergio. *J.N.L. Durand (1760–1834), Art and Science of Architecture*. New York: Rizzoli, 1990.

Vogt, Max Adolf, *Le Corbusier, the Nobel Savage: Toward an Archaeology of Modernism*. Translated by Radka Donnell. Cambridge: The MIT Press, 1998.

Wahnich, Sophie. *In Defence of the Terror, Liberty or Death in the French Revolution*, forward by Slavoj Žižek. London and New York: Verso, 2012.

Wallerstein, Immanuel. "The French Revolution as a World-Historical System." In *The French Revolution and the Birth of Modernity*, edited by Ference Fehér. Berkeley: University of California Press, 1990.

Wallenstein, Sven Olov. *Architecture, Critique, Ideology: Writings on Architecture and Theory*. Stockholm: Axl, 2016.

Warner, Martin. *Phantasmagoria: Spirit Visions, Metaphor, and Media into the Twentieth-First Century*. Oxford and New York: Oxford University Press, 2006.

Weber, Nicholas Fox. *Le Corbusier, A Life*. New York: Alfred A. Knopf, 2008.

Wiener, Norbert, *Cybernetics: or Control and Communication in the Animal and the Machine*. Cambridge: The MIT Press, 1984.

Willett, John. "Art and Revolution." *New Left Review* 112 (July/August 2018), 61-87.

Wood, Ellen Meiksins. *Democracy Against Capitalism, Renewing Historical Materialism*. Cambridge: Cambridge University Press, 1995.

Žižek, Slavoj. *Absolute Recoil, Towards A New Foundation of Dialectical Materialism*. London and New York: Verso, 2014.

Žižek, Slavoj, *Did Somebody Say Totalitarianism? Five Interventions in the (Mis)Use of a Notion*. London and New York: Verso, 2001.

Žižek, Slavoj. *In Defense of Lost Causes*. London and New York: Verso, 2008.

Žižek, Slavoj. *First as Tragedy, Then as Farce*. London and New York: Verso, 2009.

Žižek, Slavoj. "Introduction: The Specter of Ideology." In *Mapping Ideology*, edited by Slavoj Žižek. London and New York: Verso, 1994.

Žižek, Slavoj. *Less Than Nothing, Hegel and the Shadow of Dialectical Materialism*. London and New York: Verso, 2012.

Žižek, Slavoj. *Like a Thief in Broad Daylight: Power in the End of Post-Humanity*. London: Penguin, 2018.

Žižek, Slavoj. *Living in the End Times*. London and New York: Verso, 2010.

Žižek, Slavoj. *The Parallax View*. Cambridge: The MIT Press, 2006.
Žižek, Slavoj. "The Parallax View." *New Left Review* 25 (January–February 2004).
Žižek, Slavoj. *Sex and the Failed Absolute*. London: Bloomsbury, 2020.
Žižek, Slavoj. *The Sublime Object of Ideology*. London and New York: Verso, 1989.
Žižek, Slavoj. *Tarrying With Negative, Kant, Hegel, and the Critique of Ideology*. Durham: Duke University Press, 1993.
Žižek, Slavoj, Frank Ruda, and Agon Hamza. *Reading Marx*. Cambridge: Polity, 2018.
Zupančič, Alenka, *Ethics of the Real*. London and New York: Verso, 2000.
Zupančič, Alenka, "When Surplus Enjoyment Meets Surplus Value." In *Reflections on Seminar XVII. Jacques Lacan and the Other Side of Psychoanalysis*, edited by Justin Clemens and Russell Griggs. Durham and London: Duke University Press, 2006.

Index

Adorno, Theodor 146
Althusser, Louis 10, 13–14, 19, 147, 155, 167, 170–172, 175, 191, 195, 201, 220, 228, 289
anaesthetization 5, 200, 227, 257
architecture 1, 3, 5–6, 8, 11, 13–15, 18, 23–24, 26–31, 33–34, 36–38, 42, 47–49, 50–51, 53, 55, 57, 59, 60–67, 69, 71, 73, 75–79, 81, 83, 85, 87–89, 91, 93, 95, 97, 99, 101–103, 105, 107, 109–111, 113, 115, 117–122, 125–131, 133–134, 189–203, 205, 207, 209, 211, 213, 215–217, 221, 223, 225–227, 229, 231, 233, 235, 237, 239, 241–243, 245–247, 249, 256, 264, 275–276, 280–281, 286, 289, 294–295, 297–299

Badiou, Alain 4, 18, 41, 44, 63, 65, 73, 94, 103–127, 131, 161, 162, 194, 263, 277, 281–285, 286–287, 289, 290
Baron Haussmann 51, 102, 108, 114
Bataille, George 34, 38, 43, 120, 133, 295

Baudelaire, Charles 54, 59, 60, 61, 115, 116
Benjamin, Walter 3, 5–7, 18–19, 36, 43–44, 48–51, 64–65, 67, 70–74, 81, 86, 89, 92, 94, 97, 103, 107, 108–110, 115–116, 118, 131–133, 216, 225–226, 247, 290–291, 297
Bensaïd, Daniel 4, 18, 290
Bentham, Jeremy 203, 234, 235, 286
blank wall 47, 49, 51, 53, 55, 57
bonapartism 32, 37, 65, 102–103, 105–113, 117, 119, 121, 122–123, 125, 126–127, 129–133, 226–227, 290, 292
Boullée, Etienne-Louis 53
bourgeoisie 40, 42–43, 48–49, 66, 86, 89, 109, 113, 116–117, 258, 265
Borromean Knot 10, 200–201, 203, 206, 226
Breton, André 51
Buck-Morss, Susan 65, 94, 247, 291
building 23, 28, 32, 38, 40, 43, 94, 104–105, 109, 115, 119, 131, 132, 200–201, 207, 221–222, 226, 241–242, 254, 258, 292
bürgerliche Gesellschaft 267

301

Index

Caesarism 103, 110, 112, 130, 132, 290, 292
camera obscura 223, 224, 247, 294
capitalism 2–4, 6–8, 11, 16, 18, 19, 23, 29, 31–34, 36, 39, 40, 43, 67, 78, 97, 103–106, 108, 112, 119, 122, 124–125, 129, 133, 144, 159, 162, 169, 172, 181–182, 186–188, 190, 193, 206–207, 214, 228, 235–238, 240–241, 248–249, 274, 282, 285, 290, 294, 298–299
Carver, Terrell 25, 112, 132–133, 291, 196
citoyen 265, 268
civil society 38, 41, 52, 83, 92, 98, 118, 123, 125, 141, 225, 257, 225, 257–258, 267–271, 273–274, 278
Clark, T. J. 54, 58–59, 91, 93, 291
commodity 22, 146, 156–158, 164, 166–167, 172–174, 182, 186, 194, 196, 203, 207, 213, 214, 216, 217–218, 220–223, 225–226, 228–229, 234, 236, 239–242
Commune 48–49, 74, 98, 117, 225, 296
communism 2, 4, 8, 12, 67, 104, 106, 125, 145, 214–215, 260–261, 283, 286
communist manifesto 4, 49, 51, 85–86, 117, 119, 189
Copernican turn 140, 151–152, 154, 159–160, 169, 170, 193
Corbusianism 36, 42, 102–103, 106, 108, 110, 118–119, 127, 129, 131
Corday, Charlotte 55, 60
critique 1–6, 8–11, 13–19, 23–25, 30, 32, 40–41, 48, 67, 70–71, 73, 76–77, 80, 85–86, 93, 97, 121–122, 124–126, 132–133, 137–147, 149–151, 153–155, 157–159, 161–163, 165, 167–169, 171, 173, 175–179, 181–183, 185, 187–195, 197–201, 203–213, 215, 216–217, 219–221, 223, 225–227, 229, 231, 233, 235, 237, 239, 241–249, 254–255, 257, 259, 272, 275–276, 286, 290–294, 296–300
critique of political economy 15–16, 19, 23, 25, 121, 126, 144, 146, 154–155, 158–159, 161–163, 169, 171, 177, 182, 188, 192, 193–195, 198, 206, 219–220, 227, 246, 296

David, Jacques Louis 47, 49, 53–63, 76, 88–89, 91–93, 96, 99–101, 156, 268, 277, 289, 291, 293, 298
Davidson, Neil 49, 89, 99, 101, 291
de Kesel, Marc 212, 245, 291
Derrida, Jacques 4, 18, 126, 217, 221–222, 229, 246–247, 280, 286–287, 291
Dolar, Mladen 146, 189, 191, 291–292
Duchamp, Marcel 205
Durand, Jean-Nicholas-Louis 50, 51–53, 63–65, 89–91, 103, 130,134, 298

École Polytechnique 50, 65, 89, 110
emancipatory 37, 61, 67, 85–86, 140, 142, 144, 195
Engels, Frederick 8, 12, 14, 19, 33, 74, 85, 109, 117, 155, 195, 223, 247, 296
Enlightenment 2, 3, 7, 10, 16, 17, 52, 65–66, 90, 95, 99, 140–141, 143–144, 189, 207, 229, 286, 292–293, 297
equality 16, 32, 67, 71–72, 83, 88, 90–92, 196, 217, 234–235, 256–257, 260, 264, 266, 268, 272–273, 277, 286

Index

equilibrium 28, 38, 40, 119, 123, 124, 128, 233
ethics 7–8, 10, 41, 62, 142, 144–145, 154, 159, 191, 201, 203, 206, 211, 214, 226, 244–246, 255, 291, 295, 300
exchange-value 156, 157, 163–166, 182, 203, 219–221, 234, 239–242, 249

Fascism 103, 106, 112–113, 120, 125, 127
fetishism 156, 166, 117, 119, 121, 123, 125
Feuerbach, Ludwig 2, 19, 170, 193, 195, 223, 269
Foucault, Michel 66
freedom 3, 11, 30–32, 37, 41, 43, 76–77, 82–84, 100, 125, 140, 145, 167, 196–197, 201–204, 209, 234–235, 261, 264–267, 269–270, 272, 277, 286, 295
French Revolution 1–4, 9–10, 12, 16–17, 19, 29–30, 32, 34–37, 42, 47, 48–51, 53–57, 59–69, 71–73, 75–87, 89–103, 111, 256, 264–265, 272, 286, 289, 291, 292–293, 298–299
Freud, Sigmund 12, 14–15, 17, 38, 41, 62, 67, 145–147, 153, 154, 169–174, 177, 180, 188, 190, 195, 197, 206, 209, 211, 216, 228, 230, 239, 243–244, 249, 258, 280–281, 289, 292, 294
Freund, Gisela 109

generic humanity 41, 155, 263–264
Gide, André 20, 22, 24, 296
Giedion, Sigfried 32–33, 43, 64, 94, 110, 131–132, 292
Girondins 55–57, 92, 266

Goetschel, Willi 138, 188–189, 292
Gowan, Todd 93, 297
Gramsci, Antonio 1, 95, 103, 130, 244, 292

Hamza, Agon 2, 17, 18, 300
Hegel, G. W. F. 3–4, 6, 10, 14–19, 24, 30, 38, 39–42, 48, 53, 61–63, 68, 73, 76–77, 81–85, 88, 93, 98–102, 106, 111, 125, 131, 145–147, 150, 154–155, 159, 162–163, 165–169, 176, 188, 190–193, 195, 211, 215, 227, 240, 245, 257, 266–270, 271–274, 276–279, 286, 292, 293, 295–297, 299–300
Heine, Heinrich 4, 37, 63, 78, 80–81, 85, 99, 293
Hobsbawm, Eric 1, 17, 32, 34, 43, 65–66, 89, 94, 95, 119–120, 122–133, 293

Idéologues 51, 52, 90
ideology 2, 8, 11, 16, 19, 38–39, 51–52, 90, 93, 95, 100, 120–121, 126, 147, 155, 168, 171–172, 175–176, 191, 195, 196–197, 211, 213, 216, 220, 222–225, 242, 245–247, 282, 294, 296, 299–300

jacobins 56, 57, 71, 79, 83, 87, 92, 266
Jameson, Fredric 1, 2, 16, 17, 44, 93, 129, 134, 143, 197, 207, 242, 244, 249, 278, 286, 293, 294, 295
jouissance 177, 178, 179, 180, 181, 182, 184, 185, 186, 187, 197, 198, 199, 213, 241

Kant, Immanuel 2, 4, 7, 8, 9, 10, 15, 16, 17, 19, 24, 44, 53, 62, 63, 66, 68, 76, 77, 80, 83, 84, 85, 93, 99, 100, 132, 133, 137, 138, 139,

303

140, 141, 142, 143, 144, 145, 146, 147, 148, 149, 150, 151, 152, 153, 154, 155, 156, 159, 167, 168–169, 172–174, 187–193, 195, 201–215, 242–249, 254–257, 264, 267, 275–278, 286, 292–293, 294, 297, 300
Karatani, Kojin 3, 7, 15, 17, 18–19, 24, 37, 103, 112, 127, 132–133, 137, 142–159, 161–162, 168–170, 187–193, 195, 201–211, 213–216, 220–221, 228–229, 236–238, 241, 243–248, 283–286, 294
Keynes, John Maynard 18, 29, 38, 42, 91, 93, 103, 118, 119, 120–129, 131, 133–134, 237, 277, 294, 296–298
Keynesianism 18, 42, 91, 93, 103, 118–119, 121–122, 124–125, 128–129, 131–133, 237, 277, 296
Kofman, Sarah 224, 247, 294
Kordela, A. Kiarina 232–234, 238–241, 248–249, 294
Kouvelakis, Stathis 9, 10, 17, 19, 44, 77, 79, 81, 83, 84–85, 87, 93, 95, 99–101, 273, 278, 294

L'Esprit nouveaux 36
Lacan, Jacques 14, 62, 146–147, 177, 195, 197–199, 214, 229, 244–245, 247–248, 289, 291, 294–295, 300
Le Corbusier 3, 26–32, 34, 36–39, 41–44, 50–51, 63–64, 78, 99, 102–103, 106–110, 118–123, 126, 133–134, 253–257, 261, 263–266, 274–276, 291, 295, 298–299
Lenin, V. I. 12, 15, 98, 296
Leroy, Julien-David 53
liberal-industrial capitalism 32, 34, 36, 43, 104, 112, 285
Loos, Adolf 60

Lukács, Georg 168, 195
Lyotard, Jean-François 87

Maison Dom-Iino 264
Mann, Geoff 18, 29, 42, 60, 91, 93, 103, 118, 124, 131, 133–134, 264, 277–278, 296
Marat, Jean-Paul 47, 53–60, 62, 69, 76, 88, 91–93, 298
Marcuse, Herbert 169
Marx, Karl 1–20, 23–25, 31, 33, 38, 41–44, 48, 51, 61, 63, 73–74, 76–77, 85–86, 89, 92–93, 95, 98, 100–101, 104–105, 110–113, 116, 123, 126, 128–129, 131–134, 137, 139–147, 149, 151, 153–156, 147, 158–173, 175–201, 206–207, 209, 213, 215–217, 219–229, 232–241, 243–249, 255–263, 271–274, 276–278, 280, 281–287, 289–297, 300
Marxism 12, 18, 43, 95, 101, 104–105, 133, 145, 170, 181, 191–192, 194, 244, 280–283, 285, 291, 292, 293
Mies van der Rohe 63
Montagnards 55, 92

Nancy, Jean-Luc 44, 263, 277, 290
Napoleon III 36, 48–51, 64, 102, 108, 111, 115, 117, 127, 130, 225–226
necessity 3, 7, 8, 30, 31–32, 34, 41, 43, 52, 76, 79, 83–84, 86, 88, 125, 146, 167, 171, 190, 197, 201, 204, 264–267, 269, 275, 277–278
Negri, Antonio 96, 120, 134, 287, 297

O'Neill, Onora 189, 254, 255–276, 297

parallax 145–151, 154–155, 158, 161, 190–194, 209, 211, 227, 286, 300

Index

phantasmagoria 49, 109, 116–117, 131, 216, 219, 222–223, 225–226, 246–247, 289, 299
philosophy 1–4, 6, 9–10, 12, 14, 16–19, 23–24, 30, 41–42, 44, 48, 53, 56, 61–62, 68, 76–77, 79–82, 88, 93, 95, 98–102, 105–106, 131, 138, 148, 153–154, 159–160, 167, 189–193, 195, 215–216, 229, 232–244, 246, 253–255, 257, 259, 261, 263–269, 271–272, 274–279, 289, 290–294, 296–298
Postone, Moishe 162–163, 166, 194, 297; poverty 3, 23–32, 36, 44, 48, 64, 76, 92, 94, 118, 125, 257, 265, 269–271, 274, 278, 290
proletariat 3, 48–49, 66, 74, 78, 86, 88, 92, 109, 117, 172, 176, 195, 256, 257–258, 272–273, 278, 285, 292
Proudhon 3, 260, 284
psychoanalysis 62–63, 146, 153, 169, 171, 177–178, 191, 195, 197–199, 201, 211–212, 215 227, 228, 230, 244, 245, 289, 291, 192, 295, 300

rabble 125, 257, 268, 269, 270, 271, 272, 273, 274, 276, 277, 278, 279, 298
Rancière, Jacques 161, 162, 206, 243, 244, 258, 289, 297
Reich, Wilhelm 169
religion 6, 7, 9, 10, 18, 19, 62, 80, 99, 145, 159, 160, 161, 193, 215, 218, 223, 255, 290, 293
revolution 1–4, 9–10, 12, 16, 17, 19, 29–30, 32, 34–37, 42, 47–51, 53–57, 59–69, 71–73, 75–87, 89–101, 103, 111, 256, 264, 265, 272, 286, 289, 291–293, 297–299
Ritter, Joachim 81, 99, 100, 297

Robertson, Etienne-Gaspard 222
Robespierre, Maximilien 4, 29, 31, 37, 42, 55, 56, 57, 63, 67, 68, 71, 72, 73, 75, 76, 80, 82, 90, 91–92, 95–98, 264, 265, 266, 269, 270, 277, 293, 29
Ruda, Frank 18–19, 257, 271–273, 276, 278–298, 300

Saint-Simonians 32, 34, 114, 128
sans-culottes 31, 56, 269
Saussure, Ferdinand 228–232, 247, 291
Scurr, Ruth 68, 96, 298
Second Empire 36, 48–49, 51, 64, 102, 104, 106, 108, 111, 122, 127, 133, 225–226, 297
shelter: philosophy 16, 24, 32, 37, 38, 40–41, 79, 253–259, 261, 263–265, 267, 269, 271, 273, 274, 275, 277, 279, 281
Sittlichkeit 268
Sohn-Rethel, Alfred 146, 168, 190, 298
Spinoza, Baruch 14, 232, 234, 238, 248, 249, 294
sublime 91, 191, 196, 197, 200–201, 206, 210, 211–213, 245, 300
surplus-*jouissance* 178–179, 180–182, 184–187, 198–199
surplus value 165, 171, 178–187, 197–199, 232–240, 241, 248, 300
symptom 14, 119, 146, 170, 172, 175–176, 195–196, 239, 258, 291

Tafuri, Manfredo 31, 63, 119, 120–123, 126, 133, 134, 298
terror 29, 35, 42, 67, 69, 70–76, 80–84, 87, 88, 91–92, 95–97, 100, 107, 110, 289, 298
The Death of Marat 47, 54, 55, 57, 60, 62, 88, 91–93, 298

305

Index

thing-in-itself 14, 31, 72, 91, 142, 148, 150–152, 154, 168–170, 180, 181, 183, 191, 203–204, 217, 222, 233, 240–241, 245, 260, 263, 272, 275

Tomšič, Samo 172, 176–178, 180, 191, 195–196, 216, 227–228, 230–232, 240, 247–249, 298

transcendental 15–16, 62–63, 137, 138, 142, 144, 146–147, 149–153, 156–159, 161–162, 168, 170, 172–174, 187, 188, 200, 202–203, 205, 206, 207, 226, 240, 241, 244, 254, 258

Transcritique 17, 19, 24, 132–133, 137, 144–147, 149–159, 162, 167, 169, 187–193, 195, 200–201, 203, 205–207, 209, 211, 213, 215–217, 219, 221, 223, 225, 227, 229, 231, 233, 235, 237, 239, 241, 243–249, 294

unconscious 14, 151, 153, 159, 169–170, 172–173, 177–178, 180, 185–186, 188, 191, 195–197, 216, 222, 227–228, 230, 238–242, 247, 248, 249, 293, 295, 298

Urbanisme 39, 51, 106, 127, 129
use-value 157, 163–166, 184, 187, 196, 203, 217, 219–220, 222, 234–235, 239–242, 249
utilitarianism 6, 11, 203, 213, 214

Valéry, Paul 20–21, 22–24, 226, 242, 296
value form 22–24, 69, 105, 128, 155, 157–158, 163, 166, 171, 173, 180–185, 196, 198–199, 201, 203, 217–223, 226–228, 233, 235–236, 238–239, 241, 248
Vers une architecture 24, 27–28, 36–37, 42, 51, 55, 59, 61, 89, 97, 119, 225, 295
Vighi, Fabio 183–186, 198–199, 298
Villari, Sergio 51, 89–91, 134, 298
virtue 42, 67–69, 71, 73, 76, 80, 82, 92, 95, 266, 298

Wahnich, Sophie 69, 96–97, 298
Wallerstein, Emmanuel 159
Weber, Max 7, 44, 144, 159, 237, 278, 299
Willet, John 34, 43, 299
Winkelmann, Johann Joachim 52

Žižek, Slavoj 3, 11, 14–19, 39, 42, 44, 62, 67–68, 72, 73–75, 78, 92, 93, 95, 96–98, 132, 141, 145–146, 149–150, 154, 161–169, 172–176, 181–182, 187, 189–201, 206–207, 211–213, 215, 222, 243–246, 258, 276, 286, 293, 297–298, 299–300
Zupančič, Alanka 146